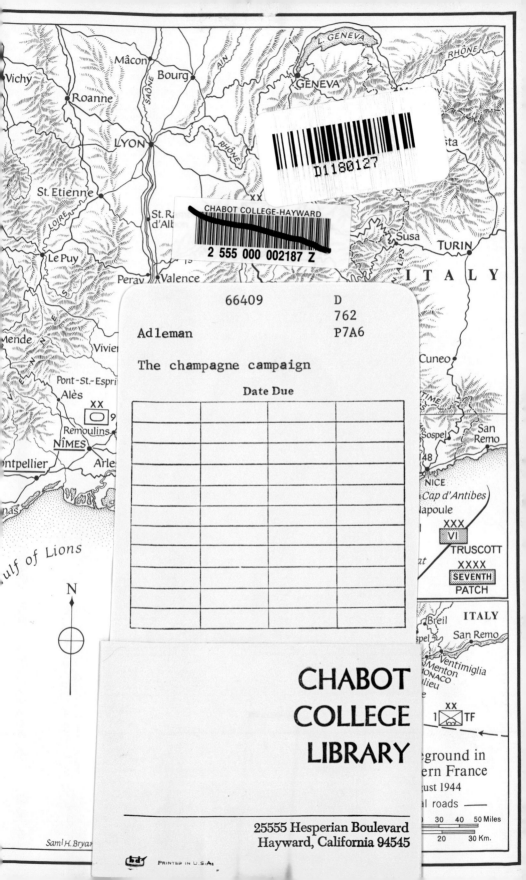

Books by ROBERT H. ADLEMAN *and* COLONEL GEORGE WALTON

THE DEVIL'S BRIGADE

ROME FELL TODAY

THE CHAMPAGNE CAMPAIGN

THE
CHAMPAGNE
CAMPAIGN

THE
CHAMPAGNE
CAMPAIGN

by ROBERT H. ADLEMAN
and COLONEL GEORGE WALTON

with photographs

LITTLE, BROWN AND COMPANY • BOSTON • TORONTO

Grateful acknowledgment is made for permission to reprint material from the following books:

Command Missions by General Lucian K. Truscott, Jr., published by E. P. Dutton & Co., Inc. Copyright 1954 by L. K. Truscott, Jr. Reprinted by permission of Curtis Brown, Ltd.

The French Army: A Military-Political History by Paul-Marie de La Gorce, translated from the French by Kenneth Douglas. English translation copyright © 1963 by George Braziller, Inc. Reprinted with the permission of the publishers, George Braziller, Inc., and George Weidenfeld & Nicolson, Ltd.

*This book is affectionately dedicated
to our good friend and editor Stanley Hart*

ACKNOWLEDGMENTS

OUR heartfelt thanks are due Mrs. Lois C. Aldridge, World War Division, National Archives, Washington, D.C.; Egon Weiss, Librarian of the United States Military Academy, West Point, N.Y.; George J. Stanfield, Librarian of the National War College, Washington, D.C.; Miss Katherine Howell and Mrs. Frances Kilburn of the Wilmington Public Library, Wilmington, N.C.

CONTENTS

ILLUSTRATIONS

ILLUSTRATIONS

A FOREWORD

COMPARED to some of the mighty battles that took place in World War II, the campaign to take and occupy the French Riviera was, at best, a colorful sideshow. Major General Robert T. Frederick had only ten thousand men in his First Airborne Task Force and when this group is considered within the context of the massed armies on both sides, it might perhaps seem worthy of only a page or a chapter in the histories of the period.

But the factor that renders the First Airborne Task Force indistinguishable in the larger canvas is also its strength: they were so few in numbers and yet they accomplished so very much.

The parachuting of Frederick and his men into Southern France on August 15, 1944, resulted in the most successful major airdrop of the war. The Force had fewer casualties, took more prisoners and reached its objectives more exactly than any other airborne unit on either the Allied or Axis rolls.

After the preliminary mission had been effected, the Force fought on with an efficiency that higher headquarters never anticipated during the planning stages. Functioning as an infantry division with far less than the number of men normally allocated to such a unit and certainly with only a fraction of the support units, supplies or transport that any division commander has a right to expect, the Force drove to the Franco-Italian border in fulfillment of the extraordinary assignment that it guard the entire right flank of the group of Allied armies thrusting northward through France.

And, while it did this, it also forged one of the most effective civilian-military relationships that existed in any theater of war throughout the world. It should be underlined that the "civilian" half of this partnership was made up of those determined individualists who live along the Riviera.

What more could anyone ask of a task force? These men not only deserve a book, they also deserve to be studied for their unblemished professionalism. We have been entrusted with the willing cooperation of almost every leader and many of the men in this group. Wherever possible, we have used their own words to carry the narrative. It is impossible to acknowledge, individually, their help, but this does not mean that we are unaware that this is their book.

ROBERT H. ADLEMAN
GEORGE WALTON

CHAPTER I

THE SOLDIERS

---

*So I guess you have a right to be known as the usually at-
tached, frequently aborted, unhonored and unsung fire brigade
of the European Theatre of Operations. And, knowing him as
well as I do, I sometimes get the impression that Terry Sanford
is as proud of the lieutenancy he had with the 517th as he is
of the governorship of North Carolina.*

— LIEUTENANT GENERAL JOHN W. BOWEN,
addressing the 1964 reunion of the 517th.[1]

DURING World War II a group of army units unfamiliar to each other were harnessed by a superb fighting general into the First Airborne Task Force.

The Force was assembled from many quarters for a specific purpose: to act as the spearhead for the Invasion of Southern France. After completing this assignment in a fashion that set a high watermark for American military efficiency in World War II, the individual units were again divided and sent to perform other duties with other organizations. The First Airborne Task Force was disbanded without fanfare.

But it is necessary to know the men and their backgrounds to really understand how well they fought, sealed off borders and handled the complicated affairs of the residents of the Riviera during the almost manic transition from military occupation to civilian government.

« 2 »

One of the largest units included in the First Airborne Task Force was the 517th Parachute Infantry Regiment, which was activated on March 15, 1943. Its initial commander, Colonel Louis A. Walsh, who had recently returned from the jungle fighting in Guadalcanal, took obvious relish in the organization's semiofficial designation, the "True As Steel Troopers."

They were almost uniformly tough, intelligent and brave men. After the war, an amazingly high percentage of the junior officers ended their careers as generals; quite a few turned into wealthy businessmen; Terry Sanford, a second lieutenant, became governor of North Carolina; and a majority of the other survivors found a comfortable degree of success in civilian life.

Colonel Howard E. Hensleigh supplied a workable description of the men who joined the paratroops in that era. "They actually fell roughly into two categories," he recalls. "One was the high school athletic type attracted by the paratroops because of the physical education and the ruggedness it required and there were the other types who came in because they were really basically tough guys. We had one man in our company who had been let out of jail with the promise that his sentence would be suspended if he would join us. He teamed up with a clean-cut young boy of the first category and, in combat, they were our lead scouts. Whenever the company attacked, those two would be at the head of it. You would go through an area and find that they had left ten or twenty dead Germans in their wake . . . in effect, they had cut a path through a whole defensive area for us to practically walk through.

"They always worked together, one would move up while the other covered, and it sometimes looked to me that they had almost the same attitude as if they were out shooting rabbits."[2]

Everyone in the 517th was a volunteer during the unit's early days. The reasons given for requesting this obviously hazardous duty ranged from a desire for adventure and the attraction of the extra pay earned by paratroopers all the way to Henry Wenerzynowicz's (his name was later occasionally used as an unbreakable password in combat) simple statement that "it seemed to me to be a good way to get some free airplane rides."[3]

[*8*]

But whatever the separate reasons the men had for joining, they lost little time in achieving a joint identity as a first-class unit that would be dependably capable in combat. During its training, the 517th established an enviable number of records for physical conditioning, foot marches[4] and tactical performance. The average IQ of the men in the Intelligence Section was 120[5] and this general combination of mental and physical excellence resulted in a unit which fairly brimmed with independence and good morale.

One of the men who had much to do with shaping the spirit of the 517th was Lieutenant John A. Alicki, who, according to one of the early recruits, an ex-Columbia University football player named Philip T. DiStanislao, "seemed to be a formidable, broken-nosed character at least eight feet tall when he met us at the train."[6] Lieutenant Alicki had just completed Jump School and Demolition Training at Fort Benning in the summer of 1943 when he was assigned to help organize the 517th. This included greeting all potential members of the unit with a classic oration which became widely known as "Boom-Boom Alicki's Blood and Guts Spiel."

Evidently, it was a memorable address. Later, in Southern France, he was walking down a village street one foggy night when he noticed two paratroopers standing in front of a cafe. They neither saluted nor gave signs of recognizing him as he passed, but as he went on, he heard one of their voices floating out of the mist, "There goes that son of a bitch who talked me into this."[7]

Dick Spencer became a platoon commander in the 517th, despite his bantam size. Now a magazine editor in Colorado, he evidently still retains the operational truculence that won him the respect of his men during the war. In 1967, for example, he was having dinner in a restaurant near his home in Colorado Springs when his attention was attracted to a disturbance being caused by a hulking, bearded young man. After loudly advising the seating hostess that "you'd better get at least three or four cops in here if you want me to be quiet," the man found himself confronted by Spencer. "What the hell do *you* want?" he asked. "My friends and I like quiet when we eat," answered Spencer and got it by punching the man into insensibility with two left-hand and two right-hand shots delivered with buzz-saw speed.

"I was majoring in journalism at the University of Iowa," says Spencer, "when war came along. We went right into OCS from our Advanced Military Course, and that's when I volunteered for the paratroopers. Luckily, it was around the time that they were forming cadres for the 517th.

"But the 517th were screening their recruits very carefully. As I recall, every man in the outfit had an IQ of a hundred or better, which is not bad for the infantry. We got together two good battalions, and then the speed-up came. They needed more paratroopers in Europe so they got the Raggedy-Ass 3rd Battalion together. I was assigned to it and we had some guys in it who had just been let out of the penitentiary, some Mexican boys who hadn't been assigned yet and some of the Indian boys that no one else seemed to want. We sure looked pretty sad compared to the other two battalions in the regiment, but when we got into combat then all the differences completely disappeared."[8]

These were some of the men of the 517th. Their leadership was just as tough and every bit as colorful.

Three battalions made up the regiment. The 1st was commanded by Major William Boyle. Richard J. Seitz, presently a major general in command of the 82nd Airborne Division, had the 2nd, and the outfit described by Dick Spencer as "the

Raggedy-Ass 3rd," was headed by a twenty-six-year-old major named Melvin Zais. A quarter of a century later, his son also became a paratrooper, making his qualifying jump at Fort Benning. And for the hell of it, his father, now Brigadier General Zais, jumped with him.

The regiment's first commanding officer was Colonel Louis Walsh. Although he was a dedicated man, part of the 517th never responded to his brand of leadership and after the Tennessee Maneuvers he was replaced by Colonel Rupert D. Graves. In the words of the Protestant chaplain, Charles L. Brown, Colonel Graves "was a courtly gentleman with a great deal of patience and the ability to bring out of each man as much [ability] as was there."[9]

Colonel Hensleigh describes the first officers' meeting presided over by Colonel Graves: "There had been many gripes over some of the things that Colonel Walsh had enforced most strenuously. One of them was the order that all boots had to be laced straight across so that only parallel lines were showing instead of the normal crisscross method. When Colonel Graves took over, one of the young battalion commanders asked if we were to carry on all of the fine old traditions of the outfit. Graves asked what these traditions were and was told that one of them was lacing the boots in a prescribed fashion. He pulled on his chin a bit and then said, 'Well, I always considered that the way a man laced his shoes was his own business.' This little thing evidenced an attitude that made a tremendous hit with the officers and men of the 517th. From that time on he could do little wrong in their eyes.

"He must have been forty or forty-five years old at the time, seemed to be a sound tactician, and had the rare ability to inspire people to do their best for him."[10]

[*11*]

Dick Spencer said that, "the first view that the men had of their new commander, Colonel Graves, was during inspection. The entire regiment was all 'spit and polished' and as he came down the ranks, we all noticed that one of his pant legs was flopping outside of his paratrooper boots. I could tell that Zais was almost physically restraining himself from grabbing him and rolling up that trouser leg for him. I tell you, it was a tough job keeping a straight face during that formation!

"But even though we referred to him as 'Old Hose Nose' behind his back, he was a good man. He never made snap decisions, he had deep respect for his troops — a real affinity for them. He was a good combat officer, maybe not the same type as, say, General Jim Gavin, not that kind of a tiger, but a quiet tiger in his own way.

"I remember once in combat when we were being heavily shelled, he and I took shelter in a basement. Just the two of us in a potato cellar. It was snowing outside, bitterly cold, and we were hungrier than heck. I found a candle stub, lit it, and we used the knives we always carried strapped to our legs to peel some of the spuds . . . and it suddenly hit me: here was a bird colonel holding a slice of raw potato on a knife over a candle, not actually cooking it, just blackening and smoking it up. His nose was running, dripping down from the cold. And I thought, 'Boy, this is the Army. Here I am a first lieutenant and if I work and work, someday I'll get to be a full colonel and get to sit in a damn cellar and eat raw potatoes with another damn lieutenant!'"[11]

The subdued quality that won the respect of the men for Colonel Graves sometimes failed to do the same job for him on higher echelons. One superior officer,[12] still exasperated after the passing of several decades, said, "The 517th was a god-damned good outfit but I really don't think its commander had much gumption. Sometimes you'd give him an order and he'd look sort of blank as if he was wondering what in hell you were telling him to do!"

When asked for his own recollection of his early days with the 517th, Colonel Graves answered, "I came there about two months before the outfit went overseas. I wouldn't say it was in good shape, it needed a lot of things done to it. I remember one day I went out to look at a unit going on guard and almost every piece of equipment they had was either rusty or dirty. I asked one of the soldiers why his gun wasn't clean, and he answered, 'Well, I've been on guard duty for four days now and I haven't had the chance.' These men had been pulling guard duty every day without any relief. Evidently, it was considered the thing to do.

"They also believed in splitting the men up when it came to moving a body of troops from one place to another. One battalion would be spread out over ten or fifteen miles with no contact or communication between its elements. It was things like this that convinced me that the regiment just wasn't in too good a shape. But, by the time we went overseas we got a little more organized."[13]

According to all reports, the spiritual leadership of the 517th was of as tough a caliber as the military one. Charles Brown, the Protestant chaplain, according to one of the men, resembled "nothing so much as an aging matinee idol. Classic features, iron-gray hair, well proportioned and at least six foot tall."

Almost every army chaplain carries a full load, but Charles Brown was even busier than most. In addition to his religious responsibilities, he quite often found himself at the top of the sixty-foot jump tower, illustrating to reluctant trainees that there really was nothing much to standing up straight and jumping out into space.

Some men would freeze on the platform at the tower top, and if the instructors found it especially difficult to pry a frightened man's fingers away from the overhead trolley line, they would say in disgust, "Oh, for God's sake, stop acting like a baby. Even the chaplain can do it!" Thereupon, Brown would dutifully scale the tower and jump in order to show the recruit how easy it all was.[14]

The Catholic chaplain would have qualified as an individualist in any organization and in any army. Father Alfred J. Guenette was described by a postwar acquaintance: "The padre is a stocky, cocky little guy who is now [1968] a missionary down somewhere in Chile where he visits the islands lying off the coast to hold Mass and to administer to the natives. He does what he can to get schools established and to set up recreational centers. He is obviously, in the best sense of the word, a good man. He enjoys drink and he enjoys conversation whether it's in English, French or Spanish. It's a delight to be in his company."

John Hollowell, a former enlisted man of the 517th, who has become the owner of a prosperous chain of dry cleaning stores in Virginia, retains vivid memories of Father Guenette. "One day while waiting to get ready for a field jump, we were shooting craps, and he came along and just knelt down and said, 'my dice,' and he grabbed for his money and shot dice with us just like anybody else. He sure knew how, too.

"One time when Chaplain Brown got hurt, the Father preached a sermon in his place. I don't know if he was supposed to do it, or even if it was breaking the rules, but he preached one of the best sermons I ever heard in my life. And I'm a hard-shelled Baptist.

"When we were embarking to go overseas, the order came down to cut our hair short. So we swiped some clippers somewhere and we all took turns shearing one another. First thing we knew, Father Guenette had slipped in and had gotten his hands on the clippers and was shearing the man in front of him so he would look like an Indian. Lucky thing that the man was a Catholic because his first reaction was to turn around and clout the guy who was running the shears over his head. You should have seen the look on his face when he realized it was the padre that was doing it!"[15]

One mishap occurred during these days that served to fix Father Guenette forever in the memories of those who were there. On a training drop, his parachute became snarled in the plane's fuselage and, after being hauled back in, he refused the pilot's offer to turn back to the field, insisting that he be permitted to make the jump as scheduled.

The veterans of the 517th offer many colorful versions of the incident, but the most dramatic is the priest's own unembellished recollection. He says, "On this particular morning I remember Lieutenant Marks (he's now a general) kidding me along . . . telling me that I was going to freeze in the door before going out and that he would have to throw me out. I told him that the reverse was probably going to happen, since I followed him in the stick.

"When we were over the drop zone and it came my turn to jump, I threw myself out as usual, but I found out that the webbing of my chute had caught, leaving me dangling down between the door and the fuselage. For some reason or other, my first reaction was to be amused over the fact that Lieutenant Marks had told me I was going to freeze in the door and here I was outside, and freezing like all get-out as that plane sped through the wind.

"I tried to do what I could . . . I tried to cut myself free by using my paratrooper's knife, but the webbing was too thick. Then I banged on the fuselage with my hand but to no avail. I yelled, but in that wind it didn't do any good. So I started to kick myself away from the fuselage and that didn't get me anywhere, either.

"Then I saw all these chutes opening far away in the distance below me and I thought, 'Well, maybe I'll have some luck . . . maybe this wind will finish ripping the webbing and I can drop, using my reserve chute.' I hadn't thought about using my reserve chute till then because I knew it would be foolish because I was so close to the tail. But nothing happened and after a while I began worrying that I'd be landing with the plane and since I was hanging like a dummy doll up there, I'd probably hit the ground first.

"So, in a cold sweat, I decided that it would be a good time to make an Act of Contrition and I guess it was the best I ever made in my life because about then a plane in the rear spotted me and called up my pilot to ask if he knew there was a man hanging outside his plane.

"So, the pilot got out of the formation and the two men in the plane who had been helping with the jump made a human chain . . . one of them using the inside of his feet against the door to hold himself while the rest of his body was outside . . . and even though the other man was securing him, neither had chutes on . . . and this was quite a heroic act. As a matter of fact, looking at him over my shoulder, I felt like hollering and calling him a little fool to get out that way without a chute. Anyway, the two of them slowly snaked me back in. It was a wonderful sensation to be walking on air back through the door!

"When I got back in, the pilot asked me how it felt out there and I told him it was pretty cold and he said, 'You know, Chaplain, I saw that silk in the plane during the jump but since this was the first time I had dropped chutists, I was wondering that maybe every chuter left a little silk behind!'

"The world is small. When we got to Rome after our first skirmish in Italy, I saw this pilot outside of a restaurant, sitting with some buddies. He recognized me immediately, and putting his arm around my shoulder, he led me back to his friends, saying, 'This is the fellow who was outside my door!' "[16]

The training was long, sustained and arduous. For the first thirteen weeks the men were not even permitted to visit the battalion headquarters day room, which was less than a hundred yards away from their barracks, except in formation. They worked day and night, training in swimming trunks and jump boots and, as training developed, carried two weapons at all times. Probably the most grueling part of this was the daily five-mile run up Mount Currahee and back. If a man fell out because of the heat or from exhaustion, he was left where he dropped. No one was permitted to fall out to help him.[17]

The few leisure hours allowed the men became correspondingly hectic. For example, Colonel Graves remembers that Dick Spencer, who was married just before arriving at the training base, used to swim the Chattahoochee River every night to visit his wife in Columbus, Georgia, and then swim back in time for next morning's reveille.[18]

They had a mountain lion for a pet. Charles M. Keen, Jr., said, "I'm not certain where we got him, but we kept him under

[17]

the first sergeant's desk. That is, we kept him there until Major Boyle came in one day and sat down at that desk. He happened to look down and there was this big long cat. He said, 'What the hell is this?' So the sergeant told him it was our pet. Boyle answered, 'I don't want B Company to have any more god-damned pets whatsoever. I don't want to see this goddamned thing again. Ever!' "[19]

Evidently Boyle relented because shortly afterward the men adopted another mountain lion. Although everyone in the camp knew about it, Boyle never acknowledged its presence until one night, after a party at the Officers' Club, the major and three other officers were struck by a sudden worry that the pet wasn't getting enough exercise.

"They had me pile the lion in the back seat of their jeep," said the animal's occasional keeper, Frank James, "and they all got in the front seat and took off. Later, I heard what happened. The lion must have gotten scared by the way they were driving and he reached out and hit Boyle on the side of the head with one of his big paws. I understand he damn near took his head off. There are some guys who claimed that Boyle hit the lion back, but I don't believe it. Anyway, right after that we had to get rid of it. But it wasn't the lion's fault. He had never been in a car before."[20]

The colorful recollections of the training period produced by Philip DiStanislao seem at a variance with his presently sedate status as a practicing dentist in Virginia. But abundant confirmation exists for every one of his stories. He describes the physical training as "tough, tough, tough. Although we didn't do too much the first few days, they made up for it by having us double-time everywhere we went. Even if someone had to go to the john in the middle of the night, he double-timed. This was a tremendous exercise in psychology. Over a period of time they convinced us that we were rougher and harder than anyone else. And it actually worked.

"Our company commander was a man named Bowlby. He was real spit-and-polish. He was everything that a West Pointer should be, had a moustache that was almost but not quite RAF, and seemed to go into a frenzy every time we failed to measure up to the standards he was setting for us.

"All of our classes were held outdoors. If you fell asleep in class, part of the punishment was that Bowlby would stick the hilt of a bayonet into the ground and you squatted over the blade pushing an M-1 rifle away from your body. Of course you strained so your tail wouldn't touch the point, but after a little bit your legs got so tired that you just couldn't help hitting the point. In retrospect, there was nothing wrong with this. No one got disemboweled that I know of, and I think things like this made better soldiers of all of us.

"Bowlby was as swaybacked as a mule but he insisted on good posture in his men. If he caught any of us slouching around, he made us stand at attention, our back pressing stiffly against the side of one of the tar-paper shacks we had out on the range. When we had sweated enough under that summer sun so that we had produced the wet outline of our body on the side of the shack, he let us go. And it was damned rare that anyone ever slouched again after an afternoon spent in this fashion.

"There was one man who was negligent about getting his hair cut to the proper degree of shortness. Bowlby took him into the supply room and shaved him with a straight razor. Next day, on parade, the action of the hot sun heating up a steel helmet on a bare head caused the guy to pass out in ten minutes flat.

"Major Boyle was another real tough cookie. I remember we had to double-time every morning the two and a half miles to the mess hall for breakfast. One time Boyle hurt his ankle, but he ran the whole distance with a sprain that I couldn't have hobbled on for five yards.

"Boyle fathered us, he beat us, he carried us and we were scared to death of him and we loved him. He could do anything we could do, but faster and better.

"I remember once I went AWOL and part of my punishment was a week on KP. Well, we all hated the cooks, anyway . . . and when one of them told me to clean out the grease trap, I told him it would be a cold day somewhere before I stuck my hand down into that slimy mess. He threatened to report me to Boyle and one word led to another until I hit him. So Boyle heard about this and called me out and asked me, 'You think you're a tough paratrooper, don't you?' I said, 'No sir.' And he answered, 'Well, I've heard that you do. Do these leaves (pointing to his major's insignia) bother you?' Then he took his jacket off and said, 'I'm going to beat the hell out of you.' At that I took off and ran all the way back to the company . . . and I could hear him laughing most of the way.

"We hated the cooks, anyway. I remember one time í was on 'Shoot Patrol.' This was an outfit we made up of our own men to go in and check the town for any of our guys who might be getting into trouble. If we came across any, we brought him back to our outfit before the Military Police could get their hands on him. Well, anyway, I was on patrol one day and I caught one of the cooks wearing jump boots, which were practically a sacred symbol to us. I made him take the boots off right there on the street and let him get back to the base any way he could. We sure were psyched up over those boots!

"One time one of our boys had bought a new tropical worsted uniform and it was stolen before he had a chance to wear it.

When it was reported to the first sergeant who was a good man . . . not inspired or intellectual, but a darn good first sergeant . . . he went to the Mail Clerk to see what packages were being mailed out. In one of the packages he saw the uniform. He called a company formation, set us up in two rows and then told the man whose name was on the package as sender to come forward. After telling the rest of us what this guy had done, he sent him between our rows like running a gauntlet. When the man got to the end, where the sergeant had put a footlocker with its lid raised up, he forced the man to put his hand on the edge and brought the lid crashing down on his fingers. Afterwards, he sent the guy to the hospital along with all of his gear. We never saw him again and we never afterward saw anyone in our outfit steal from anyone else in the outfit either!

"Another time, I remember we had two of our boys in the stockade. I had been detailed to guard them while they were straightening up the warehouse. Since I knew them, I believed it when one of them told me not to worry, just go ahead over and sack out while they did their job. But when I woke up I found they had swiped my rifle and hid it on me. They had me begging and pleading with them to tell me where the rifle was. They finally relented because it would have been curtains for me if I had gone back to the stockade without my rifle. When I finally marched them back, we must have presented a funny sight. I was cursing them every step of the way and they kept roaring with laughter.

"After getting busted a few times, I finally made some kind of a name for myself. As one of my friends later told my wife, I was the only acting temporary corporal the 517th ever had who went out and bought himself a swagger stick.

"Finally," DiStanislao concluded, "we finished up and left

[*21*]

for overseas. We went aboard the *Santa Rosa,* and all went down into the hold to go to sleep. In the morning everybody jumped down out of their cots and then jumped right back up. Believe it or not, there was a line of Wacs, messkits in hand, lined up for breakfast, threading through our sleeping area!

"So it turned out to be a delightful pleasure cruise. We all met some very nice girls and had dancing up on the fantail every night. We had one officer who got extremely close to a good-looking gal and the two of them finally got caught in a rather compromising position in what had used to be the ship's library. This brought chagrin to more than the two people involved because every shift of the guard detail had been watching them through some holes they had bored in the library doors."[21]

According to Colonel Hensleigh, the trip was highlighted by an elaborate prank played on a young officer who fancied himself a lady killer. He said, "We came over on this converted pleasure cruiser with three detachments of Wacs aboard. So Dick Spencer and some others decided to play a joke on Mac who was our resident Romeo. They started sending him notes, ostensibly written by a Wac who confessed in very warm tones how handsome she thought he was, that she had been watching him on deck and had fallen madly in love with him.

"So they kept passing notes back and forth for some time, leaving them to be picked up by each other in a place that the 'Wac' had declared was safe. This kept up for a few days and Mac started to get damn near into the panting stage. Finally, one day, the 'Wac' said she'd meet Mac in his room.

"Spencer was a rather small boy. Although he was very wiry (he'd been a wrestler at Iowa University), he had the innocent look of a young girl. They dressed him all up in borrowed Wac clothing, brassiere and all, painted his face with makeup, and planted him in Mac's quarters. When Mac walked in, Spencer rushed over, threw his arms around him and gave him a big kiss in what Mac must have rather smugly thought was uncontrollable passion. Just at that point, the Captain whom we had detailed as the ship Provost Marshal, and who was in on the gag, burst in. He grabbed Mac by the arm and hauled him out of the room, yelling, 'The Colonel is going to hear about this!'

"As they went up the stairs they bumped into Colonel Zais, who was also in on it. Zais said to the Provost Marshal, 'Captain, Mac here is a pretty good boy. Don't you think we can talk this thing over?' The Captain shook his head vigorously, saying, 'No sir, I got my orders and I've got to report anyone caught with a Wac and that's where Mac's got to go.' The Colonel said, 'Are you sure you have this story right?' And the Captain answered, 'Well, sir, I saw it with my own eyes. He practically had her down on the floor!' And Zais said, 'Well, where is the Wac?' and the Captain said that she was back in Mac's room and for all he knew she was probably still there. At this, Zais put on a very stern face and said, 'Let's go back there and have her confirm or deny it once and for all.'

"So, between the two of them they pulled Mac back to his room, so befuddled and scared that he didn't know what was going to hit him next. Of course, when they opened the door, everybody who had engineered the gag was in there and when they all screamed 'Sucker!' at him, he almost had a heart attack right on the spot."[22]

Perhaps the most concise description of the 517th's journey to the combat zone was inherent in the question asked by one of the men, "Who in Heaven's name was stupid enough to send us to Italy with a boatload of Wacs? No wonder the captain of the ship told one of our officers, 'If I had thought that my ship was going to be turned into a seagoing whorehouse, I would have scuttled it in Newport News!' "[23]

Anecdotes of the training of the 517th have been retold at length because these men later became one of the largest single units in the First Airborne Task Force when it dropped into Southern France on August 15, 1944, as the Invasion's spearhead. But there were others who were just as colorful.

<< 3 >>

The 509th Parachute Infantry Battalion was a combat-hardened outfit by the time it became a unit of the First Airborne Task Force. Its commanding officer, Colonel William P. Yarborough, was a seasoned professional who probably knew more about airborne operations than anyone else in the Army at the time.

In recalling the unit's beginning and end, Yarborough, now a major general stationed in the Pentagon, said: "The unit was disbanded after the French experience. I had run into General [James] Gavin in Washington just after it had happened and he told me about it. Well, this really floored me, because I felt that the very least they could have done was to have inactivated it and sent its colors back under a Guard of Honor.

"It was such a gallant unit, starting as it did: the very first parachute outfit to be sent overseas. It also made the longest flight in parachute history when it went from Land's End, England, to participate in the American invasion of North Africa. It had been known then as the 2nd Battalion of the 503rd, but it was redesignated the 509th in the way that only we in the United States Army do . . . we keep tampering with names and numbers.

"It went to England early in 1942 and became a part of the British 1st Airborne Division for training and indoctrination. It fought its way all up through Italy, jumped into Southern France and was part of the Battle of the Bulge, so I thought it was a damn small return for dedication and devotion to be disbanded."[24]

General Yarborough, the son of an Army colonel, graduated from West Point in 1936. His first post was the Philippines where for three years he served as a member of a scout regiment. Upon returning to this country, he was sent to Fort Benning, where he was posted to the first parachute battalion being formed in the Army.

In July 1942 he went to England as Airborne Advisor to General Mark Clark, joining the 501st as Executive Officer in time to make the flight to North Africa. He dropped into Tunisia and fought with the infantry and the remnants of a French regiment which was then reassembling.

In 1943 he was given command of the 2nd Battalion of the 504th Parachute Regiment. He led this unit in the invasion of Sicily, went ashore at Salerno when the decision was made to invade Italy, and took it through the bitter battles up the Italian peninsula until the day he was given command of the 509th, which he led with such distinction that higher echelons decided to include it in the forthcoming Invasion of Southern France.

Without exception, every one of Yarborough's associates has considered him to be a remarkable man. For example, Gabriel Rafael, one of the Frenchmen who joined the OSS detachment which became part of the Force, spent a considerable length of time with him in the fight along the Riviera. "Bill was an exceptional person," Rafael says, "and the first thing that struck me when I met him was his extreme youth for the rank he held. I was twenty-four years old at the time and barely a second lieutenant in the French Army. He was just a few years older and he was a lieutenant colonel.

"I was surprised that he never asked any questions of me. He took me at face value, which was most gratifying because it was strange under the circumstances to be trusted so much so quickly.

"He seemed to have tremendous control of his troops. There was one incident that occurred only a few hours after I met him. As we were going into Cannes, the parachutists were walking on either side of the road, close to the French people, who were so overjoyed to see them that they were all offering bottles of wine. Naturally, the soldiers accepted this and drank as they marched. When we went by in our jeep, Bill would just say in a very quiet voice to the parachutists to get rid of the bottle. He never raised his voice once. But the fellows all dropped their bottles as soon as he talked. There was not one who tried to hide his bottle or even showed a trace of resentment. I pictured to myself how different this would have been if it had been in the French Army! The very least our soldiers would have done would have been to shake their heads in mute dissatisfaction. But not Bill's men. They just dropped their bottles without any comment when he told them to do so.

"There were many other glimpses I had of Bill in that campaign, but they all amounted to the same thing . . . Bill Yarborough was a very admirable and very brave man."[25]

Major General John S. Guthrie, who was one of the planners of the Invasion of Southern France, when asked about Yarborough, said: "Unusual man. He ran the Green Berets Center at Fort Bragg when President Kennedy was in office. A very colorful fellow. Imaginative. As a lieutenant, it was like working with one of those fellows from whom ideas just bubbled forth. Anything Bill set out to do, he did with flair and imagination. He was exactly the kind of man we needed for the airborne drop in Southern France. He was fiercely proud of his battalion and I think that perhaps he was less than enthusiastic when it was suggested that it be attached to the outfit that Rupert Graves had, since the 517th hadn't had any combat experience."[26]

Major General Kenneth Wickham, the chief of staff of the First Airborne Task Force, described Yarborough as an outstanding leader in combat, a tremendous liberator of territory, and one who was able to maximize the strength of his unit by all sorts of devices and, occasionally, by all kinds of ruses.[27]

The commanding officer of the First Airborne Task Force, the almost legendary Robert T. Frederick, agreed that Bill Yarborough was an officer with outstanding qualities. Frederick, who habitually used a yardstick which differed from that recognized by most regular Army men, says, "I don't know whether I should mention this at even this late date, but I do remember that when we were assembling our supplies for the drop, I began to grumble about the lack of motor vehicles that had been included. Yarborough was there and he said, 'Well, just give me tonight and I'll get you all the vehicles you want.'

"That night he sent some of his men into Rome to the Military Police Vehicle Stockade where they kept all of the stray automotive equipment they had come across in the city. Some of the men distracted the attention of the guards while the others crept inside and, lying on their bellies in the dark, they wrote down lists of all of the vehicles, their numbers and the unit names stencilled on their bumpers.

"The next morning, Yarborough, who had in the meantime assembled all sorts of unit patches and insignia, issued one patch to each of his men. Then the men went down to the vehicle stockade and asked the guards if they had vehicle number so-and-so from such-and-such outfit. The guards, after running down their lists, of course saw that they had and released the vehicle to the man with the patch.

"And that's the way Bill Yarborough improvised and operated!"[28]

« 4 »

Among the remaining handful of units awaiting inclusion into the First Airborne Task Force were two of the most genuinely dramatic collections of soldiers in World War II.

The first of these were the Nisei who had been gathered into the 442nd Infantry Regiment. During the first days of the war, the use of weapons was denied to second-generation Americans of Japanese descent, and it was not until January 1943, that Nisei were assigned anywhere but to post exchanges, service installations and the like. The injustice of this discrimination was underlined by the magnificent fighting records established by the 442nd after its activation in February 1943. Their accomplishments in Italy are highlights of that campaign and the part that the men of the 100th Battalion and the antitank company of the 442nd played in the fight for Southern France certainly entitles them to a substantial portion of the operation's remarkable record.

Unfortunately, these soldiers had a twin fight confronting them. As it turned out, dissipating the ethnic prejudice against them proved to be only slightly less difficult than winning against the Germans. Pat Harrison, one of the best combat leaders in the First Special Service Force, noting this, observed: "I just have to put in a word for those little fellows from the Japanese-Hawaiian unit. In my opinion they were at least the equal of any U.S. infantry outfit and a hell of a lot better than most.

"We had the good fortune to work fairly close with them on a couple of occasions and I just don't think that enough good things can be said about them. I always felt particularly bad over the way they were discriminated against when out of the line and again when they came back to the States.

"I was at the reception desk of a rest camp in Nice one night when some bloody jerk of a captain was refusing them rooms instead of trying to give them a break as anyone would who had any knowledge of their heroics in combat. I couldn't keep from putting in my two-bits' worth which, of course, didn't go over too well with this armchair hero who then tried to send me back to my unit too."[29]

Colonel Edwin Walker's outfit, the First Special Service Force,* did not join the First Airborne Task Force until a few days after the Invasion. Although they were qualified paratroopers (they also received intensive training as ski troops, mountain fighters, demolition experts and, in particular, in killing quietly through unarmed combat), they functioned solely as the first infantry assault wave for the Invasion troops who came by sea into Southern France. After accomplishing their initial mission of silencing the German coastal batteries which might have torn great holes in the massed Invasion fleet, they were quickly shifted over to the Riviera sector to become a part of the FABTF.

This organization has been widely described as "the best small force of fighting men ever assembled on the North American continent."[30] It was activated in 1942 after the Allied high

* The forerunner of the Special Forces known today as "The Green Berets."

command became convinced that the German occupation of Europe could be seriously disturbed by dropping a trained group of saboteurs into Norway. As an experiment in continental unity, it was decided that the combat echelon of projected force would be composed of approximately sixteen hundred of the toughest men that Canada and America could find. The Canadians contributed some of the best soldiers in their Army, but the Americans picked out a mixed bag of brawlers, miners, trappers, lumberjacks and, in an excess of zeal, some of the harder-nosed inmates of their military stockades. To this was added a sprinkling of idealists looking for an exciting way to prove their manhood.

The name "First Special Service Force" was selected for them because it sounded close enough to the Army's entertainment branch to mask their real identity, and for maximum security the unit trained in an obscure post near Helena, Montana.

The Force so far exceeded the expectations of the planners that the Norwegian government in exile, after being apprised of the destructive efficiency of the unit, refused to let the men be dropped in their country, saying, in effect, that they had less fears of the effects of a continued German occupation.

The Force was finally given its opportunity in Italy. Although the men were never dropped in combat as paratroopers, and never used the more esoteric skills drilled into them by their instructors, they proved to be such ferocious warriors that the Germans, who were not given to unrealistic appraisals, rated them at the strength of a division (which is approximately sixteen thousand men) and promised a generous furlough to the personnel of any of their units who succeeded in capturing a Forceman alive.

At Anzio, where the Force held one third of the total defense perimeter, they earned their name of the "Devil's Brigade." A diary was found on the body of a dead officer which contained the entry: *The Black Devils are all around us every time we come into the line, and we never hear them come.* This was a reference to the Forcemen's habit of gliding, black-faced at night through the enemy lines, slitting the throats of all sentries in their way.

They were a ribald and irreverent group. Their antics in battle provided the correspondents with some wildly funny high spots in what was essentially a grim and dispiriting campaign. For example, one platoon found an abandoned village well behind the German lines. They elected their lieutenant its first mayor, converted the houses into bars and billets, farmed the adjacent area by day and deployed on intelligence patrols at night. They would dig foxholes large enough to accommodate their livestock as well as themselves. Sometimes they went out on patrols simply to steal supplies for their farms from the Germans.

Nor did they confine their looting activities to the enemy. Once, hearing of the existence of a huge supply of wine stored in a cave, they disarmed the Allied sentries on guard and appropriated the cache for their own use. It made no difference to them that the cave was also the headquarters of the VI Corps commander, Lieutenant General Lucian K. Truscott.

They were first-class soldiers, who seemed incapable of respecting any officers other than their own, but, to a man, they stood in awe of one individual: their commanding officer, Bob Frederick.

« 5 »

One of the dictionary definitions of *hyperbole* is "an obvious and intentional exaggeration." And it might seem as if the foregoing descriptions of the men and units who constituted the First Airborne Task Force approaches at least hailing distance of that description. But it must be remembered that these were especially picked units assigned to execute the first massive airdrop on German-held territory. Inevitably, they would be fighting men of high potential and accomplishment.

But there is absolutely no way for the historian to describe Robert Tryon Frederick without provoking an immediate accusation of hyperbole stretched to its outermost limits.

And yet, it is all true. After twenty-five years, the men who served with and under him still speak of him with such unqualified admiration that it is difficult to believe that he or his accomplishments ever existed. Winston Churchill, in describing him, once said, "If we had a dozen men like him, we would have smashed Hitler in 1942. He's the greatest fighting general of all time."[31]

Frederick was wounded nine times in action, incurring most of his wounds *after* he had reached the rank of general. His staff and aides lived in unending fear of the possible consequences of his habit of going off on a patrol behind enemy lines accompanied only by one or two enlisted men. On one occasion his men, after a particularly bloody battle for an objective, found that Frederick, preceding them by hours, had already infiltrated the enemy lines in order to get a closer look at the reactions of his junior officers in a sticky combat situation.

He never attempted in any way to impress the members of his command. In fact, he rarely spoke with them unless it was to issue an order. They knew that in whatever mission he undertook, the odds were strongly against survival for any of them. And yet these incredibly tough soldiers not only followed him unquestioningly, but quite a few of them had tears in their eyes

Major General Robert T. Frederick at his headquarters in Nice, October 1944. (From the collection of Joseph W. Welsh)

when he informed them that he was leaving the First Special Service Force for the command which turned out to be the First Airborne Task Force.

Although he was a West Point graduate, his unorthodox approach to military situations led many of his brother generals to refer to him in terms in which the phrase "that crazy son of a bitch" was always prominent. Their dislike either seems to have been inspired by their inability to understand him or was simply rooted in envy. In 1944, at the age of thirty-seven, Frederick had become the youngest major general in the American Army.

Physically, he was slender, of medium height, wore a moustache, and in the words of a baffled Canadian officer who saw him for the first time, "looked like a bloody goddamned actor." The Canadian later became one of the most devoted men in the cult which had respect for Robert Frederick as its focus.

Resembling nothing so much as a gentle, retired high school principal, he now lives quietly in Palo Alto, California. His wife, a woman of fragile beauty, calls him "Bobby" and he seems light-years away from the instinctive master of guerrilla tactics who killed so many of the enemy with his own hands.

This was the man who put together, briefed and led the First Airborne Task Force through much of its short combat life.

« 6 »

Another of the men who played a significant part in the success of the First Airborne Task Force was an obscure OSS captain named Geoffrey Jones. He had parachuted into Southern France two weeks before the Invasion.

CHAPTER II

BEFORE THE DROP

The OSS had to improvise quite a bit as it went along. But the point is, everything went well for us on this one. Everything meshed. Everything went so well that everybody thought it was just a ball. When I got back here to New York after the war I found out that the people who had seen me on the Riviera with the girls had spread the word that Jones was having a hell of a nice war in Southern France.

— GEOFFREY M. T. JONES[1]

MOST of the men with whom he served in World War II have settled into comfortable niches, but Geoffrey M. T. Jones remains an exuberant, shaggy-haired and handsome man who prowls like an impatient cat through his cluttered New York apartment while waiting for another of those ambiguous telephone calls that seem so essential to his profession of "Management and Communications Consultant."

He is a tall man given to wearing plum-colored slacks and electric-blue turtleneck sweaters. He appears to know most of the people who operate the control levers in New York and other centers of influence. Open and friendly, talkative to the point of being garrulous, he rarely offers honest clues to his actual train of thought.

Except perhaps for the addition of twenty or thirty pounds, he is almost the same as he was that day in early August 1944, when as an OSS agent, he parachuted into occupied Southern France. Even then he might have described himself as a management consultant. His orders were to weld the splintered Resistance fighters into a service arm for the oncoming First Airborne Task Force.

Since the French are quite sensitive to titles and rank, this was the kind of job that the American Army would have ordinarily assigned to someone carrying much more impressive insignia than the captain's bars that Jones had been wearing in the Algerian headquarters of the OSS.

"But you must remember," he explains, "I had more experience than anyone. The only trouble was that I had been moving around so goddamned much that I never had the chance to stay long enough in any one spot to get a promotion. Let me tell you about it.

"Five days after graduating from Princeton as an ROTC artilleryman in 1942, I received orders sending me to the Artillery Replacement Center in Fort Bragg. But somewhere along the way I got wind of the news that parachute units were being put together . . . and I figured that if I was going to fight a war, I might as well fight a good one.

"So I volunteered for the parachutes, but being an artilleryman they didn't know what to do with me. Well, lucky enough, right about then they were also in the process of deciding that parachute artillery units were feasible. You see, they had figured out how to take the old seventy-five millimeter howitzer apart, drop it in pieces and put it together again. So just by being in the right place at the right time, I got into the first class at Fort Benning for parachute artillery.

"When I graduated, I was assigned to a parachute battery . . . . there's one in each airborne division. Well, evidently because I was one of the few officers in parachute artillery who had graduated from college, I was made assistant G–2 [Intelligence] at division headquarters.

"Next thing that happened, Joe Swing was given command of the division. He kept shuffling me around and at various times I think I served as everything from garbage collector to G–1 [Personnel] and G–4 [Supply] . . . it seemed as if anytime anyone got sick I was detailed to take over their job. Also, for

Captain Geoffrey M. T. Jones, 1944

some reason or other, I was sent to the Command and General Staff School during this period. This was highly unusual because I was still a first lieutenant . . . and it was very rare that a lieutenant found himself in *that* school. As a matter of fact, up until the time I graduated, some of the instructors insisted on referring to me as lieutenant colonel in their records!

"Then Joe Swing appointed me as his aide, although he had the reputation of hating anyone who had this particular assignment. Obviously, while in this job I met a number of men who turned out to be quite helpful later on.

"All of this gave me a background in staff work as well as parachute and artillery. As a matter of fact, during this period I

[*39*]

designed the first airborne jeep. General Swing told me to go ahead and strip down the standard jeep . . . which, in effect, meant that I pulled off the bumpers and a lot of other things in order to make it light enough. Of course, this got the regular Army Ordnance sore as hell . . . they wanted to court-martial me for tampering with U.S. property and the general had to go up to Washington to get me off the hook.

"Later, when I got into OSS I found that I was the only man in the whole outfit that had my kind of experience. But while I was still in the States they caught up with me and sent me off to the Artillery School at Fort Sill. At the time that was a necessary requirement for every Artillery Officer. But when I got out there, I found that I was more familiar with the parachute artillery than anyone else in the school. The general who ran it used to ask me to come over to his quarters at night to tell him something about the airborne because no one knew anything about it in those days.

"This is when I heard about OSS. Although General Swing was visibly annoyed when he heard that I wanted to volunteer for the 'super-spy' outfit instead of going to the Pacific with him, he okayed my request for assignment. But what the hell, like everybody else I wanted to liberate Paris.

"Incidentally, I had been hoping that I would get into the fight for France. You see, I had been brought up in the South of France. I had even gone to school in Caen when I was a youngster. Funny enough, when the Invasion force landed in the south, they were within a mile and a half of where I had lived on the outskirts of Saint-Tropez. My family had a villa there.

"Anyway, I passed all the OSS tests and after some fairly rudimentary training was issued my cloak and dagger. This was in March or April of 1944, and within a week I was on my way to my first post, Algiers.

"On the plane going over, someone told me that the man sitting opposite me was the baseball star, Moe Berg, a catcher for one of the big league teams. I looked him over and when I saw his wristwatch, in spite of myself, I started to laugh. Naturally, he wondered what I was laughing at, but then when my watch caught his eye, a big grin spread over his face too. Although no one was supposed to know that we were secret operatives, all of the graduates had been issued the same kind of special watch. The OSS might as well have hung tags around our necks. Later on both of us got away from the VIP's in Algiers in favor of a billet of our own. We had quite a time there for a while.

"Anyway, my background must have come to the attention of someone on a higher echelon because my first assignment in Algiers was to the inter-Allied group in charge of all the sub-rosa activities in Southern France. This turned out to be a two-edged blessing, since I found the operational work so fascinating that I kept volunteering to go in with the groups dropped . . . but my superiors wouldn't let me go because once again I was the only guy in the unit with the kind of specific knowledge of military tactics needed to help train the groups going in.

"Finally, when my chance came, it was brought about by another of those flukes that always controlled my military career. My outfit had the official designation, *Special Projects Operation Control*. We were under General Sir Harold Alexander's command and our specific function was to take a group of fifteen neophyte operatives off to some barbed-wire-enclosed headquarters and put them through a four or five week basic course in map reading, living off the land, the use of plastic explosives, night marching, telegraphy, reading the stars . . . you know, everything you ought to be proficient in when you are going to work behind enemy lines.

"Although I was terribly anxious to go in with any one of these groups, I realize now it would have been a foolish thing to do. Because of our being in on the big tactical picture, I had a great deal of information about the Invasion of Southern France that was going to be shortly launched out of Italy. If I had gone in and been taken . . . and this was always a fifty-fifty chance . . . I might have been able to fool a German interrogator but I certainly would have been turned up if I had been questioned by one of their local collaborators. After all, no one is sure how well they are going to stand up under heavy pressure and this was something I wouldn't have known until the Germans tried out their brand of persuasion on me. And then, if I was wrong, it would have been too late.

"But as I say, I didn't give this too much thought during that period. I really wanted to get away from this barbed-wire and paper-pushing assignment. I was getting awfully tired of waving good-by to these guys.

"My chance came when we lost an operative named Donalde to the Gestapo. Later we found out that he was tortured and killed, but all we knew then was that he had been taken. When he went, we were in trouble. We had been telling the high command that we had a topnotch guy over there to help when the Invasion force came ashore, and that he would have the local Resistance already coordinated. So my immediate superiors made a decision not to tell anyone about it but to send someone else in right away to do the same job. He had to speak French, be aware of the size of the job to be done, and be familiar enough with the

Invasion plans to work intelligently on his own. Since this was somewhere around the end of July and the Invasion was slated for the middle of August, there wasn't much time to train anyone from scratch. That, as I kept pointing out to my superiors for two straight days, meant me. So I got the job. And this is when I began to fully realize that if I ran into bad luck, it could have some awfully adverse effects on the whole operation.

"They attached me to a French Naval Mission that was already scheduled to go in to help keep the French fleet from steaming out of the harbor at Toulon when the Allied landings took place. My specific mission was to have the French Underground clean out the glider landing areas and then meet the airborne troops coming in. You see, the Germans had sunk large poles at five-foot intervals in most of the open spaces and connected them with barbed wire. If we didn't get these out of the way, the barbs ripping through the flimsy floors of the gliders would have torn the balls off of an awful lot of Americans . . . not to mention the hazard the wrecked gliders would have been to the planes unavoidably landing on top of them or crashing into them.

"In order to give me added weight with the Underground, I was officially appointed a *Délégué Militaire* of General de Gaulle, whose name was sort of the rallying point for all of these groups. Also, I finally received my promotion to captain.

"When we went in, we wore the blue civilian type of thing and brought a certain amount of equipment with us. We also were given some sort of a password . . . you know, the kind of thing like 'The strawberries in the spring will come out green,' meaning that the Allied landings would take place on such and such a date.

"For some time prior to this I had been flying over with my trainees because many of them didn't speak any English and the crews of the Lancasters and Sterlings that were transporting them didn't speak anything else. So I already had some experience in flying over and looking for drop zones. We used all kinds of gimmicks on these flights. For example, we would go in with a bombing group and then peel off like we had gotten lost, knowing that it would be only one small 'blip' on the unsophisticated radar screens in use during that period and that, anyway, the Germans would be more worried about where the mass of the bombers were going.

"We almost didn't drop when I finally got to go in on my own mission. You know, one of the worst things that can happen to you is when everybody says good-by and then you don't go in and you have to meet everybody again at breakfast next morning. There's a very strained feeling. I guess everyone is wondering whether or not you chickened out and you know that this is what they're wondering about and nobody, because of security, is allowed to say anything at all. So when we got over France that night and our pilot sent a crewman back to tell us to look at all the vehicle lights down there and that they were probably German patrols out to greet us, I didn't feel very good. I wasn't sure that if I went back I would ever get another crack at it.

"Our landing zone was Mont de Malay, the last big mountain going south in the Basses-Alpes, and we were right over it so I sent word back to the pilot to circle around once or twice. Then I finally made out a couple of signal flares and I knew that my people were down there waiting for me . . . and I said to one of the Frenchmen, 'What the hell, I'm not going to be ducking my head down tomorrow at breakfast, let's go in anyway!' This Frenchman, he was an older man being in his forties and I was only twenty-five or twenty-six, was good and tough and he smiled and agreed. At the time we were sitting by the hole in the ship through which we would jump.

"But the pilot, evidently afraid that he might lose his ship in addition to losing us, turned off the small light above us that was the signal to go. At this the Frenchman nodded to me and pushed himself down through the hole. He was the senior officer and by protocol was entitled to go first. I went next. Later I learned that some of the English crew grabbed the next man, who was supposed to have been my radio operator, and kept him from following. This later scared the hell out of Algiers because I had no way of getting in touch with them during the next four or five days and they didn't know what had happened to us. All that they knew was that we had jumped right in the middle of all the German patrols moving down below."[2]

« 2 »

There are some American veterans of the forces which invaded Southern France who still retain the impression that the French Resistance consisted of really not much more than isolated pockets of temperamental individualists. Even Geoffrey Jones rarely hints that it was anything else, but in his case, this represents discretion. His work in the Algerian OSS headquarters left Jones intimately aware that inside France there existed a complex mass of movements and organizations united into a temporary pyramid by a common determination to oust the Germans from their country.

Since everything splintered and sank into a morass of selfish interests after the Invasion had succeeded, the maneuverings of these organizations are pertinent here in only enough detail to clarify the situation into which Captain Jones was jumping.[3]

With only a few exceptions, the dislike that existed between each independent group and the scorn that all of the independents felt for members of the regular French Army, and which most of the Army heartily returned towards them and their American allies, remained hidden. A few of the more perceptive journalists were aware of the situation, and only a small number of these had the courage to report it during this era of strange bedfellows.

A. J. Liebling, the highly respected correspondent for *The New Yorker*, was in this last group. Not long after he had reached North Africa he recorded with amazed repugnance that he had found that most of the officers in the French Army headquarters were paying only enough lip service to the doctrine of Allied unity to insure a continued flow of supplies and support. He reported that French officers who were suspected of favoring the Americans were "practically ostracized. Liaison officers assigned to American units were scolded for 'fraternizing' with the Americans — nearly two months after we had officially become allies [this was after the landings in North Africa]. Most of the officers above the grade of battalion commander were a sad lot: those not definitely hostile, because they owed their promotions to Vichy, were apathetic because they had never expected to fight again and they hated the prospect.

" 'They are selfish!' a friendly Zouave major told me, 'they are in love with their pensions. Let it pass. But the blasphemy is that they do not want to fight.' "[4]

General Jacob L. Devers, who commanded the Sixth Army Group during the Invasion of Southern France, recalls, "We needed officers badly [during the campaign up the Rhone Valley to link up with the Allied forces fighting their way east]. De Lattre [General Jean de Lattre de Tassigny, the French corps commander in that campaign] was very shorthanded, and we tried to pick up all these French officers that had stayed behind in France after the surrender. But de Lattre was considerably handicapped in trying to get these approved because the Maquis had to okay them . . . whether they had helped in the Resistance . . . and, oh, we had quite a little problem!"[5]

However, it is important to say immediately that the shenanigans of the political leaders and the reluctance to fight that characterized many soldiers and officers of the regular French Army[6] did not extend to those civilian patriots who elected to face the dangers of torture and death in order to harass the German forces in their country. Almost every social and economic class contributed to the grim total of approximately twenty-four thousand Resistance fighters, men and women, executed by the Germans in France.

Of course, there was also a picturesque side to these clandestine operations. For example, Colonel Ullmann, alias Urban, who had been a tank officer in the regular French Army, was the chief of staff of the Secret Army of the Alpes-Maritimes which was the department of France that would be the scene for much of the activities of the First Airborne Task Force. Prior to the Invasion, he had been contacted by a staff officer of the Italian Army of the Alps who sent word that since "he liked champagne and hated the Nazis" he was ready to cooperate with an officer of the French Underground forces.

A meeting in the American bar in Grasse was arranged. The Italian was to be in plain clothes and Ullmann was to carry a newspaper in each of his side pockets as a recognition signal. Ullmann showed up early and, to his horror, he was immediately recognized. Before the war he had been a film producer and, as luck would have it, a film company had come to this Riviera city in order to make a musical. Many of the players were in the bar. Seeing the Frenchman, they immediately clustered around, offering drinks, companionship and, in the case of one particularly noticeable starlet, a much more comprehensive invitation.

Monsieur Ullmann masked a quick decision by an outward gallant eagerness. He rose, took the startled (but flattered) girl by the arm, and headed for the door. Outside, he explained to the girl that he was devastated by the recollection of an urgent prior commitment and beat a hasty solo retreat up the street. As far as he was concerned, both the girl and the Italian could wait for another tryst.

After a few days, he contacted the Italian again and, after explaining the delay, reached an agreement with him. It was arranged that every Italian soldier who joined the Maquis with his arms would be given civilian clothes and a set of false identity and ration cards. He also negotiated the purchase of two trucks loaded with light weapons for one hundred thousand francs. As a result, when DRAGOON, which was the final Allied code name for the Invasion of Southern France, took place, Ullmann's group amounted to three thousand men who were ready to help the Allies during the Riviera campaign.

Another officer of the Secret Army operated a newspaper in Nice as a cover for his activities. At a dinner party one night he was seated next to a talkative Vichy official who admitted that he was worried over the activities of Allied agents along the Riviera. With every glass of wine he grew more confidential. Finally, he asserted that it would not be long before he had dealt this nest of traitors a back-breaking blow. From one of his informers, he said, he had learned that an English submarine was arriving at a coastal point near Nice in three days with a crew of trained saboteurs. He intended to be there with a strong reception committee.

The newspaperman agreed that such a coup would probably entitle him to a commendation from Pierre Laval, and probably earn him a dazzling promotion to boot. But the newspaperman neglected to tell him that he was the man to whom the saboteurs were supposed to report.

That night the clandestine radio sent out signals arranging another landing point at a later date. One job remained to be done; to find the traitor who had betrayed the plan to the collaborationists. This was a job for "Colonel Vautrin," commander of the Secret Army in the Grasse section.

Vautrin was a subtle man who could be depended upon to explore human frailty for whatever elements that would help speed the ultimate day of Liberation. It was he who had perfected the technique used by the Underground to examine the baggage and papers of German and Italian officers holidaying along the Riviera. Shortly after arriving at the Hotel Martinez or the Hotel Royal, the alien would invariably be met by a stunning blond or brunette who quickly would find him to be irresistible. No document was ever stolen. But microfilms of everything of military value in the visitor's possession generally arrived promptly in London.

It was easy for Vautrin to arrange an invitation to the next dinner party the Vichy official attended. Again, his tongue lubricated by wine, the collaborationist bragged of his efficiency and was predictably delighted when the bemedaled Vautrin said, "You are just the man to help me organize a counterespionage ring. Will you do it?" There was an immediate and enthusiastic assent. Seeking to impress Vautrin, who seemed to have the highest and firmest connections with Vichy, the man proudly announced that he already had a skeleton network of informers, including a man named Chambret who had just tipped him off about a proposed submarine landing.

Two nights later, the collaborationist and his crew lay on their bellies until dawn on the sands. The submarine never came. The official returned home, so tired, frustrated and angry that he found it difficult to sleep.

An hour after he finally closed his eyes, his superior called from Nice. He was being transferred away from the prized Riviera assignment to one of the dreariest departments in the north.

His superior was also a member of Vautrin's ring.

And a few days later the local newspapers carried the story that M. Roger Chambret had been accidentally killed while bicycling down the Grasse road. He had apparently been going too fast and had run into a tree in the darkness, resulting in a fall which had fractured his skull.

« 3 »

There were others awaiting the parachute descent of Captain Jones. Isabel Pell, for example.

She was an American expatriate who had been living on the Riviera because, it was rumored, her family was willing to grant her a generous annual allowance on condition that she stay abroad. The most widely accepted explanation of her family's attitude among her French neighbors and the American troops to whom she later attached herself as they swept over the area was that she never troubled to dissemble the fact that her tastes in companionship ran more to women than men.

But she was a big gusty woman whom everyone loved. Possessed of courage, humor and impeccable social position, she is indelibly associated with the Riviera campaign in the minds of everyone who was there.

One of the semiofficial descriptions of her Resistance activities is found in a letter by a Capitaine François addressed to the Civil Affairs Detachment concerned with the American military administration of the Riviera communities. In part, it reads:

At the end of 1943, in North Africa when the battle was over, belonging to the Air Force I was designated to be parachuted in France so as to form reception groups, establish a liaison by radio between France and Algeria and generally organize the Resistance.

The 21st of October, I was parachuted in the Drôme, where I met another group which had arrived before me. Together we got to work. I stayed there till the end of December.

I was then ordered to go with my radio-man in the Alpes-Maritimes. After some personal investigations I decided to settle in Puget-Théniers.

I found there a number of trustworthy men who had been inspired with the spirit of Resistance by Miss Pell. Together with these men we started work in January 1943. There was no time to rest. We had to receive arms and supplies that had to be hidden till we could deliver them in the towns where it would have been impossible to parachute.[7]

Colonel Bryant Evans, who was in contact with Miss Pell while temporarily in command of the First Airborne Task Force, recalls: "The French referred to her as 'The Girl with the Blond Lock' because I seem to remember that she had a blond streak in her hair. She had been wild in New York and it was said that her family was paying her twenty-five thousand dollars a year to stay out of the country. I also have a recollection that she held the record for the fastest automobile trip between Grasse and Paris.

"Of course, I must say quite emphatically that this is all hearsay on my part. She was a dazzling woman and there were hundreds of stories floating around headquarters about her.

"She had a farm up near Grasse which she left as soon as we got to Nice in order to offer us her services as an interpreter. We later found out that she had been one of the chief executives of the FFI in that region and had been responsible for the storage of all the ammunition and supplies that we and the British had dropped for the Underground before D-Day."[8]

One of the first to avail himself of Isabel Pell's knowledge of the area was Geoffrey Jones. "By a peculiar coincidence," he remembers, "Colonel Robert Thompson, who helped start the Navy League with Theodore Roosevelt, was Isabel's grandfather and was also a classmate of my grandfather at Annapolis. Because he helped bring up my mother, she selected him as my godfather. So we knew all the Pells and what's more, I knew that I could trust anyone okayed by Isabel Pell.

"I had heard that the people up at Puget-Théniers . . . a little town north of Nice up in the mountains . . . adored her. She protected quite a few people who were hiding out from the Gestapo. On one occasion the Nazis raided her farm, and although she had four people down in the cellar at the time, she swore that there was no one there. In my opinion, things like these take more guts than shooting a gun off in battle. I mean it really takes nerve to stand up to a German officer with a squad of soldiers coming in to search your house, and be able to act with such self-assurance that they go away.

"She was one of those strange people who came out of the flapper era. She might have been lifted intact from a page written by F. Scott Fitzgerald. She was quite tall, built huskily, but was rather attractive-looking, wore her hair in a flapper cut . . . you know, bangs in front and a few curls on the side. Quite pleasant with an enormous zesty laugh. She was one of those Americans who never got to speak French very well but whom everyone understood because she was on their wavelength.

"She was a maverick. Never tried to hide her way of life, but she certainly had complete acceptance in Europe. In America we'd consider that she should be severely ignored . . . but in France she was only regarded as, well, eccentric.

"Another thing. You've got to remember that although the French aristocracy has been away from power for many generations, in the small villages they still show great respect for the 'seigneur.' His château might be quite small, but it is still the only one in the area and although he might not have quite enough money to support it, he certainly has the manners and air to go with it.

"Isabel had this kind of bearing and background and she instinctively understood how to treat these people. She used a sort of benevolent intelligence that never got in the way of her sincere liking for these people.

"Before the war, she . . . oh, I don't know how to explain her life unless you say that she just sort of existed. She painted, did some sculpture, raised money for the local orphanage . . . that sort of thing.

"The point I'm making is that she was a loved person and a character because of these different facets in her background. When I knew her she was in her late thirties, wore suits and flat-heeled shoes, had this tremendous drive and didn't make any bones about what she was. She was the big Saint Bernard that comes into your house with muddy feet and romps with your kids and is so damned lovable that all you do is to make yourself a mental promise that before it comes in next time you're going to make sure that her paws are wiped off.

"Isabel was just one of those people who sweep down the road without worrying what the people on the sides are thinking."[9]

« 4 »

Of course, the Germans were not aware that they were waiting for Geoffrey Jones. Their information, although quite accurate as to the time and constituency of the Invasion force, rarely extended to the identity of individual operatives since the round-the-clock pounding by Allied bombers now kept their patrols from sifting through the civilian population with their former vigor.

But the Germans were there and it is a matter of record that they considered Southern France as vital territory.[10] The route northward, the *Route Napoléon,* up the Rhone Valley has always been the principal avenue of entry from the Mediterranean into the heart of France. To defend this lifeline, the German Nineteenth Army had stationed nine divisions along the Mediterranean coast and at strategic points in the interior. Two of these, the 244th and the 242nd Infantry Divisions, were garrisoned at Marseilles and Toulon, which represented excellent defensive positions for the area. In the Cannes-Nice area, the 148th Reserve Division was considered strong enough to secure the area from any enemy movement along the coast. These last three units were at almost full strength and the only question they presented to the German command was their comparative lack of combat experience.

There is no evidence that the German Army offered any

[54]

gentler treatment to some of the people of the Riviera section than they did to the inhabitants of any of the other areas they occupied. For example, one American officer recalled, "After we landed in Southern France, one of our young officers struck up a romance with a girl who had been put into one of their officers' brothels by the Germans. Very much against her will, of course. This had been her introduction to sex. Although this girl seemed to care a great deal for this lieutenant, she would hardly even let him touch her . . . because of this previous experience. Later, when our outfit went up to the Bulge, he got a letter from her that was so passionate it practically melted the snow for yards around. Apparently, she was only able to think of sex in the distance. You sometimes wonder what happens to people like that."[11]

That this was not unusual treatment was underlined in an interview an American correspondent secured on August 15, 1944, with Mme. Emilienne Moreau, a member of the French Underground and a delegate to the French Liberation committee's consultative assembly.

Mme. Moreau was positive that the women of her country hated the Germans even more than their men did. They sabotaged trains, gave information to Allied Intelligence teams, served as liaison agents in the secret distribution of anti-German propaganda, and hid members of the Maquis from the enemy. She remembered one young girl who had bones in her face shattered by a kick from the hobnailed boots of her interrogator when she refused to answer his questions about the Underground. In another case one hundred and fifty-two prisoners were shot by German officers who then retired to a nearby farmyard to eat cherries in the spring sunshine.[12]

Pierre Galante, now editor of *Paris Match*, became a member of Geoffrey Jones's OSS detachment after the Allied landings. Remembering that the occupation grew increasingly brutal towards its end, he described two men being hanged on the main avenue of his village: "They were driven up in separate trucks, a rope around the neck of each. The other end of the rope was thrown over a light pole and secured. Then the order was given for the trucks to drive away. The men were snapped out and strangled. The Germans left them hanging for twenty-four hours as a lesson to the villagers.

"There were many massacres. I also remember them shooting ten or fifteen men in a quarry near my home. Of course, we of the Underground always retaliated. After a while the Germans had to issue orders to their men that no soldier was allowed to walk anywhere by himself and that even pairs of soldiers were not allowed to go anywhere except on the main streets. They were afraid that if a soldier should get out of a truck and walk off the road to relieve himself, we would knock him off. Everyone was doing what he could. The ones that were a little stronger in the stomach than the rest of us naturally did more."[13]

« 5 »

When Captain Jones landed on the Mont de Malay, he found himself without the company of the Frenchman who had preceded him through the opening in the floor of the Sterling bomber.

"I landed on one side of the mountain" he recalls, "and Alain landed on the other. He got hurt rather badly, getting a piece of rock in his ankle bone and another in his knee. When I landed I got bashed up too. Actually, the German patrols were further down, but it looked from the air that they were standing just where we were headed. This was such mountainous territory that the time to worry wasn't when they were in their cars but when they got out of them.

"Since I had jumped second and landed on the other side of the mountain, and no one had come to pick me up, I spent a very uneasy night. I had made the decision not to carry any armament because I felt that if I got caught during the early stages I would have found it easier to bluff through that I was what I was supposed to be.

"You see, I had let my hair get shaggy and grown a moustache to lessen the Anglo-Saxon look. My pose was that I was a mute itinerant French laborer in an old blue suit who, because of his disability, was of no use to the Army and was only good for working the land. I had the proper identification cards, of course . . . so it made sense not to risk carrying a gun.

"I had sewn a penknife inside my pant leg and this was the only weapon I had. However, I've got to admit that when I started to hear footsteps and other sounds that night I really cursed myself for trying to be so goddamned prudent!

"The Maquis picked me up next day and that's when I found out that the Frenchman was badly hurt. He was delirious for the next two days. Although we had some morphine, we had no other medication. Finally, we piled him on a mule and carried him to the Maquis mountain headquarters.

"All of them in that group were Communists, having been trained by the people who came over from Spain. There were maybe a hundred and forty or a hundred and fifty men there out in the middle of nowhere on this mountain. We had a beautiful view because from it you could see all the way from Italy down to Marseilles. You could see the whole coast of Southern France, a lovely view if nothing else.

"The Germans had left these people alone because it was so far away from the road. There was nothing, absolutely nothing else up there. The only way the Germans could have gotten to them would have been by helicopter or using parachute infantry. And then we could have seen them coming long enough in advance to have melted into any one of the caves that pocked the sides of the mountain. So we had good security there just so long as we didn't harass the Germans too much.

"We ate fairly well too. We had goats and periodically we'd send a few men down to the village to get some other food and then it would be picnic time. We could even have a campfire, so long as we made it in one of the small valleys up near the crest.

"These Maquisards were quite impressed with our identities as de Gaulle's delegates. And of course that helped me get their cooperation. One time, after I finally got radio contact, I had Algiers drop us some supplies . . . just to show them that the Great White Father could bring down the parachutes. Unfortunately, however, the villagers got to the supplies before we did and stole half of them.

"Early in my stay, one morning they had a formation to honor me. They all drew themselves up and sang the 'Internationale' and then they sang the 'Marseillaise.' They were really carried away with the idea of being Communists. They called each other 'Comrade' and had a political commissar for each one of their three battalions. But, again, I ought to stress that they had been trained by the veterans of the Spanish Loyalist outfit who had drifted back over the border after that war ended. Later when I took about twenty of them into a small action, and the guns started going off, I looked around and I only had two left! Not that I blame them . . . they really didn't get much military training . . . they seemed to think it was more romantic just to live up there on the mountaintop and call each other 'Comrade.' As a matter of fact, I must admit that I really didn't see too many bona fide Resistance people until after the Allied forces came ashore. Of course it was much different up in the north where a lot of former soldiers and their officers were hiding out. Those boys could fight alongside anyone!

"After about a week one of the fellows was able to get me a radio and I could signal back to Algiers to let them know that we were okay. Well, I finally did get together enough real Resistance people to form an organization. One of our first jobs was to knock out the radar installation in Fayence, which we did, using small mortars.

"We were getting instructions via the BBC. They'd tell us what to do, using all the kinds of melodramatic codes we had set up. It got really exciting when the code came through that the landing was scheduled for the early morning hours of August 15. This was just a few days away so I got my people together to start pulling down those long pointed poles called 'pikes' that had been erected in the open fields as obstacles for the gliders. Actually, this turned out to be an easier job than I had expected. The Germans had used local labor to erect these poles but the Frenchmen, instead of digging holes for them, just stood them upright and piled rocks around them. We knocked over quite a few of them with just a light push.

"It turned out to be quite exhilarating. Although Alain still felt quite badly and I had gotten hurt in one of our small actions, it didn't bother either of us. I guess it's the adrenalin popping through your veins. I've seen a parachutist jump from a plane, take his chute off, wrap it up, walk a hundred yards and then when he's told to stop he finds out he's got a broken leg. It's the adrenalin."[14]

« 6 »

The others who would meet Geoffrey Jones in Southern France had now been assembled into the First Airborne Task Force in Italy.

CHAPTER III

THE TRAINING

Early in July, Frederick — recently promoted to Major General — was relieved from command of the First Special Service Force, and assigned to organize and command the Provisional Airborne Division which comprised the British 2nd Independent Parachute Brigade, the 517th Infantry Regiment, the 551st and the 509th Parachute Infantry Battalions, the 550th Glider Infantry Battalion, the 406th and 463rd Parachute Field Artillery Battalions, the 602nd Glider Pack Howitzer Battalion, and a number of service troops attached from Army elements. All these contingents had to receive airborne training in the limited time available. This force, trained on airfields near Lido di Roma not far from Rome, was transported in 535 C–47's and C–53's, and 465 gliders of the Provisional Troop Carrier Wing, commanded by my old friend Brigadier General P. L. Williams.

We went over all details of the Corps assault plan with Frederick, and from them he developed his plans for the airborne mission which was to be dropped in the Argens Valley near Le Muy to block roads leading toward the beachhead and then to attack the defenses of Fréjus from the rear. The troops were to parachute into three drop zones at first light about 0430 and eliminate resistance before the glider-borne troops were brought in on scheduled flights beginning about 0930.

Frederick's feat in organizing and training this composite force and perfecting the operation within a period of less than one month is one of the remarkable exploits of the war. It was one of the most successful airborne drops.

— LIEUTENANT GENERAL LUCIAN K. TRUSCOTT, JR.[1]

WITHOUT question, the looming Invasion of Southern France was the worst kept secret of World War II. Security violations were so flagrant that, for some time, many believed that it was simply a gigantic hoax: that the loose talk was being deliberately encouraged in order to draw attention from a strike in another area. However, by late July, it became apparent to all that the high command had actually committed beyond recall the participating units to a landing in the Riviera sector.

And the security leaks still continued. A Roman priest, in the first days of August, asked his congregation to pray for the success of the coming attack. The more seasoned war correspondents, aghast at the freedom with which military secrets were being openly discussed on street corners, cafes, hotel lobbies and bars throughout Italy, reported the occurrences to their friends among the higher ranking officers. They were assured that the men responsible would be disciplined or, at the least, cautioned. But the babbling stream continued.

Speculation began to center around the actual date of the Invasion and the number and identification of the troops involved. Several enterprising junior officers, borrowing a technique from the football games back home, created a betting pool around these vital points.

On July 20, Seymour Korman, correspondent for the Chicago *Tribune*, reported standing in a crowd of soldiers and Italian civilians and hearing a Red Cross worker blurt out, "I've got to get to Naples by August first, because I'm going to be in on the Invasion of Southern France a few weeks after that."

Korman also heard a soldier in Naples naming the American divisions which would participate in the attack and his horror was deepened when another in the group continued the narrative by detailing all the warships that would take them there. Korman was shocked by the accuracy of both lists. He knew that they were accurate because earlier, in a supposedly ultra-secret briefing, a select group of correspondents had been given this information by one of the highest ranking American officers who had then gone on to warn them that the disclosure of any of this information would inevitably result in an appreciably higher casualty rate.

Another correspondent purchased a *Guide to Southern France* in a Roman bookshop. The proprietor, noticing that the news-paperman was attempting to mask his purchase by burying it in the file of papers he carried, commented, "You are being more careful than the American officers. They come in and ask for maps of Southern France and talk of Toulon and Cannes."[2]

In all fairness, it would have been an impossible secret to keep, even under the most stringent security precautions. Sustained concentration on a further battle for Italy inevitably would have met the law of diminishing returns[3] after the success of the June 6 Allied landings in Normandy.[4] The machine-like precision with which General Eisenhower sent his men and matériel flowing out of England already had the Channel ports operating on a twenty-four-hour basis and there simply weren't enough ships available to bring additional forces directly into Normandy from North Africa or other areas.[5] All of this indicated an urgent need to almost everyone[6] for another major gateway to the arena and this inescapably meant Marseilles and the other convenient points of entry in Southern France.

The only questions left in the minds of the German commanders were precisely when and where to place their thinned-out forces.[7] Although the fighting in the north had drawn away many of their divisions and almost all of their air power, they were guarding a coast that was favorable to defense. Rocky promontories overlooked the small beaches and the many coastal artillery batteries positioned long ago by the French had been substantially reinforced by the Germans through the addition of some four hundred and fifty heavy and twelve hundred light antiaircraft guns, most of them along the shoreline.[8]

The German command, contemplating their experiences in Africa and Sicily, felt that they could not prevent the Allied landings, so the decision was made to keep their forces mobile enough to reassemble and mount a counterattack against an enemy beachhead, wherever it occurred, in the shortest possible time.[9] Although Generaloberst Johannes Blaskowitz, the commander in chief, southwest, felt that his forces in Southern France were "only static and often immobile combat units,"[10] General Wiese, the man who actually commanded the German Nineteenth Army, told his Allied captors in 1948 that "the troops of the [German] Army were well disciplined and in good order, even in the rear Army area."[11]

But generals are not famous for understating their opposition or overrating their resources when recounting battles. As nearly as can be determined from the vantage point of history, there is no question that Hitler, while insisting that Southern France be defended, had agreed to withdraw a substantial part of the force necessary for its defense. But what was left was well led and capable of inflicting substantial casualties on the invaders while executing an orderly and strategic withdrawal to the main perimeter of strength.

And so the primary assignment of the First Airborne Task Force became to cut communications, isolate units and to raise enough hell behind German lines to disrupt the German plan to race mobile units to wherever the Invasion lance was to be inserted in Southern France.

« 2 »

General Frederick described his initiation into command of the First Airborne Task Force: "After I left the First Special Service Force, I went to the 36th Division, but I was only there two days when I got a radio message to come back to Fifth Army headquarters. They acted very mysterious there and told me to go on to meet General Devers in Algiers.

"When I got there, General Devers said, 'You're going to command the airborne troops in the Invasion of Southern France.' We talked about it for fifteen minutes or so and I finally asked, 'Well, where are the airborne troops?' And he answered, 'So far, you're the only one we have.' "[12]

General Jacob L. Devers qualifies as one of the most overlooked military leaders of World War II. Although he reached four-star rank, his assignments invariably left him on a plateau between the Army commander of successful campaigns and the unit commanders who put together dramatic victories in the field. During this period he was deputy Supreme Allied Commander in the Mediterranean Theater, and later, when given the command of the newly organized Sixth Army Group, he found that his peers were Generals Bradley and Montgomery, two men who seldom lost the unwavering attention of the public.

Nevertheless, Devers had an almost Byzantine ability to assess and motivate the men around him. His maximum use of the talents of the brilliant but difficult French general, de Lattre de Tassigny, and his productive relationships with the always touchy Charles de Gaulle are almost all the evidence needed to indicate that he was a commander with a constant ability to recognize and use whatever would work best in a combat situation. He was indisputably the man who picked General Frederick (who had very little actual experience with airborne operations) to train and lead the First Airborne Task Force although another commander had already been slated for the job.

He recalls, "We promoted Frederick to major general and I brought him back to Rome. Then I picked some officers off my staff who could work with an airborne operation and got a few more from some of the commands in the States. When I brought Frederick back, I also brought in Paul Williams to command the air arm, set them down in a little town outside of Rome towards the sea and married them to this operation. I told Frederick that he could choose one or two men from his First Special Service Force, but since it was going to be used for a specific operation going into the South of France, I preferred that he select his staff from the people we now had available. I wanted him to build his own staff because I've always felt that in order to get an efficient team, you've got to have the rhythm that only comes when everyone has picked his own assistants. This way you can largely eliminate the resistance that arises from adverse personalities. You're making sure that you have people willing to give in when the situation demands that the other fellow should win.

"I remember when I told Frederick he was to be commander of this operation, he thought for a while and then turned to me and said, 'General, I think you think that I'm a paratrooper . . .

that I've jumped out of quite a few airplanes.' I said, 'No, Frederick, I have no idea that you've ever jumped out of *any* airplane . . . but I know that you sure as hell are going into Southern France by air, whether it's by glider or by jumping . . . and that's what your men are going to do, too!' "[13]

John Guthrie as Operations Officer of the Seventh Army was one of the principal planners of the Invasion. He described the assembly of the Task Force's staff by saying, "One of the first things I remember Frederick doing was to get rid of the chief of staff we had picked for him, a man named DeGarve. DeGarve was a good man, but Frederick, I'm sure, had the feeling, 'Well, DeGarve and some of these others are nice guys but they've never had combat experience and I have, and what's more, I want the same kind of people around me.'

"I might add that practically the whole Seventh Army staff was in the same situation as DeGarve. We didn't have any experience in this sort of thing either. And it wasn't easy dealing with guys like Truscott at a briefing and seeing in their eyes the feeling of 'what the hell do you squirts know about all this, anyway?' Believe me, it was damned painful. Frederick was this way, too.

"Well, anyway, DeGarve ended up as an 'orphan.' The general who had picked him to help him run the operation wasn't brought over, which is sometimes the way the dice rolls. Frederick decided to bring in Ken Wickham who had been his chief of staff in the First Special Service Force. Wickham was Frederick's exact opposite: the methodical, conservative kind of a guy who keeps the show on the road.[14] And, what's more, he knew Frederick intimately.

"As I say, Frederick was not without temperament either. He sort of gave us a hard time on occasion . . . nothing very serious, of course, but he was unquestionably a difficult man to control. But everyone was for him. Because of what he had done in Italy, they felt he was the ideal man for the job."[15]

The recollection of Michael M. Isenberg who, as a major became Provost Marshal of the First Airborne Task Force, furnishes a more specific illustration of the mechanics used in selecting the staff. "While I was in North Africa," he recalls, "I was told that I was one of a small group who had been earmarked for the Force. When we got to Italy, it became clear to us that General Frederick was favored by the Army as no other general had been favored before in that Theater. He had been permitted to select the major portion of his staff which was highly unusual. He apparently had screened an enormous number of individual records in order to get the officers he considered most competent for each staff position. As a result, he felt sure that he had the best available man for each job. This was, as I say, quite unusual because in most cases at that time, the staff for a particular unit was almost invariably chosen for the commander by higher headquarters."[16]

It turned out that there was much wisdom in placing so much stress on the careful selection of the staff. It took something approaching an administrative miracle to translate the restless urgings of a firebrand like Frederick into a smooth harnessing of the wildly disparate groups that became the First Airborne Task Force.

There are few senior officers who would not instinctively review their command abilities at being told: "You have one month to consolidate, train and lead into the largest airborne operation of the war the 9732 officers and men of the following units:

2nd Independent Parachute Brigade (British), with the 2nd Chemical Battalion attached.

The 517th Regimental Combat Team composed of 517th Parachute Regiment, 460th Parachute Field Artillery Battalion, 596th Parachute Engineer Company, attached: Company D 83rd Chemical Battalion, and Antitank Company, 442nd Infantry Regiment.

509th Parachute Infantry Battalion and 463rd Parachute Field Artillery Battalion (Combat Team).

550th Airborne Infantry Battalion with one platoon of the 887th Engineer Company attached.

551st Parachute Infantry Battalion with one platoon of the 887th Engineer Company attached.

602nd Pack Howitzer Field Artillery Battalion.

"Later," the directive might have continued, "will be added the First Special Service Force and a group of Civil Affairs specialists to help you administer the activities of all the people of all the nations who have gathered along the Riviera."

« 3 »

The Force was activated on July 11 and by July 15 almost all of the units plus the general staff ordered by General Frederick had assembled. Two days later, he moved his headquarters to the Lido di Roma airfield outside of Rome.[17] Within another week the tactical plan for the Force was approved[18] and the unit, under the code name RUGBY,[19] was incorporated into the master plan of attack which bore the name Operation DRAGOON.[20]

Many official descriptions exist in the archives which explain how RUGBY's mission evolved, but Colonel Bryant Evans, the artillery commander under Frederick, needs far less space and is infinitely more graphic when he says: "Seventh Army headquarters planned this airborne task force invasion, but where they got their tactics and techniques, God only knows. They had us dropping in small groups all over the South of France.

"One of the main principles of airborne combat is to drop en masse, not fritter away your forces by separating them. Put one big glob in one place. So, after we demurred, the search went on for a big glob in one place . . . one place to put the whole outfit.

"If you look at a map of Southern France, you'll see that the town of Le Muy is in a little valley about fifteen miles inland from the coastal town of Fréjus. It's a center that controls all the roads from the north, east and west leading to the coast. So that was the deal: block those roads and you had the Germans so that they could not reinforce at the beaches nor could the beach troops get out because our force would be in between them. This was so obvious after it was pointed out that the plan was changed immediately. We would drop on Le Muy."[21]

General Guthrie offered the conclusion that much of the revised plan was the work of Colonel Yarborough: "We got him from Rome down to Naples [where Seventh Army headquarters was located] in order to work it out with us. Then, in effect, Yarborough presented it to Frederick whom he knew quite well. With some very minor changes, Frederick bought it because it not only fitted in with his own concepts, he also had considerable confidence in Yarborough."[22]

In a description supplied by the writer of a military monograph who had chosen the activities of RUGBY Force as a subject, "General Frederick [now] had the gargantuan task of making his composite group into a close-knit fighting force within a month's time. Before 15 July 44, all his assigned units had been operating as separate forces, and in some instances had not had airborne training."[23]

But since his shaping of the Devil's Brigade, crash training programs no longer had a capacity to induce self-doubt in Bob Frederick. Using an area near Rome placed at his disposal, he began the twin jobs of merging the airborne and troop carrier units into a unified command which could rehearse the actual Invasion and, at the same time, setting his staff to work on the final plans for the airborne assault.[24]

A substantial part of the Force was scheduled to go in by glider, a form of transportation which inspired such distaste that more than a few officers were promptly sent back to replacement depots. The rest attended a newly established glider school where they learned to load and lash their equipment in place. Many of the casualties that the Force subsequently took were due to a failure to properly absorb this instruction.

Each regimental and battalion command post set up its own war room, where sand tables duplicating the rocky terrain of Southern France were set up. Then, tactical exercises were scheduled and missions similar to those expected in combat were executed.

By August 10, all officers had been given the complete plans and every unit down to squad level had begun briefings on their actual mission. The men were informed that the Nineteenth German Army had nine divisions in the area. Intelligence estimates (many of them smuggled out of France by the Resistance units under Geoffrey Jones) indicated that in the Le Muy area, the German forces to be expected were: 1000 Officer Candidates of the Antiaircraft School, 500 Labor Troops, one battalion of Infantry, one Antitank Battalion, one Armored Tank Battalion and several Assault Gun Units.

HEADQUARTERS
PROVISIONAL TROOP CARRIER
AIR DIVISION
·U.S. ARMY AIR FORCES

FIELD ORDER
NO. 1

FOR OPERATION
DRAGOON

7 AUGUST 1944

REG. NO. 60
COPY NO. 40

TS-358

The cover of the actual plan which contained the orders for the Invasion of Southern France

Forces like these, plus the German divisions in the area, indicated another problem that might not have occurred to a group less confident than Frederick and his men: with so many of the enemy available, the odds seemed strong to the Task Force that the number they would capture could grow to unwieldy proportions. So the Provost Marshal, Major Isenberg, was sent out on a search mission.

"I had no trained military policemen except for a small cadre," Isenberg remembers, "so just before our takeoff into Southern France, General Frederick asked me to pick up some more men at the replacement depots in the area. Up until that point I had always felt that they would furnish me with regularly trained military police . . . but now I just had to go out and interrogate men, mostly paratroopers, who were waiting for assignments.

"I picked up about fifty or sixty in this way and then faced the job of making military policemen out of them in a few weeks. It was real tough, but as it turned out, they were certainly needed. All of them. During the first few days after our drop the Force captured great numbers of prisoners, and we had to take care of these as well as do the other jobs generally assigned to MP's, like regulating traffic and guiding vehicles to command and supply depots."[25]

By this time, the enlisted men were almost completely conversant with every detail of the operation except the exact date, and this was supplied by someone definitely not a part of the organization.

"We knew what we were rehearsing," Sergeant Virgil L. West remembers, "the only thing we didn't know was *when*. But once when we went out on a practice mission wearing grease paint like we would in combat, we came back to our bivouac area through a built-up portion of Rome. This was unusual because most of the times we stayed on the back roads and out of public view.

"That evening we heard Axis Sally, the gal who broadcast each night from Berlin, commenting over the radio about the men of the 517th practicing their mission for Southern France and telling us that we needn't worry about it being dark over there before the dawn on the 15th because they would have it lighted up for us. So, when we actually did board the planes on the evening of the 14th, this is one of the things that came to mind."[26]

There was one other problem that seemed to bother the enlisted men during the pre-drop period: the paratrooper "jump boots" that appeared so important to Philip DiStanislao during his training days back in the States. Lieutenant Dick Spencer described the way it was solved by a few of them: "Some of the men didn't have jump boots and that figured to make a paratrooper pretty mad . . . especially when Mark Clark [commanding general of the Fifth Army in Italy] had his MP's wearing them on every street corner in Rome. That caused quite a bit of static on the enlisted man's level and, as a second lieutenant, I heard most of it. They used to tell me that it wasn't fair to make them jump in these combat boots that had buckles on the side that could catch on almost anything . . . you know, they invented every reason in the world why they should get the high-laced boots instead of the shorter, standard-issue combat boots.

"Finally one of them, a corporal, came to me one day and said, 'Lieutenant, I can get jump boots for all the men in the platoon if you get me a pass into Rome.' I answered, 'I can get you the pass, but I really don't want to hear about whatever you're going to do once you get there. That's strictly between you and Rome.'

"I got passes for several of them who went into Rome and next morning everyone in the platoon had jump boots. Of course, I finally learned what happened: the boys went around the city together until they came across an MP who looked like he had the right size feet. They'd ask him directions and everything while they checked to make sure the foot size was right. If it was, they would keep talking to him while one of them would amble around and hit him behind the head with a bar of soap wrapped in a sweat sock. This didn't break any bones, but it would put him to sleep for a while. In every case they left the guy with a new pair of combat boots, after they took his jump boots away.

"I guess this kind of burned the high brass up because they had quite an investigation going on afterwards. As a matter of fact, they actually knew the names of some of the men involved. I found this out after the war when I met the colonel who had been in charge of the investigation. He told me that the only thing that saved our outfit was that it jumped into combat right then and that there was more trouble waiting for us in Italy than we ever found in France!"[27]

« 4 »

His insurance and real estate operations in Miami, Florida, have made Duffield W. Matson, Jr., a millionaire,[28] but in 1944 Duff Matson was apparently a bad egg whom only a Robert Frederick would trust. The story of how he came to join the First Airborne Task Force illustrates one of Frederick's colorful ways of exercising command:

"I had already been court-martialed several times," Matson says, "but the last one, the one that led to my getting into the Task Force, resulted from a fight with an MP lieutenant. I had had paratrooper training in the States and was stationed in Sicily. One night, this lieutenant found several of us in a bar after curfew and told us to go back to our barracks. But we didn't, we went to a whorehouse instead. When the man who owned it opened the door, he saw we were drunk and he tried to stop us. But we hit him in the face and went into the girls' quarters and proceeded to attempt to do business there which, for some reason, seemed to be against their wishes.

"Right at that moment, damned if this MP lieutenant who was over six foot tall, didn't come in with a forty-five pistol in his hand. I could see that he was an inexperienced combat man by the way he was waving it, so I knew I could hit him and get away with it before he did anything, which I did and he stretched out on the floor. But I underestimated him because as we stepped over him on our way out, we were met by five MP's that he had stationed outside. These fellows looked like they knew how to use their guns and they said, 'You can stop or you can continue running.' So I said, 'Well, I think I'll stop.'

"So they put us in this jail in Trapani. Our cell had a steel door and a little window vent about ten foot up off the ground. Because I was still drunk, I told the rest of the fellows, 'In the Boy Scouts I learned how to build a fire without paper; if anyone has still got a knife I'll show you how.'

"One of them offered me a knife he had hanging on a chain dangling around his neck down under his shirt and I whittled off some splinters which I built into a pyramid and set fire. Then we broke up the rest of the benches and pretty soon we had a real nice fire going against the door which, in our alcoholic state, we had all overlooked that it was made of steel. But the smoke had trouble getting through the little window vent in the wall and it got so horrible that we were beginning to suffocate, so I suggested something that seemed quite logical to me at the moment. 'Let's piss on it,' I said.

"This didn't put out the fire but it did result in such a stench that pretty soon we were all gagging. One guy vomited and it wasn't long before the rest of us followed suit. And they didn't let us out all night. They kept us there in this little cell until late next day when they took us out for a court-martial and I guess this is the first time anyone ever went to their trial with a feeling of relief!

"Actually, in a sense, I was quite innocent. As I explained to a parachute officer that came in to see me, 'Captain, you know how they are treating paratroopers in this area. It's a rigged up charge and, besides, the guy I hit was only a leg soldier.'

"Well, this officer got me off pretty light, I think maybe it was a year, which isn't bad for hitting an officer.

"But once in the stockade, it didn't take long for me to figure the hell with it and another fellow and I escaped. This wasn't difficult since I wasn't considered a violent prisoner at that time. As a matter of fact, some of the people there, including a few of the guards, looked on me as a liberator because I had hit an MP lieutenant.

"The first thing we did after getting out was to stuff a barracks bag full of the socks, underwear, towels, blankets and things like that that belonged to my friends. We knew they would understand. In those days you got enough money on the black market for a pair of dirty socks to stay drunk for a day.

"We took off for some mountain that had on it the highest

[*78*]

village in Sicily. It's so high that no cars could get to it and that's why we went there. We got about two hundred dollars on the black market for our barracks bag load and we went on to Palermo where we lived like kings in a hotel for quite a while.

"Meanwhile, the MP's were looking for us all over. But no one ever bothered us in Palermo. You see, we stayed in uniform, which kept us from being deserters, and we had a whole stack of blank passes which we made out to ourselves. As a matter of fact, we spent quite a few nights drinking with some of the MP's who were looking for us. 'We're going to get those paratrooping sons of bitches,' they would tell us and we always agreed that they would.

"Next we went to Taormina, which is about ninety miles north of Palermo. Here I developed into a great procurer of hand grenades from various places. We'd sell these to the fishermen for a few dollars apiece and the fishermen would drop them in the sea where they would go off and stun all the fish around. Then the fishermen would scoop in whole netfuls at a time.

"Things went so well that I moved to the Taormina Hotel where I hired the local bandmaster to teach me Sicilian. I figured that if I was going to make all this money on the black market, I wanted to know how to count it in their language.

"Finally, we thought we'd better go back since there was a war going on and we'd been having a good vacation for about a month. So I went back and an MP sergeant said, 'Why you son of a bitch, we're really going to give it to you this time. You wait right here while we get a truck. But this time you'll get ten years!'

"While they were over at the motor pool, I said to my friend, 'I think maybe we ought to get another barracks bag full of stuff.'

Which we did, including the belongings of the sergeant who had threatened us, and we took off again. We figured that if they were going to jail us for ten years, the least we could do is take a longer vacation.

"But after a couple more weeks, I finally figured that it would be better to go back and take what was coming to me. So I went back and this time they didn't say, 'Wait here.' They said, 'Come with us.'

"I tried to defend myself at the court-martial by saying, 'Look, gentlemen, you didn't catch me, I came back of my own will. If I hadn't wanted to come back, I could still be living up in the mountains with my Sicilian friends because I've got plenty of them.'

"No matter, I got a long sentence in the stockade outside of Rome near Lido di Roma. This place was for the tough cookies. I was told, 'If you stick your nose out of the door here, we blow it off! You're here only to exist . . . not to live, merely to exist.' They used to get us up at 4:30 in the morning, work all the daylight hours, and sleep in pup tents in the mud and the rain. It was just plain terrible.

"I was in there for a few months when, one day, some men from Frederick's headquarters came down. One of them was named Leonard Cheek, an Apache Indian, who gave the head of the stockade a receipt for me and said that Frederick's people wanted me. And they took me, with a Thompson submachine gun in my back, to the Task Force headquarters. At that moment I had no idea what it was all about. I knew no one with Frederick, who was a legend among combat men even at that time.

"So we rode in a jeep to the Intelligence Section at headquarters. Captain Pysienski, who was in charge, met me. I found out that he had gone through the records, saw that I had a high IQ, a decent family background and had been to college, and was therefore good potential for the G–2 section of the First Airborne Task Force.

"Pysienski said, 'You have a choice: you can stay in that stockade or you can come with Frederick.' And, of course, I immediately agreed that I wanted to be with Frederick. And the men dropped their guns and I was free. At this, he brought me inside and introduced me to everyone, saying, 'Here's Matson. He has a wealth of talent. He's with us now.'

"Everything was wiped off and no one pointed a machine gun at my stomach any more.

"I have no idea why Frederick sent for me other than the fact that he had taken men out of a stockade before and had been very successful with them. I never heard of him ever having a failure with this kind of man and he certainly didn't with me because I never had another court-martial. I made a good record in the Intelligence Section where, for the first time in my Army career, I was allowed responsibility. As a matter of fact, later I was recommended for a commission.

"Among my other duties I was assigned to clean Frederick's office, which isn't as menial as it sounds. One of the most stringent rules in headquarters was that every scrap of paper that Frederick wrote on or received should be destroyed after he had discarded it. Frankly, I was very proud of the job: coming from a stockade background, to be entrusted with this duty, because obviously anyone given this job just had to be considered reliable.

"Many evenings he'd be sitting there alone when I walked in and he'd chat with me. Oh, I don't mean a family get-together kind of talk, don't misunderstand; Frederick was never one for aimless conversation, but he'd say just a few words that showed he was interested in me as a man.

"To be honest, this kind of treatment was a godsend at this particular point of my life. Just before they took me out of the stockade I had made up my mind to bust out come hell or high water. I didn't give a damn if I had to shoot anyone or if anyone shot me, but I was going to get out. So Frederick's willingness to take me changed my whole life.

"It was as if someone had come along with a wand and made everything fine. One week I was living like a pig in the mud and the next week I was a member of an elite group, completely trusted with a gun and everything else.

"Finally, when it came time to jump, I had apparently communicated this feeling to the people around me. The night before, Captain Pysienski came up and told me that I was going in on the same plane with Frederick and that I would act as a sort of bodyguard for him. Pysienski said, 'Your only duty is to see that Frederick lives, that's all you have to do, *make sure he lives.*'

"I would have done that, no matter what."[29]

« 5 »

Late in the afternoon of August 14, the order came to assume battle readiness. The men of the Force climbed into their jump suits, put on their netted steel helmets and battle webbing. Pistols appeared and long knives of all descriptions were strapped onto hips and legs. Filing by companies, the troopers made their way over to the service area where they were sprayed into anonymity with camouflage paint.

The next step came almost immediately. A convoy of trucks

pulled up to take them to the various dispersal airfields scattered along the west side of Italy's boot.

Upon arrival, the necessary last-minute preparations were initiated: chutes were fitted; equipment bundles were packed and checked; ammunition and emergency rations were issued. Every paratrooper received a set of paper scraps upon which, imprinted in French, were such disquieting phrases as: "I am an American parachutist, I am wounded"; "Where is the enemy, how many of them are there?"

Then came takeoff time. The first wave left for the coast of France at approximately 3:00 A.M. on the 15th of August.

CHAPTER IV

THE DROP

The pilot of my plane had studied his sand tables just as we had studied ours. Before we took off, he even mentioned this grape orchard in which we were to land, seemed to know it intimately. This was good, because this thing was supposed to go like clockwork: so many minutes to land, assemble and get off the drop zone because next they would be dropping heavy equipment . . . and if any of the chutes had failed to open, you know, you wouldn't want a mortar baseplate coming down on your head. So, as we talked this over with the pilot, he said, "Now you remember there's a little bitty shack down there on that sand table right in the grape orchard, and I'm gonna drop you right on that shack."

And, of course, since I parachuted, I never got to tell him that he missed it by twenty-two miles.

— LIEUTENANT RICHARD SPENCER[1]

« 1 »

THE German defenders had been feinted out of position by many of the Allied ploys. They believed, until the last moment, that there was a strong possibility that the invading force was heading for Genoa.[2] A token drop of six hundred dummy parachutists northwest of Toulon[3] offered them another temptation to disperse their admittedly slender reserves. The invitation was promptly accepted and on August 16, Berlin newspapers carried graphic accounts of the fight in which the phantom force was beaten off.[4]

But nowhere did the Germans misread their situation so completely as in their estimate of the help they could expect from the French. Almost every German general, in statements given to Allied captors after the war,[5] stresses two points: that the huge holes in their supply and communication lines torn out by unchallenged enemy air power made the job assigned them by Hitler an impossible one; and that the unbelievably perfidious French failed to give them the help that they had been promised.

These assertions indicate that a sense of reality was frequently missing from their preparations, executions and explanations. They delayed their plans to destroy major supply dumps[6] until it was too late, they failed to pull back to a workable defense perimeter until sizable elements of their Army were engulfed and destroyed,[7] even losing a corps headquarters complete with commanding general in the process; and, as for the French help, it was obvious that they never came close to understanding that a Frenchman's only loyalty is to his country, a feeling inevitably projected to a personal dimension by almost every Frenchman.

There is no question that the overwhelming majority of the French population refrained from Resistance activities during the occupation by German troops. Utterly pragmatic, most of them refused to do anything that could affect the well-being of their families or themselves so long as they were convinced that the gestures would be largely quixotic. But when the Allied armies appeared in strength, they saw no inconsistency in joining what was obviously going to open a quick route back to prewar normalcy.

If this historical truth is kept in mind, the remarks made by Generalmajor Ludwig Bieringer in 1947 further illuminate the German view of the pre-Invasion scene:

I should like to mention that fighting the French Resistance Movement, so far as it necessitated commitment of military forces, as in the case of sabotage, raids and attacks, belonged entirely to the mission of [our] Corps. For this purpose, the Corps Hq had assembled a special company which had the mission of fighting against the Resistance Movement, [but] it was engaged on only a few occasions. Perhaps its presence sufficed to suppress the activity of the Resistance Movement. . . .

In the last week of May, I succeeded in making an extensive patrol trip into the rear area of the department [which] did not reveal any activity or presence of armed Maquis bands. The same results were attained by other patrol trips, which were carried out at regular intervals. . . .

In reality, during the Invasion by the Seventh U.S. Army . . . none of [the] measures planned for the event of an invasion were put into effect. The inhabitants remained in their lodgings, wel-

comed their "Liberators" with shouts of joy and [treated] the German soldiers in American custody led away before their eyes, with
scornful laughs, fits of rage and acts of violence. On my drive into
captivity on 17 August 1944, to the headquarters of the Seventh
U.S. Army, I was protected by the commander of the First Airborne
Task Force and two American soldiers from being bodily injured
by bloodthirsty Frenchmen.

During the weeks prior to the Invasion, the entire attitude of the
French police . . . disclosed passive resistance. Contrary to the stip-
ulation of the terms of Armistice concluded between Germany and
France in June, 1940, the French policemen did not even meet their
obligation to greet German officers and functionaries. Repeated
representatives to Prefects* produced but short-lived effects. . . .

The attitude of the civil population toward the French Militia was
neutral, so no conflicts were observed. Likewise, the inhabitants of
the Var Department never showed a hostile attitude toward the
German occupying troops. The friendly attitude shown toward German officers and soldiers during the first months of the Occupation
had changed into a passive reservedness. One of the reasons for this
change was the permanent anxiety of the inhabitants of being
watched by the Underground Movement and being openly branded
as *Collaborateur*. Open clashes or conflicts of any kind between German military personnel and French civilians had never occurred.
. . . Up to the very last time prior to my capture, I was often riding
in my car, distinctly marked by a general's flag, through the Department and was never molested. The Command Hq at Draguignan,
the District Command Hq at Toulon, and the outlying stations were
always frequented by French civilians, who full of confidence, applied to our authorities, concerning their wishes, anxieties and complaints, asking for assistance and help from the FK,† and its sub-

---

* The chief administrative officer of the French political division known as a
department. France is separated into departments as America is divided into states.
† District Command.

[*89*]

ordinated offices. It was not necessary to assign Security Guards to the entrances of the Hq Buildings or the quarters of the District Commander up until the day of the Invasion. . . .

Until the very day of the Invasion, a certain cooperation could be observed on the part of the population in the Var Department. Employees could be obtained for internal work as artisans, kitchen personnel, drivers, etc., as well as men for outside work. Thousands of Frenchmen were placed at the disposal of the Infantry Battalions in order to carry out all kinds of earthwork in fortnightly shifts. They were used in the rear area for building anti-landing obstacles, dugouts for riflemen and tank traps, on either side of the main communication road under the supervision of the French administrative center. Except for a certain part of the population, which, as a principle, refused any collaboration, the majority of Frenchmen were willing to cooperate, primarily for the reason that once a day, besides a fixed pay, they received a hot meal, which in those days of extreme scarcity of food undoubtedly was the determining factor, never failing in its purpose.[8]

Only a slight objectivity is needed to supply the missing dimension in General Bieringer's report: the Germans mistook French cooperation for agreement and misread perfidy for the surprising degree of resistance on August 15. But the inhabitants were neither passive nor perfidious. They were simply being Frenchmen. Insensitivity to this point was almost as serious a handicap to German plans for the defense of Southern France as the missing or inaccessible stores of men and matériel.

The Operations and Intelligence Sections at Seventh Army headquarters had neither discounted, dismissed, nor relied too heavily on the part that the French would play in the Invasion.

They had correctly estimated the number of armed and unarmed members of the FFI available to render active service to the Allied forces[9] and then, just as accurately, gauged the quality of the help that would be offered. The Frenchmen digging the anti-tank obstacles and dugouts, whom General Bieringer thought to be only interested in the hot meal ladled out to them each day by the Germans, were the originating source of the rich stream of intelligence reports that units like the one captained by Geoffrey Jones sent back to the Allied planning groups on a daily and, sometimes hourly, basis.

The beaches of Southern France became as familiar to the planners as those back home, not through estimates, but by actual photographs. Admiral Samuel E. Morison described the process by observing:

Over the shoulders of a smiling couple in bathing suits taking the sun on the Île de Porquerolles, one observes a pier suitable for tying up PT boats. The man who snapped Mademoiselle standing on the ramparts of an old fort inadvertently chose a background which helped an Intelligence officer to make a panoramic sketch of that part of the coast. . . .[10]

The responsible clarity of the intelligence factor, combined with the ability of General Frederick and his staff to fashion a smooth unit out of dissimilar sources, insured the success of the drop by the First Airborne Task Force. The 509th Battalion Combat Team dropped into France at 4:30 in the morning of August 15. Five minutes later, the 517th Regimental Combat Team parachuted into its zone and the British 2nd Independent Parachute Brigade followed thirty-five minutes later. As the day dawned the first glider elements began to arrive. They were

First Airborne Task Force paratroopers making their Invasion jump near La Motte, France on D-Day. (Signal Corps Photo)

followed by other serials making precisely spaced appearances until nightfall.

By 6:00 P.M. almost all of the Force elements were in contact with each other and a functioning command post had been set up. By the end of D-Day the villages of Le Mitan, La Motte, Clastron and Les Serres had been occupied and a protective screen had been established over the road net connecting the Invasion coast with the interior.

On the charts of the planners in Seventh Army headquarters, this all appeared as a nicely engineered mechanical performance.

But this is only the way it appears on the charts of the planners or in the pages of history. These were ten thousand men of flesh and blood, the representatives of ten thousand families, each of whom had varying quotas of doubt and insecurity, curiosity and bravery.

Some of the men, plunging down toward the heavy fog which covered the area, thought they were going into the sea and grew panicky at the recollection of the weight of the equipment they were carrying and the difficulty that could be involved in struggling free of it.

Innumerable investigating officers and groups have never produced an answer to why Colonel Bryant Evans's injunction that a parachute force should be "dropped in one big glob" was ignored, and why some parachutists or glider troops landed as much as thirty miles from their targets.[11]

The reactions of just one of the thousands of young men, reconstructed from notes made at the time, are enough to illustrate that the tally of results kept at a headquarters are quite often abridgements of original copies written in sweat and blood.

« 2 »

Terrell E. Stewart, of the 509th, graduated from a Columbus, Georgia, high school in January 1943. A few weeks later he was in the Army and was busy filling out his application for paratroop duty. Within approximately thirteen more months, he had been sent overseas and was wounded while assaulting an enemy objective on the Anzio beachhead and, after six more months, had recovered and was taking off in the dark hours of the early morning of August 15 for his sixth jump from a C–47.

A literate and sensitive man, his evocation of the flight and the jump is a synthesis of what almost every member of the Task Force must have felt: "We had not been in our plane long before the motors turned on. They warmed up for a while, the roar making conversation almost impossible. The plane finally began to move, taxied slowly down the field, turned, hesitated a moment, then charged down the runway, gathering speed — and suddenly we were airborne. The crew chief came back and replaced the door, and this shut out some of the roar. We were told we could smoke until further notice and also grab some sleep if we felt like it. I soon saw glowing cigarette butts describing patterns across from me. There was little conversation now. Each man was alone with his thoughts.

"The steady droning of the plane's motors was lulling to a degree. But there was that in each one of us which could not be lulled. Each mind must have been filled, at one moment or another, with lively speculation about the coming events: What kind of a reception would we get? Would we be permitted time to organize? Would we be dropped where we were supposed to be dropped? Mistakes had been made before now. I had heard that during the Avellino jump, some of the men had been dropped in a German tank park. So there were imponderables, and it was not easy to consider them dispassionately.

"Once or twice I looked out the windows and could see the dark shapes of other C–47's flying nearby. I couldn't see anything below. Our plane seemed to sway gently on its cushion of air, and to hit air pockets occasionally, when it would drop ever so slightly. I had a touch of anxiety early in the flight as I briefly considered what we might encounter on the ground. But I quickly realized that such thoughts were not good for me. I temporarily made my mind a sort of kaleidoscope in which it was allowed to rest on no one subject at all for any length of time. Eventually I grew rather philosophical and fatalistic. There was nothing I could do about events, I told myself; I would just have to accept them, whatever character they might assume.

"Once during the flight, 'Blackie' asked, 'How're you doing, Stewie?' 'Okay,' I said. What else could I say?

"At last the crew chief came back and said, 'Cigarettes out!' This meant we were nearing the coast! A thrill shot through me. It wouldn't be long now! We began making last-minute adjustments. Straps of the parachute harness which had been left unhooked for comfort during the flight were now hooked. The crew chief removed the door, and the roar of the plane's motors became more audible.

"The procedure in all the planes was basically the same. I think something like this took place: the crew chief reappeared and said, 'Five minutes to go!' We sat expectantly on the edge of our bucket seats, our snap fasteners in our left hands, ready to rise on command and connect these to the anchor cable running the length of the ship above us. We knew Lieutenant Ruyffelaere was waiting for the small red light next to the door to come on.

"It came on and he shouted, 'Stand up and hook up!' We rose. There was a shuffling of boots and a series of rapid metallic clicks as the snap fasteners on the ends of our static lines closed on the anchor cable. We stood in a tight file, each man crowded closely front and rear, maintaining his balance by his left hand on the anchored static line. There was, I noticed, no cut-and-dried procedure such as had always taken place at Benning. We knew what we were supposed to do — examine as well as we could the chute of the man in front of us to see that there was nothing wrong with it as far as the eye could tell and to see that his static line was securely anchored.

"Lieutenant Ruyffelaere placed himself in jump position at the door. I felt the pressure in front of me ease as the next three men moved up. I followed them and we became a tight little bunch at the door. Since I was fourth man, I was easily in a position now to see out. As it was night I didn't experience the somewhat breathless sensation of height which the sight of the sunlit ground often gave me. I saw that we were following the coastline. The completely black land contrasted with the lighter sea. We flew over small islands. All the land seemed wooded; I couldn't distinguish any buildings at all. Upon the shores of the islands and the mainland beat a lazy surf. The billows were remarkably luminous, seeming almost phosphorescent in the moonlight. As I now watched the surf rolling in far below us, I marveled at the exaggerated slowness with which it seemed to move, and I reflected that distance must somehow create such an illusion.

"We were all, I'm sure, keyed to a high pitch of excitement.

The moment of moments was fast approaching. I decided I mustn't let my mind entertain another vagrant thought. I kept it filled with just one idea: 'When the green light comes on — go, *go, GO!*' Suddenly the red light went out. A brief pause, no light at all. Then — green!

"Lieutenant Ruyffelaere disappeared. The rest of us were instantly galvanized into action. Lieutenant Ruyffelaere's place was quickly taken by the little medical captain. My mind was a blur. Go! Go! I felt the pressure in front of me ease as Hall moved up; the medical captain had jumped. I slid my snap fastener down the cable, released my hold on it and faced the open doorway. Hall's form filled it briefly. Then he was gone. Hardly daring to think, just pure movement, I took Hall's place in the doorway, paused momentarily, my hands on the sides of the doorway — and jumped.

"I tried to follow prescribed body procedure learned at Benning, made an effort at a quarter turn to the left as I went out the door, bowed my head, clasped my reserve chute with both hands, and tried to keep my feet together. The instructions learned at Benning, and followed there on every jump, still had a strong hold on me. The propeller blast caught me rudely, and gave me the violent familiar push rearwards. I dropped downwards, as if in a funnel of air, my body seeming to incline now left, now right.

"Suddenly I was jerked up sharply — *very* sharply. My chute had opened. I was suspended peacefully in the night air. For a moment, so violent was the shock of the chute opening, I saw a small galaxy of spitting lights around me. I thought, 'This is known as "seeing stars." ' I had never had such an experience, though I had seen it depicted in comic strips often enough. The lights gradually faded.

"I could still hear the drone of the planes, but growing fainter. I looked around. On both sides of me chutes were drifting softly downward, as if in a kind of dream world. The chutes were companionship. I was glad they were there. As the plane drone finally died, we were engulfed by complete silence.

"I looked below. At first I could see nothing, and for several seconds continued to see nothing. I accepted this as normal and reflected that the ground would show up eventually. Then, as I continued to fall, a dull whitish expanse began slowly spreading below me. It grew larger and larger as my chute descended. 'What is it?' I wondered. I wasn't disturbed, just curious. The whitish mass gradually expanded to such a degree that I was able to see that it had no density to speak of; it looked like a kind of vapor. Then suddenly I knew what it was — a cloud! We had jumped above the clouds. Gently the friendly mass received me. I was encompassed by a dull, damp whiteness, surrounded by a pleasant glow as from subdued fluorescent lighting. Refreshing moisture caressed my cheeks. Innumerable tiny crystals seemed to break against my skin.

"My buddies, of course, likewise passed through this cloud. But the effect of the cloud's first appearance produced on some of them a terrifying effect. Some of them later told me they immediately took the cloud for open water. A deadly fear of drowning seized them. They began frantically divesting themselves of every disposable item of equipment — the reserve chute went first. Such a frightening thought had not occurred to me. I'm certainly glad it didn't. What I took to be a cloud was, of course, the heavy fog or mist which Jacques Robichon [the author] often mentions — *brouillard*.

"The passage through the cloud was swift. When I emerged from it, I saw no more chutes. Now I was truly alone. But the other men, I knew, were still somewhere near and I would meet them on the ground. I kept my eyes glued below. It must be nearly touchdown time — this long chute drop couldn't last forever. Out of the darkness under me details began to form a coherent picture. I saw I was landing in the countryside. Good — no city buildings. A cultivated field lay below. Good — no trees with tearing branches. I could see everything extremely well. There was a small farmhouse and an outbuilding. At first I was confident I would miss the farmhouse. Then, as I continued to descend, I seemed to be headed straight for it, and my mind struggled vigorously against the idea. Then, happily, the house seemed to move out of the way, almost as if of its own accord.

"Now I was rapidly coming in. I hadn't realized how fast I was falling as long as there was no close ground to judge by. But I was falling fast. I tried to relax and keep my feet together. I plummeted in, and hit — *hard!* The impact threw me off my feet. I had expected the landing to be rather rough, as many are. But it was not unusually so. I wasn't stunned or hurt. I raised myself to one knee and at once went about the business of getting out of my parachute harness.

"The need for swiftness here is obvious. One must get free as quickly as possible from this encumbrance, so one can engage the enemy if he is about. I didn't yet know the situation. A Jerry might surprise me at any second. I quickly discovered that it was not going to be easy to free myself from my harness. The fly in the ointment was a wide belt part of the harness known colloquially as 'the belly band.' There was a buckle on the belt, but I couldn't manage it. The belt had too much pressure against it. I worked at the buckle for several seconds while sweat poured out on me. To no avail. I saw clearly there was no hope at all of undoing it. There was only one thing to do — cut the belt. I drew my trench knife and easily sliced 'the belly band' through.

"Before I had had a chance to wonder long about what to do next, I heard sounds of movement in the area to my left which I had judged to be our men. I knew my buddies would be active around here somewhere, and I expected them before I expected a Jerry, since everything had been so peaceful thus far. I felt that if there had been any Jerries in the immediate vicinity, there would have been fireworks by now. But I had heard no firing. So as the figures approached, I made no effort to conceal myself. I was seen, and the first word of the password was flung at me in a hoarse voice — 'Democracy!' 'Lafayette!' I answered, equally hoarsely.

"I then emerged fully into the open and joined the others in the grassy area beyond the ditch, for grassy it proved to be, or rather weedy. The man who had challenged me was a noncom from my company — Corporal Colbert. I was glad to see him and to become a part of his group. He had about three other men with him."[12]

« 3 »

Carefully timed to coincide with the seaborne attack, the infantrymen arriving in gliders either consolidated the positions taken by the paratroops or mounted new attacks in nearby areas. Then everyone turned to the next job of preventing the defense forces from reaching the beachhead. To the C–47's flying back overhead it must have seemed as if the operation was as smooth as parachute silk but this is more of a tribute to the skill of the glider pilots than a description of the actual conditions.

The glider pilots performed with enormous courage. Their target area, described in the briefings as a group of fields broken up by hedgerows and low stone walls, was actually surrounded by rows of trees, rising to heights of forty and fifty feet. The fields, appearing on the photo overlays as cleared land or covered with wheat stubble, were filled with *Rommelspargel* (Rommel's asparagus), the tall wooden poles joined by barbed wire and mined.

The glider pilots had been trained to come in on low approach "blitz" landings. Expecting to clear three-foot hedgerows, they found themselves forced to hurdle fifty-foot trees. Many just didn't make it. Those that did found their approach too high, overshot the next field and washed out in a farther row of trees. Very few gliders landed without crashing and, unavoidably, casualties were high. But, in spite of these obstacles, the troops and equipment were delivered on schedule.[13]

Some of the pilots paid a fearful price for this efficiency. General Frederick once graphically described how, in a misjudged attempt to go beneath a section of strung wire, both the pilot and the copilot of one ship were completely decapitated.[14] Colonel William Blythe, his Intelligence Officer, remembered another aspect: "We landed in a vineyard while firing was going on all around us. But the men were so sick [from the motion of the ship while trying to maneuver into a clear spot] that many of them simply fell out of the glider on their faces, lying there vomiting. It took a while for their officers to get them up and moving."[15]

After the war, some of the veterans of the Japanese antitank company met one night in Kailua, Hawaii, to rehash the events of that glider flight. One of them, Yuki Nakahiri, had an especially memorable moment on the flight to Southern France be-

(ABOVE) *Gliders that landed in France on D-Day. The tall poles are the obstacles erected by the German defenders.* (BELOW) *First Airborne Task Force troops inspect a glider damaged in the D-Day landings. (Signal Corps Photos)*

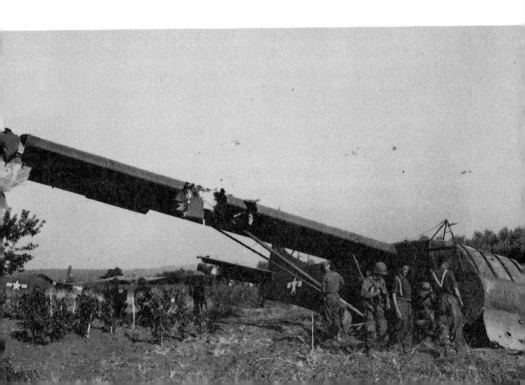

cause of his almost unmanageable curiosity. Bored by sitting in the dark waist of the ship, he had torn a small hole in the canvas side of the plane in order to see what it looked like down below. But the strong wind force continued the tear along the weave and he spent the balance of his journey pinching the canvas together before the running tear in order to keep the ship from turning into a tattered kite in mid-flight. "Even so," he said, "it was fun. We were all happy that we were going to France and we weren't too concerned over the problems we'd find when we hit the ground. The fellows on my glider sang Hawaiian songs and cheered on the pilot and copilot during most of the flight.

"But when we got there, the fun and games stopped. I think that the photos we had been shown of our drop zone weren't as recent as they could have been because they didn't have the tall trees and the vineyard terraces that confronted us. There was a heavy mine field in the pasture next to us so the glider scheduled for that spot pulled up and landed in an uncleared alfalfa patch just beyond. The boys in his ship got pretty well disorganized."

"There were other problems, too," Jack Kaguni reminded the group, which had gathered at the home of Edward Sakai, "especially in those gliders where the loads broke loose from the retaining ropes during the force of the landing. Quite a few of the pilots got hurt by being rammed by a shifting load."[16]

Edward Sakai, now the principal of a Hawaiian public school, traced the development of this unit into one of the most valued components of the First Airborne Task Force by saying, "We had been in combat in Italy, and just about the time we were heading up the coast to Leghorn they pulled us out of combat. Since we were an antitank company, and were obviously needed in the push, the rumors began to fly and they didn't stop (and some of them were pretty wild) until, at a base near Rome, they briefed us on the mission. Well, since none of us had flown in gliders before, we weren't without trepidation. But we were willing to go wherever they assigned us and after a few of our practice flights, we found that it was exciting and interesting and we began to look forward to it.

"The flight over was just about the way Yuki described it and, after we landed near Le Muy, we really got into the swing of things. As I understand it, the paratroopers who landed before did a lot for us by deactivating the traps that were set up for our gliders. We were quite grateful and I know that throughout the campaign we were buddies with each other . . . we sort of morally supported each other in such a way that we each felt more comfortable. I know that they felt more secure with our big guns right alongside of them. We'd share rations whenever any-one ran out . . . that sort of thing."[17]

« 4 »

Although the planning for the mission had been scrupulously exact, there was one problem for which no one had made provi-sions: what to do with the glider pilots after the troops were on the ground.

The ribald and unrepeatable names they had given to most of their ships indicated that the fliers had an even more unorthodox concept of military conduct than those who flew conventional aircraft and their actions after the landing did nothing to weaken the indication.

Colonel Blythe, the G-2, first attempted to organize the glider pilots into a perimeter defense of the headquarters, "but it was soon evident that the pilots were more interested in getting souvenirs."[18] One paratrooper said that all the pilots he saw were running around machine-gunning chickens in order to get a first-class meal together.

Colonel Guthrie, back in Seventh Army headquarters, put together the first reports trickling out and saw that "the glider pilots posed a problem because once their gliders got down, they were no longer under the command of the people they carried. So some of them tried to absorb all the wine that they could corner in that part of France. Others actually joined the units they had carried and did very well as infantrymen until we caught up with them. I had a hell of a time rounding them all up and getting them back to Italy."[19]

General Frederick agreed about the problem: "Oh, that was terrible. After they landed we just tried to round up as many as we could and march them down to the dock to go back to Italy. They were just sort of running wild all around France. I think there are still some over there."[20]

It fell to Major Isenberg, the Provost Marshal, to shepherd the locatable fliers out of the area. He did it by making them guards over the prisoners of war captured the first day. "They all had forty-five automatics," he said, "and we also gave rifles to some of them, and then just assigned them to groups of prisoners and sent them marching off down to the beaches. In that way, neither the prisoners nor the pilots could go anywhere but where they were supposed to."[21]

« 5 »

General Frederick jumped in the first wave. Duff Matson, who was with him, described the flight and the drop: "I got out to the airfield in the middle of the afternoon. The planes were like ovens from sitting in the sun, so we didn't go in them, but hung around a tent that Frederick had thoughtfully erected there in order to serve us white bread and jelly and things like that while we were waiting to emplane.

"Frederick didn't get there till around eleven o'clock that night in a command car. He had gone into Rome for a rubdown and a steam bath that afternoon. I remember thinking how great that was. If I were a commanding general, that's exactly what I would have been doing.

"It was a fairly good flight. Frederick sat up at the front by the door and Captain McCall, his aide, was by him. Another man, myself and a newspaper reporter sat next. This reporter lost his typewriter later during the jump . . . evidently the snap with which his chute opened jolted it out of his arms, and he almost got killed running around looking for it. Everyone else kept telling him to stay down, but he kept running and yelling that the whole thing was no good if he didn't have his typewriter!

"The going-over part took several hours. It was dark in our C–47 and we just sat there. When we got near the coast, Captain McCall looked out and said, 'There's antiaircraft fire coming up at us. They know we're coming.' We looked and saw the spurts of flame coming up from the ground but none of it came near us.

"Then we stood up and Frederick who, up till that time hadn't said a word, stood at the door. He was wearing a jump suit, a white silk scarf at his neck and a forty-five on his hip. In his hand he was carrying the blue flashlight that he was going to use for signaling. He looked out and then said in a conversational tone, 'Alright fellows, follow me,' and then he jumped. The rest of us followed."[22]

The story is picked up from here by Frederick: "I had told the air corps to drop us from six hundred feet but, because the area was covered by clouds, we were dropped from about twenty-two hundred which I think was a mistake because it really had the effect of scattering us.

"When I hit the ground I looked up and around for other parachutes but didn't see any and I thought that maybe I had jumped too soon. So I got out my map and by the light of the blue flashlight I tried to orient myself. I looked over to the west where there was a hill on which Bill Yarborough and the 509th were supposed to land, but saw nothing. Over to the east I made out a little town which seemed to be the one I had selected as my command post so I started down the path toward it. Before I had gotten more than a few hundred feet, I saw in the mist what I thought was a German. Circling behind him I jumped and got my arm around his throat and began to break his neck in the fashion we had learned back in the Special Service Force.

"Finally the man spluttered out 'Jesus Christ!' in an English accent so I relaxed my hold and said, 'Who are you?' He said, 'I'm from the 2nd British Independent Parachute Brigade,' so I answered, 'Well, go on about your business, but you'd better be careful. Your helmet in this mist looks like it's German.' And he said, 'No, I'm going with you. I lost my rifle in the jump and you've got a forty-five and I'm not taking any more chances.'

"So we went down the trail and just then McCall and another man joined us. As I understand it, Matson broke his leg in the jump and had to be evacuated.

"When we got to the CP we found that all of our equipment, including the radios, had been dropped thirty miles away. There was nothing else I could do, so I just lay down and went to sleep for a few hours. I had been up for three days before that."[23]

« 6 »

After the war the chief of staff, Kenneth Wickham, observed that: "The fact that the units were unintentionally scattered during the drop over a wide area was extremely confusing to the Germans. It caused them to exaggerate the total airborne effort being made."[24] General Zais, then a lieutenant colonel in command of the 517th's 3rd Battalion, agreed. "It contributed greatly to the success of the operation," he said. "Enough people landed on the main road nets to blunt the movement of the German forces, and enough people landed in other places to completely confuse the defenders. They didn't know which way to turn."[25]

Of course, it must be admitted that the first Americans to land in scattered patterns were almost as badly confused as the Germans. A French writer, Jacques Robichon, in describing Zais's predicament, said:

[The young colonel] was bent on reassembling his battalion which had been air-dropped in three areas, over a distance of ten kilometers or so, between the towns of Seillans, Fayence, and Callian. . . . Zais had covered [some of the distance] when his small group was unexpectedly joined by 80 paratroopers of the Second English Brigade. . . . It took one long day and night before this brave little unit, isolated in a foreign country, reached its goal.[26]

Robichon also relayed the impressions of two French children when they first saw the Americans that night:

In the dimness, the two soldiers seemed literally painted in black and green. Their machine gun gave them a savage, cruel look; their

Le Muy, France, August 15, 1944. The paratroopers move along a dusty country road toward their initial objective on D-Day in Southern France. (Signal Corps Photo)

helmets were covered with branches, and two large yellow "eggs" hung on their chests. Jacqueline learned later they were grenades.

At that moment, following the order of the older, one of the soldiers walked to the back of the room and cut the telephone wires. Seeing the little girls, the other who had "a funny nose, red and hooked" took Jacqueline on his lap and gave her a stick of gum. She had forgotten the taste for years, but it removed the child's doubt immediately — these men could only be Americans and the landing had taken place.

On the Lavals' table, the man with the gun had spread a huge aerial picture, taken a few weeks before, and the owners of Ste. Roseline were amazed at recognizing their property in all its detail — the castle (château) included the ruins of a famous Abbaye of the 11th century. Long ago, in the Allied plans, the old residence of the Lavals had been picked to serve as Hqtrs. to a regiment of American paratroopers on the night of August 14.

The mischievous Jacqueline and her sister burst out laughing on noticing that the American had half of his mustache black, the other green, and under his hooked nose was all scratched up. But the paratrooper explained to their parents that his landing had not taken place in the best of circumstances; hitting the ground, he had accidentally "fallen nose first in the grapevines." It was Col. Rupert D. Graves, head of the 517th, whose troops were, at the moment, spread over more than 40 km.[27]

Colonel Graves does not disagree that confusion dominated that night. He said, "I think we landed fairly close but not right on the drop zone at all. We ended up on a mountain or a big hill. It was a wooded area, rocky and everything was so black that you just couldn't see.

"We wandered around and waited a while. In the dark you could hear people sort of thrashing around but we didn't know

*On D-Day an American paratrooper stands guard at a country crossroad.
(From the collection of Robert T. Frederick)*

who it was. We picked up a few people here and there, maybe a half a dozen or so.

"When daylight came, I sent out some units to establish road-blocks, and I remember that one group came back with this big old black car. There had been a German staff officer and a chauffeur and a couple of other people driving in it and our men said they had had to take it away from them. We didn't have any transportation, of course, so I thought it was very thoughtful of them. Then I took a look at it. The back of the car was full of blood. When I didn't say anything, one fellow said, 'Alright Colonel, we'll take care of that,' and he took his gun out and shot a hole in the bottom of it for the blood to run out. Then he told me, 'There it is, it's all fixed.' "[28]

And, as in training days, the spiritual leaders of the unit were right up in the thick of the activity. Father Guenette dropped early in the morning into an area completely surrounded by Germans. He remembers: "I was rolling my chute up in the darkness when suddenly I heard a rustling nearby. I gave the password which was 'Demo' but got no answer. But I could see some kind of a silhouette against the sky so I came up a bit closer and found out it was two men. Again I whispered 'Demo,' but again no answer. I decided that there might be a danger of some-one being trigger-happy under these circumstances, so I walked up to these two fellows and pushed their guns away and said, 'What's the matter with you guys, don't you know the password?' It turned out that these were two of our boys, so scared that they had forgotten how to answer.

"At dawn we met another group and we all walked down the road until we saw a house. Being French, I told them that I would go in and ask where we were.

"When we got there, this young girl in pajamas was waving at us. We were all painted up . . . the camouflage goo all over our faces . . . we all looked the same. She asked, 'Are you Americans, are you really Americans?' And I told her that we were. At that she jumped at me, threw her arms around my neck and started hugging me.

"We went into the house where there were approximately twenty other Americans who had already gotten there. They were looking at a map on the wall trying to orient themselves while the girl's mother kept trying to tell them that they were not where they thought they were but thirty-five miles inland, instead. None of them spoke French so I explained to the men that we were pretty far away from our drop zone.

"They were upset by this news, so to relieve the strain I turned to the mother and said, 'You know, you've got a pretty impetuous daughter here. We met her outside, she hugged me, a Catholic priest, right out in public. I think the best thing to think about right now is penance for her.' When the girl heard this, she began to blush, so I went on and said, 'So the best thing for this kind of terrible action is a very special penance . . . I think she'd better hug and kiss every one of the men in this room so it will be clear that nothing special was intended.'

"So she did, and after she was through she was thoroughly smeared with all of the camouflage goo, but all the men were laughing and felt easier. It relieved the tension and we started out in good spirits to find the rest of our outfit."[29]

Chaplain Brown, the Protestant clergyman, broke his leg on the fall and was left with a group of French women who hid him in a hayloft. "I stayed there for most of the rest of the day," he recalls, "and perhaps half the night. Men kept coming and I acted as sort of a relaying point. Whenever a paratrooper came by, I'd say, 'They went thataway.'

"That afternoon the people in the village held a funeral service which I attended. It was for a child who, like a few of the other children, had found some dynamite that the Allies had dropped for the FFI bands. Only this child, thinking it was food, had eaten it. At this funeral service, when the priest found out that I was a chaplain, he asked me to say something. I hobbled upright and said a few words as a kind of a gesture of American respect for the child and the people of the village."[30]

One paratrooper had his chute caught in a tree during the jump. Thinking that he was teetering on the edge of a cliff he had seen on the sand tables during training, he did not attempt to get out of his harness until the morning. When daylight came, he found that he had spent most of the night dangling a foot off the ground.

Other groups had password trouble. An Englishman attached to an American unit using "Billy the Kid" as a code was fumbling around in the bushes when his outline was spotted in the dark by another paratrooper. The paratrooper brought his machine gun up and whispered "Billy," but there was no answer. The American tried again, "Billy." Still no answer; just the Englishman thrashing around in the bushes trying to get rid of his harness. Finally, the American tried once more, at the same time unlocking the safety on the gun. Hearing the bolt click, the Englishman called out, "I say, chap, don't do that. It's some goddamned American cowboy or another!"

Albert F. Goerler of the 550th took part in one of the fire fights that took place soon after the jump: "We were dropped outside a small town and although we tried all night long to take it, we had to fall back. By the next morning, the Germans sent word that they only had three hundred men and five officers and would surrender if we would stop firing on them. They let us get almost

into the town and then threw everything they had at us. We lost
quite a few men before we could get into a covered position. But,
by the end of the day, we had killed over two hundred Germans
and captured hundreds more. The French stayed right by us,
telling us where the Germans were hiding and in what buildings
they were concentrated.

"My machine gun, I remember, was red hot. The grass above
my head was being cut off by bullets, almost as if I were lying by
a lawn mower. A woman was firing at some of our fellows and
one of our machine gunners, with a glove wrapped around the
barrel so he could handle it, cut her in half from a second story
window.

"The only funny note was that while bullets were bouncing
around off the sides of the building, the women kept trying to
give us wine and flowers. But we were too busy trying to stay
alive. My assistant gunner and I got twenty-seven Germans captured in one building. We were there for three days before the
American beachhead forces got to us."[31]

Another FABTF soldier, Frank James, was a leading actor in
what turned out to be one of the most dramatic sidelights of the
entire Invasion. His factual version of it still retains the impact
which put it on the front pages of almost every American newspaper during the period.

"We landed on the top of a house about four or five in the
morning. Some old French lady and gentleman came running
out when they heard Henderson and me hitting and scrambling
around on the roof. Of course, I couldn't speak a word of French
so all I could do was show them the American flag sewn on my
left shoulder.

"They took me inside the house and the old gentleman went
off to fetch some people from the local Underground. They came

in about fifteen minutes later and they hid our parachutes and took us five or six kilometers down the road to a little town named Lorgues. There they took us into this big mansion and introduced us to this elderly lady who turned out to be a German countess who hated the Nazis. She hid us in her hayloft.

"We stayed there for two days; French girls would bring us our food and plenty of wine. The second day, a young Frenchman came in, bringing along another American named Doyle Gray. That made three of us up there.

"A bit later on, the FFI men came back to ask if we would go on a patrol with them to the town of Le Thoronet. Of course we agreed. They had a broken-down old French truck with a battered cab in front and a bed strapped to the top. I got into the cab with the young kid who was driving and Henderson and Gray got in the back with three other Frenchmen.

"Traveling down the road to Le Thoronet, we came to a fork where we were supposed to make a right turn to get into town. There was a hedgerow and woods sitting right at the end of the road. As we approached the turn, antitank guns began firing out of the woods at us. One round hit the road and ricocheted into the truck, blowing out the radiator. We jumped out of the truck and into a ditch beside the road. The windshield had shattered and I had pieces of glass in my chest.

"Lying there in the ditch, we heard all hell break loose. They started firing machine guns and all types of small arms at us, trying to lob hand grenades in the ditch, and just about everything else. All I had was an old French pistol which turned out to be too rusty to fire.

"Finally, we just took Gray's rifle butt, tied a part of his T-shirt onto it, and raised it into the air. The firing then stopped and they all converged on us. It was a whole German outfit: an artillery unit, a battalion of infantry and quite a few others. A German major was in command who spoke perfect English.

"The major kept Gray and myself with him and had the poor fellows from the FFI dig their own holes and had them shot. They just fell over into the graves they had dug for themselves.

"This German kept asking us about the Invasion, what we had and where it was, and so forth. I had a trench knife strapped onto my jump boot and he pulled it out of the scabbard and wanted to know when I had used it last. Of course I couldn't tell him I had used it to kill Germans so I said that I used it to open cans. He got a big charge out of that. I asked him about his English and he said he had been educated at Oxford.

"That night we moved out in the middle of a pouring rainstorm, headed for another position. Early next morning the unit set up on the top of a high hill. But they had no sooner gotten established than a French armored unit had the hill completely surrounded.

"Gray and myself knew that they were about to get the hell knocked out of them by this French outfit so we started running around amongst the Krauts telling them that if they would drop their arms and surrender, we would make sure that they would be treated okay.

"So we talked to the German officer and since he, too, knew he didn't have a chance anyway, he agreed. We had all the Germans pile their weapons up: sidearms, small weapons, machine guns, everything in a pile. Then I got a white flag and went down the hill with Gray and the German commander in between us.

"Some French soldiers met us and took us into custody back to their general commanding the division. We identified ourselves and told him what we had done in talking the German unit into surrendering and that it wasn't necessary to throw any tank or artillery fire up on the hill.

"He sent us back to line up the German unit in a column, which we did. We marched them down the hill and had them surrender to his outfit. After this was accomplished he had us transferred to the closest American unit to him.

"When we reached the Americans, the commanding officer, after hearing the story, sent out a hurry-up call for the press. Then they took us all the way back to the coast where the authorities had us record the story of what we had done and it was broadcast back to America.

"Then they gave us a few days off on the coast and sent us back to our unit."[32]

Predictably, Phil DiStanislao contributed impartially to the confusion on both sides that night: "I was lost, is what I was . . . my compass had been smashed on the jump and so I tried to obey the advice they had given us to follow the directions of the planes. But the planes were going every which way and I couldn't tell if they were coming or going, so I was lost.

"I finally ended up with about thirty or forty troopers traipsing around after me. I had two British soldiers and a British medic in the group and when we got into a fire fight with some Germans a little later on, I told the Britishers to try and flank them. The Germans were hidden behind what seemed to be a lot of bramble bushes, but the Englishmen nevertheless tried to get through them in order to do what I said. I think that if I had told them to jump off the moon, they would have tried to do it, that's how rattled they were. Anyway, these guys kept pushing their heads into the bushes and trying to get through, and they just

August 16, 1944. Frederick's paratroopers escort a group of captured German soldiers to the POW collection point. (Signal Corps Photo)

couldn't. I finally told them, 'Let's do it some other way.' Which we did. We killed the Germans and then went on.

"When I got to my platoon, we were all sent down to road-block. This roadblock turned out to be quite successful. After a little while it looked like we were running a secondhand garage. Staff cars — all kinds of German vehicles coming down the road from assignations elsewhere, who presumably hadn't heard that we had landed. They kept coming blithely down and we, just as blithely, kept blasting the heck out of them. We just rolled the bodies aside, moved the cars over into the woods and set up shop for our next customer. We ended up with a whole fleet of vehicles.

"Later on that afternoon we were told to get over to a field to neutralize some mines and some shells that were triggered by wires from poles, because the glider boys were coming in. We did as much as we could before they got there, and then we sat up on the hillside and watched them. What a sight! They just poured in . . . those gliders came in and the wings would shear off — it looked like nobody could possibly be left alive. Then you'd hear a jeep motor gun up and out it would come. We went down and saw that the pilots had taken one heck of a beating. There were a lot of dead pilots up in the noses of those things."[33]

« 7 »

Less seasoned soldiers might have lost precious days in reassembling for their primary mission, but the officers and men of the First Airborne Task Force had brought too much experience to Robert Frederick's unit to squander their time. Men finding themselves splintered into a small group fought or tracked their way to other groups in the vicinity and the combined force, like iron filings pulled by a magnet, went directly to assigned positions.

By the late afternoon of August 15, they had been substantially welded back together, communication had been established between all elements and orders for the following night and day had been issued.

The 517th Combat Team took the high ground west and south of La Motte and was in command of the Draguignan–La Motte road, the Trans-en-Provence–Les Arcs road and the road net to the south of Les Arcs. These positions, representing the western perimeter of the Task Force defense area, became almost impregnable after Major Bill Boyle and fifty men started to take Les Arcs away from the German battalion which was occupying the town.

The 2nd British Independent Parachute Brigade, although failing to capture the key city of Le Muy, was nevertheless in possession of the main road into it.

Colonel Bill Yarborough had been permitted to pick the drop zone for his 509th and "had selected the high ground above Le Muy on purpose because it was rugged and difficult — it had been burned over, it was rocky, but it had the high ground that overlooked the city and the road net . . . and I preferred that to the flat place that you normally think of a parachute unit as going in.

"Surprisingly, we only had a small number of casualties on landing. But it was as dark as the inside of your pocket. When dawn came, we were in a very fine position indeed: we could see the Germans backing and filling, trying to get out of Le Muy. So we attacked down that hill. In short order the German resistance kind of folded in the middle and withdrew back into the town.

"However, we were minus one company which had been

August 15, 1944. La Motte, France. A wounded paratrooper receives a glass of wine from a French woman. (Signal Corps Photo)

dropped along the coast at Saint-Tropez. This turned out to be a good thing because it gave the illusion to the Germans that there were a lot more parachute troops than there actually were. You see, there are all different kinds of parachute operations; if you want to get a regiment or a division in to operate as such, then you try to put as many in as you can in one place. Special forces drop in small groups on purpose on drop zones that aren't supposed to look like drop zones, so that they can get their matériel together and get out of there. You have to figure the environment and circumstances. Here, the scattering of the troops worked for us."[34]

Captain Jess Walls, who took command of the group (consisting of elements of the 509th and the 463rd Parachute Field Artillery Battalion) which fell between Saint-Tropez and Cannes, made immediate contact with the FFI forces in the area and then elected to seize the smaller city.[35] Lieutenant R. F. Ruyffelaere of the 509th was with him and his account of the taking of Saint-Tropez is both graphic and colorful:

"It was pitch dark when I landed in a soft vineyard. I could hear others hitting tiles on the house roofs. The first man shot was one of our own who failed to respond in the darkness with the proper password when one of his buddies challenged him.

"We assembled by the flashing of lights as we had planned and found that we had been dropped on the outskirts of Saint-Tropez. Captain Walls did a fine job of organizing us once he found out what the hell the score was. A Frenchman called Rafael, who was in the FFI, pointed out a hill to us which was the alternate position for the Germans in the town to use as protection against a landing on the beach. This was tough luck for them because we occupied the alternate position right in the beginning.

"Then we find out that the Germans in town now know that we

are in their alternate position and are deciding to take off. Rafael told us this. Incidentally, he had a very pretty girl friend with him who was also a member of the FFI.

"We headed for the town and the first thing you know, we had the citadel [a large hotel] surrounded and what ensued thereafter was something out of an old cowboy and Indian war. The Germans would run across the top of the citadel . . . I don't know why because they had beautiful thick stone walls to stay behind to shoot at us . . . and our fellows would knock them off as they ran back and forth. They'd fall off this roof just like in a cowboy movie."[36]

It remains for Colonel Bryant Evans, the artillery commander of the FABTF, to complete Lieutenant Ruyffelaere's description of the taking of the town: "I think it was the A Company of the 509th who were dropped by inadvertence on Saint-Tropez. They were able to capture the hotel which was the headquarters of the German division and then take the town. However, in the middle of their scurrying around [after their victory] someone realized that there was only a half hour remaining before our naval bombardment of the place was scheduled to begin. Accordingly, their officers rushed them back of the sand dunes along the shore where they dug in. When the navy guns started firing, the men had very few casualties. It was, however, something to sweat out because they all had been briefed that the bombardment was coming.

"When the first units of the ground forces arrived on the beaches and came ashore, Company A came out from behind the sand dunes and very ceremoniously thumbed their noses toward the advancing American troops!"[37]

The other units went about their jobs in so methodical a

manner that there is little to report except that they reached their assigned objectives and began to funnel prisoners of war into central points for interrogation. Unfortunately, the prisoners could contribute little information except that an airborne landing had not been expected in the area. The explosive attack of the Force had thoroughly disrupted communication between German units and, as a result, the officers and noncoms could tell their captors next to nothing about present positions. At that time on D-Day their forces were reeling back in a way that was far removed from the normally efficient German defense tactics.

This information was analyzed and sent back to General Frederick at 5:00 P.M. that afternoon. He made the immediate decision to keep on the offense in an effort to cause further deterioration among the enemy forces.[38]

This is what the First Airborne Task Force had been formed to do. At 8:00 A.M., the Allied seaborne forces, consisting of the U.S. Seventh Army, the U.S. VI Corps and French Army "B," came ashore on the chain of beaches stretching from Cannes to Toulon. Their way was blazed by the First Special Service Force, which had landed earlier and subdued the defender's big guns on the key coastal islands.

The Invasion's first phase was a success.

CHAPTER V

THE LINKUP

---

*That operation was the most successful airborne operation
of the whole war. When you don't land on your objective, you
just can't sit there and wait . . . you've got to get busy!*

*That's what the Task Force did. Some of them landed on a
German corps headquarters and destroyed it completely . . .
knocked out all of their communications, which was most helpful to the entire Invasion. They were able to pick up a lot of
Maquis, get information which we'd use and always needed,
and get it to the right units. This is the way you fight wars —
we didn't have to issue orders.*

*I can't say enough for Frederick and that command. They
were magnificent.*

— JACOB L. DEVERS,
Commanding General, VI Army Group[1]

« 1 »

BY 8:00 P.M., August 15, almost all of the other headquarters officers, including the chief of staff, artillery officer and surgeon, had reported in to Frederick's command post. They were too late to have contributed to the success of the initial operation, but there were few soldiers who did not consider that the brass had been having one hell of a day. In traveling to the CP from their drop in the mountain foothills, they had intercepted thirty German soldiers, killed nine of them and wounded most of the rest.[2]

An hour later, a tall sandy-haired man in his early twenties, dressed in rumpled khakis, was brought into headquarters. Obviously irritated by the demands of the soldiers escorting him that he completely identify himself, he kept demanding that he meet with either General Frederick or the intelligence head of the unit. Since the war he is mentioned "for security reasons" in various memoirs of the period as "Captain Sanders"[3] or "Geoffrey Stanley"[4] but he was actually Geoffrey Jones, the OSS agent who had parachuted into this part of France two weeks before.

He describes his membership entry into the First Airborne Task Force: "The two things that we did that night were to first knock out a German radar installation and then get down to clean out the landing fields where the planes were coming in. When we got there, we found that another of our groups had been working all night taking out the poles that the Germans had put

[*131*]

up. There was a company of enemy soldiers in the vicinity who might have possibly interfered with the work, so we attacked to distract them from the work being done on the landing fields.

"I had gotten the message the day before . . . it was on our late afternoon broadcast . . . that the Invasion was going to take place. I had all the Resistance leaders up there in the mountains with me at the time, but I couldn't take them all down because there was a danger of getting too careless at the last minute.

"So I went down to the drop area with seven gendarmes, each of whom was thoroughly familiar with his own section of the area. This represented a complete coverage: between the group of us we pretty well knew everything that could influence the military actions in almost every drop zone.

"We came down that night in a truck. Because the Germans had several roadblocks along our route, we acted as if we were the prisoners of these gendarmes. We had a major close call because we had our headlights on (so that we wouldn't attract suspicion). Seeing our lights, some American aircraft tried to bomb us. One bomb landed about twenty yards behind our truck and a couple of our fellows were hit by the shell fragments.

"But the most hair-raising event of the night happened to me. It seemed that I was in the wrong uniform. When I took off my blue civilian suit, I was wearing khakis underneath, and everyone in the invading force was wearing olive drabs. Almost every soldier we saw wanted to take a shot at me. You see, these parachutists were landing all over the place instead of being exactly where they were supposed to be, so, understandably, many of the Americans were quite jittery. Many of them shot at each other rather than at the Germans. The first few Americans I saw were convinced that I was a German spy, but I got away. Finally, I made my identification by yelling through the fog to some sergeant. We got to the point where he was willing to let me come over so long as I held my hands up as high as they would go. Somehow or another I talked the sergeant into telling me the name of his unit, and to my relief it was a parachute artillery battalion where I was quite familiar with many of the officers because they had been with me in either the 11th or 82nd Airborne. After throwing their names around, he agreed to take me back to meet some of these fellows. After I established identification, I brought out my gendarmes.

"When I finally met up with Bob Frederick, I said to him, 'What do you want to know?' I could say this with assurance because between my gendarmes and myself, we knew where everyone was, the conditions of the roads and bridges, the location of the electric power lines, and just about everything else he had to be sure of that night.

"Then I flopped into a hayloft and had my first real sleep in three or four days. It was a good feeling to know that there were Americans all around me."[5]

« 2 »

The section of Southern France into which the Force had been dropped rises rapidly into a series of hills which then become the Maritime Alps. There is a high ridge running along the coast from Marseilles to Nice, broken by very few valleys leading to the interior. About thirteen miles from the sea, the town of Le Muy commands the pass into one of these valleys, sitting astride a good cement road leading from the landing beaches at Saint-Raphaël and stretching on up to the north.

By holding onto Le Muy, the Germans felt that they would be

in a better position to contain the Allied forces landing on the beach. So the commanding officer of the Nineteenth Army detached his "Regiment Bruendel" from the 244th Infantry Division, coupled it with the motorized antiaircraft battalion, "Tyroller," and sent them to Le Muy on August 15. Unmistakably indicating the importance of the small town to his defense plans, he also assigned parts of the 148th Reserve Division nearby on the eastern perimeter.[6]

The same reasoning caused General Frederick to assign an equally pressing priority to the taking of Le Muy. The job was first given to the British parachute brigade, but he admitted in a postwar conversation, that "I began to worry about the English back in Italy during the planning stage. They seemed to be devoting more time to getting together all the creature comforts to take with them than they were to tactical readiness."[7]

This estimate seems to be partly confirmed by Dick Spencer's recollection: "I still have a British beret that I took from a dead Englishman. When I first landed I came across two dead British soldiers lying by a big equipment bundle. When we opened it up to see what they had been after, we found that the damned thing was about fifty pounds of tea. Nothing else. That's what these guys had been after when they were killed."[8]

Colonel Blythe, who sat in on the planning sessions as a G–2 officer added: "The British brigade, which I believe came up from Greece, was commanded by Brigadier Pritchett, an immaculate, professional-type soldier who had his own opinions and his own way of doing things . . . Also, some of the questions that [he] brought up during the planning stages, perhaps, didn't impress those in charge."[9]

The artillery officer, Colonel Evans, confirmed that there was a generally skeptical feeling about the British contribution: "I had told Frederick what was going to happen because before we jumped in I'd been over to see Pritchett to arrange artillery support, and he told me that there was no necessity to discuss it because he didn't intend to fight after he had landed. I was perfectly furious about that!"[10]

But a partial explanation of the puzzling attitude of the British during the Le Muy engagement is supplied by Major General John Guthrie: "I have the feeling that Jumbo [Sir Henry Maitland] Wilson, the theater commander, was reluctant to get the British into the operation. When he did lend us the brigade, he had them on a string of some kind to be sure that they would be returned: in other words, he wanted to be sure that the British participated, but he wanted to get his paratroopers back again as soon as possible.

"In any case, we gave him what we considered to be the simplest part of the operation and we expected that once he had landed and consolidated that he could exploit the operation as did the others in the area. But I suspect that Pritchett had [private] instructions to conserve his forces."[11]

But General Frederick, unconcerned with the niceties of Anglo-American relationships, saw only that he had depended on the British to do a job and, when they failed to do it on the first day, got rid of them. "They didn't even try to take it on the first day," he said, "and when I asked Pritchett about it he said, 'Well, we jumped.' 'But why don't you go in and take the town?' I asked him. 'No,' he said, 'there are Germans in there.' So I thought, the hell with it, and I immediately sent them back to Italy."[12]

This conversation took place on the afternoon of August 15 while the British were holding the bridge over the main road into the town. Frederick then ordered the 550th Glider Battalion to

August 16, 1944. The First Airborne Task Force moves into Le Muy on the second day of the Invasion of Southern France. (Signal Corps Photo)

August 16, 1944. The Japanese-Americans of the First Airborne's antitank company move into Le Muy to meet a counterattack on the second day of the Invasion of Southern France. (Signal Corps Photo)

August 17, 1944. Major General Robert T. Frederick receives the flag of Le Muy from its mayor after the liberation of the town. (Signal Corps Photo)

do the job which was completed by noon of the following day.[13]

Frederick's peremptory treatment of the British and his cool decisiveness during the battle for Le Muy provided the men of the First Airborne Task Force with their first real insight into the character of the man who commanded them. Until that time he had been a remote and withdrawn figure.

"Something happened at Le Muy that caused me to understand General Frederick a bit better," said Colonel Blythe. "When the Germans felt they could no longer defend the town, they raised a white flag and sent an emissary who told Frederick that if he would have his artillery cease firing, they would surrender. Frederick told the German officer that he was going to increase his artillery fire and for him to tell his commander that he had better figure out his own way to surrender as soon as he could. Without any further palaver, the Germans surrendered."[14]

« 3 »

The narrative report of the operations of the 517th Parachute Infantry Combat Team for the period reads in part: *The greatest enemy threat was from the vicinity of Les Arcs and northwest of Les Arcs. This threat was held back by a gallant group of fifty men under Major William J. Boyle, commanding officer, 1st Battalion, until reinforcements arrived from the 2nd Battalion.*[15] One of those in the "gallant group" was Charles Keen and his story of what happened to them after being dropped tells more than just the way the fight went: it also offers a rare look at enlisted men judging their officers in combat:

"Shortly after we landed, we came across a Frenchman who had a big old truck. He offered to help us so we all bundled up into it and barreled into the center of Les Arcs. When we got out, we noticed that there weren't any Frenchmen around on the street. And this was the start of the Les Arcs mess.

"Finally, one guy came up to us. He was an American soldier from World War I who came from Boston. He said that the Germans had the railroad bridge covered from across the block. He said, 'Les Arcs is the key to the whole valley; the Germans can't withdraw because the seaborne forces are coming up and the seaborne forces can't get up through the valley unless they come through Les Arcs which is right at the bottom with hills on both sides.' He repeated again that the Germans were right across from the bridge and were all set up and waiting for us.

"So our captain then says, 'Everybody in the truck. We're going to storm the roadblock!'

"And there we were. Idiots. In this big high truck, going to storm across the bridge, sitting ducks for the Germans. We looked at it and looked at each other and just then an old retired French Foreign Legionnaire — he must have been about seventy and he had put on his uniform for the occasion — came up and told our captain that 'this is suicide. You'll never make it. You'll all be killed.'

"I thought, 'Well, the Captain is an officer and he's in charge of us, but this old guy seems to know what he's talking about.' The guy from Boston chimed in and also said it was suicide trying to get across the bridge.

"So the Captain reluctantly got us away from the truck, formed us into two columns, and we started moving up toward the bridge on foot. And this is when the scrap started because we were then able to get close enough to the Germans to get a fire fight going and we drove them away from the bridge. Then our captain decided to check it. He went up to the bridge, which was concrete and had little peepholes in the side. He was looking through them at the German positions when a sniper (everybody who has a rifle is a sniper — a rifleman doesn't kill anybody, it's always a sniper) snapped a bullet his way and it ricocheted, chipping off pieces of concrete. One of the chips hit the Captain in the side of the face and he jumped up screaming and running around. Well, hell, I can see where he would be startled, I guess anybody would. But he was really carrying on!

"Holding his hand to the scratch on his face, he turned to come back to us but took the wrong street, which was a fork leading off to where the Germans were. Somebody yelled, 'Get the Captain, get the Captain!' and I thought, 'Oh my God, he's gonna get me killed because being a medic, I've got to go after him.' And I went running down the street trying to catch him. But he apparently came to his senses before they got the chance to shoot him, so we came back and all of us pulled back into the town.

"The action was more or less sporadic for the rest of the night. They weren't sure how many there were of us and we didn't know how many there were of them. So both sides just kept a little sniper fire going back and forth until daylight.

"That night, Major Boyle and three or four other soldiers joined us and I thought, 'Thank God Boyle's here, that gives us a shot in the arm because we have such respect and love for him.' We didn't have much at that time for the Captain because he had sort of panicked. I guess he was a good guy, I know he can't be all bad because after the war I heard that he and his wife raised ten orphans. But he sure panicked in Les Arcs. He could have gotten us all killed. As a matter of fact, this was his last time in combat because when Boyle heard how he was going to send us through that roadblock in a truck he got rid of him. He never trusted him again.

"The next morning Boyle checked the defenses and found that we were straddling the railroad going up into the valley. But in the daylight, when the Germans saw us, they realized that we were only forty or fifty men and set out to get us. I understand now that they had a whole battalion. They came right down the tracks, through the side streets on our flanks and the fighting got real heavy.

"We held on till midmorning and then we saw we had to get out. Al Ernst was on machine gun at the edge of the bridge covering the junction of the streets and he got hit. He was lying there on his side but still at his gun. Across the road was an old '34 Ford with its windows all shattered. Ernst was trying to figure out how he could use it as a shield to drag himself out of there. Major Boyle was standing up right beside me, looking up the road. Then he started to walk towards Ernst who was bleeding, although he still was able to fire some covering bursts to protect the Major. You could see the blood coming down Ernst's face. Then Boyle called back, 'Keen, come on over here and let's help Ernst.'

"As I started to step out, I looked through the back window of the car and saw a German down on one knee waiting with a machine gun to get a good bead on Boyle. Boyle didn't notice him, but I saw Ernst grab the Major by the shoulders and heard him say, 'Don't get out, Major, there's a German right out there in the middle!' Boyle swung and jumped back and another man behind Ernst threw a smoke grenade up the street towards the German. It startled him enough to give our boys a chance to get back across the bridge.

[*143*]

"We lost the bridge, but we didn't care. We were just trying to stay together. But Boyle knew the Germans might come out at us through the other street so he called everybody back in a group while Ernst, who could hardly see for the blood, stayed right there to cover our withdrawal.

"We went back across a little garden, over a fence and assembled down alongside the railroad. Then we headed out of the town. Boyle had an ironclad rule never to abandon any of our wounded so, being a medic, he made me be the last one out. He stayed with me.

"Boyle is real tall and as we left they were firing at us from every direction. I think I developed a permanent crouch from that trip. I was crouching as low as I could to keep from being a target as we went through that garden. But Boyle was standing up tall, looking all around . . . I don't know what he was looking for and I kept saying, 'Get down, Major, stay down! They're shooting, stay down!' I realized later that he was looking to see if we had left any of our wounded behind.

"We went maybe three hundred yards more and we ran smack into a German machine gun crew. This was just barely on the outskirts of town and here we were being fired on from the front, and we knew there were more Germans on the right and that the rest of them were pushing us from behind. So Boyle has us turn to the left where in about a half mile we came to a small farmhouse. To get to it we had to go across an open field. Boyle, adhering to this strict rule of never leaving the wounded, tore down two fence posts with wire between, rolled them together and made a stretcher for some of the guys like Ernst. So, in spite of all this fire fighting, we took our wounded with us. To be perfectly honest, I know now it was the right thing to do, but I sure didn't feel like it then. I just wanted to run.

"When we got to this old stone farmhouse we got our wounded inside. There was no sign of life anywhere until we heard some commotion down in the cellar. All the French people were down in there.

"So this is where we holed up. It was just a matter of small fire fights from then on. We knew that troops were all around us, but we didn't know if any of them were Americans. It turned out later that our boys were up on the hill facing the town.

"Some of these troops, hearing the fire fight we were in while in the town, sent out a patrol of seven men to see what was going on. Their major, who was in our battalion, sent out the patrol and then with the rest of the group watched them wind their way down the valley floor. As they went, the group up on the hill saw that the Germans had seen the patrol coming and set up an ambush. The fellows ran up to the Major, but he would *not* let them fire at the Germans, even though they had their machine guns trained on the Germans. But *he would not let them fire*. He didn't want to give away the positions on the side and the top of the hill.

"Well, this major was a West Pointer who knew a hell of a lot more about the military than I did, and he was probably right about not giving away his position, but all seven of those boys walked into the ambush and were killed. They're still buried in Southern France.

"I know now that he was right. He knew that a lot of Germans would be coming down that valley because he had been in contact by radio with the command post who had gotten the information from the Underground. And those Germans later walked into an American ambush and those that weren't killed were captured. But we didn't know any of this then.

"All we were trying to do was to survive. There in that farm-house we were low on ammo, had water, and that was about it.

"But the next morning we saw the gliders coming in and we knew if we could just hold onto this piece of land we were bound to get help. That afternoon our scout, Perkins, got through to the headquarters up on top of the hill and told them where we were and that we had wounded. Perkins, who seemed to have a charmed life, got back to us still during daylight and through all the enemy patrols and lost Germans (who were as confused as we were), leading a group of the Japanese boys from the anti-tank outfit. These fellows had no reason on earth to come with him to us. They were an antitank company but they volunteered to come down through where the heaviest fighting was just to help us. They picked up our wounded and we all got the hell out of there. And, once again, I saw Boyle wandering around in the rear, a big moose at the end of the column, making sure that none of his boys would be left behind. I kept saying, 'Major, please get out of here!' Twigs were snapping and leaves were rustling and I kept thinking, 'Oh God, get me and this big moose out of here!' Boyle just ducked, just bent his head a little and kept looking backward as we crept away.

"Finally we got back, but what we didn't know was that Zais and our 3rd Battalion came into Les Arcs from the other end and if we could have held on they would have met up with us in the center of town. But Boyle didn't want to lose the thirty-five men that were left."[16]

The taking of Les Arcs was almost a textbook operation. The three battalions of the 517th worked together like the infield of a major league baseball club. Major Boyle had been leading elements of the 1st Battalion during the opening stages of the fight

[*146*]

and now the 2nd Battalion commander, Colonel Richard Seitz, picks up the narrative: "We arrived at our objective at about eight in the morning on August 15. I received word from Colonel Graves to go to the assistance of Bill Boyle and a handful of people from the 1st. My orders were to take over the position that Boyle and his men were trying to hold. They were getting a lot of probes by the Germans who were building up in that area. I moved my outfit over into position but it was in a real thin line because I had taken over practically the whole regiment's objective. Remember, the 3rd Battalion had landed almost twenty-five miles away.

"They came up, I think on the second day, to reinforce me, but this was while the Germans (who had been probing the day before) started to really get some mortar rounds in on us. By the end of the second day I had quite a bit of heat in on me and it seemed to me that the Germans were about to make a real push.

"It was about this time that the 3rd Battalion arrived. During their march up I had had the best radio communications I've ever had in my life with their commander, Mel Zais. I gave him a play-by-play description of what was going on and told him where I'd like to have him move, which he did."[17]

Colonel Zais concludes the account: "I only had about eighty men from my outfit drop together. I formed them into a unit and decided to follow an electric power line cut which went in the direction I had to go. But the other elements of my unit had all been so well briefed that we all kept meeting on the line of march. By the time I got there, the entire outfit had assembled together without any delays or loss in time.

"But the going was too slow. It was August in Southern France, we had been up all night, a lot of the adrenalin had gone, and since we had no vehicles we were carrying all of our equipment on our backs. It was very tiring, so I decided to get the men up on a hill and sleep till night. Then we'd abandon the power line cut and march on the roads under cover of darkness.

"I did just that and when we got in, I reported to Colonel Graves, who told me to take my men to rest in an assembly area because we were probably going to be used the next morning. But before we got to the bivouac area, we received word to counterattack that night up towards Les Arcs through the vineyards. Artillery support was provided by some 4.2 mortars which had come in by glider and some elements of the 406th Field Artillery commanded by Lieutenant Colonel Raymond Cato who had seventy-five pack howitzers.

"I deployed my battalion, two companies abreast, preparatory to moving across the railroad embankment and screening up through the vineyard into the valley in order to insure that we caught the Germans coming down through the valley.

"We went up the valley with a little pot-shooting here and there and finally arrived at Les Arcs. When we were counterattacked a few times, we called for Ray Cato's artillery, who got right into action after they landed and did a great job. We took very light casualties but we did inflict severe damages. During the course of that night they broke off and when daylight came there weren't any Germans around . . . just lots of bodies and lots of wounded. So all we had to do then was just sort of police up the area.

"By this time my men were pretty tired and I was too. We had been going strong for two days and two nights with just a little sleep late one afternoon.

"The following morning Colonel Graves came up to see me

and I can remember sitting up in the backyard of a little farm-house with my feet in a pail of water, eating a fresh tomato, while we chatted and made plans for consolidating the de-fenses."[18]

« 4 »

These first few days were crammed with colorful incidents which when pieced together and viewed from a distance present the picture of the way it was.

Sergeant Edward Sakai of the antitank company, for example, found himself at one time with a group of men looking at a safe they had discovered in a farmhouse. They were all wavering between the memory of the lectures they had received concerning attractive booby traps and intense curiosity about what was on the other side of the locked door, when two paratroopers brushed their way to the front, pulled out some plastic explosive and blew the safe. Inside were several thousands of American dollars which the paratroopers matter-of-factly stuffed in their pockets and then left without so much as a nod in the direction of Sakai and his friends.[19]

Colonel Hensleigh speaks of a new man in Lieutenant Dick Spencer's outfit observed during the first day of combat: "Spence noticed this man shooting a German, then after the man dropped, running over and bashing his face in with the butt of his rifle. After the fire fight was over, Spence hunted the man up to tell him that there was really no reason to take the German more than one way . . . he didn't have to beat him to death, too. The man reached in his pocket and pulled out four gold teeth and said, 'Lieutenant, this is the best gold in the world.' "[20]

In turn, Dick Spencer describes the actions of two more of his men: "They happened to be little fellows. We had just issued rifle grenades which were so new that they were still painted bright yellow instead of the olive drab camouflage paint we were used to. This one trooper had one of these and his buddy had a Thompson submachine gun; they were walking down this road and coming right smack into them from around the bend were two Germans on motorcycles. The one with the rifle grenade took quick aim and hit the German square between the eyes — the yellow fins were still sticking out of the guy's head. The other one got smeared by a burst from the first trooper's tommy gun.

"Then the two boys, who I think had been drinking a little bit of *vino,* turned around and began taking each other's picture. Just think of it, those Germans were laying there bleeding and these kids were snapping photographs as if they were at the beach!

"The one that fired the grenade was complaining; he said that it was pretty damn poor equipment that they were issuing, that the grenade didn't even go off. His buddy asked him if he had pulled the pin and the first man answered, 'What do you mean, pin? What's this old *pin* stuff?' So the buddy pulled the grenade out of the dead German's head and showed him the pin (there was this little wire pin up on the front that you had to pull on the rifle grenade). The first man then asked, 'Oh, you mean it's still good?' and the other one answered, 'Yeah, it's still good.'

"At that the first man wiped the grenade off and put it back in his carbine and the two of them went whistling down the road."[21]

There were other revealing patches of action during the period. Most of them were so brief and transitory that little mention was ever made of them in the dispatches filed by the correspondents. But they belong somewhere in the records. As one member of the 551st Parachute Infantry Battalion wrote home: "On this subject of classifying military operations as 'major engagements,' 'light patrol activity' and 'scattered clashes' . . . terms which you have often seen in the news . . . I would like to make one observation: when one guy starts shooting at another guy, it's a major engagement as far as the guy being shot at is concerned. As a matter of fact, one might say it's a helluva big battle!"[22]

One such "helluva big battle" received almost no attention in the newspapers back home. If the capture of Draguignan was mentioned at all, it was only as an item in a roundup list of the day's accomplishments. And yet, this taking of an obscure little French town had a direct effect on the entire Southern France campaign. Colonel William Blythe begins tracing the link which had its origin on August 16 when the 517th Combat Team and the 551st Battalion jointly stormed the objective:

"The German LXII Corps had three or four divisions in the area but it was badly disorganized by the quick thrust of our attack. To help the confusion along, when we took Draguignan we also captured the complete corps headquarters, including the commanding general. This left the German divisions in the field badly rattled and they got shot up pretty badly whenever our paratroopers caught them on the road. Also, I remember the German corps commander saying that the airborne Invasion was [dropped in] such a crazy quilt pattern that he couldn't figure out what the airborne units were doing or trying to do and that's why their defense was so confused."[23]

The corps commander was General Ferdinand Neuling. Under him, as district commander, was Generalmajor Ludwig Bier-

Major General Alexander Patch (seated) and Major General Robert Frederick (standing) interrogate the German Major General Ludwig Bieringer immediately after his capture by the First Airborne Task Force on August 18, 1944. (Signal Corps Photo)

inger, who described the capture of the command post in early Errol Flynn terms. When he spoke about the corps staff's attempt to protect itself, he said:

[It] was assembled in a strong point which was improved by barbed-wire entanglement, mine fields, etc., on a mountain slope [just northwest] of Draguignan, ready to offer resistance to the enemy. [Other] quarters and offices were likewise encircled by barbed-wire fences. They merely offered some protection against the Maquis [French Underground fighters], just as in the time of early American settlement the stockades and log huts protected the settlers against attack by Indians. . . . On the afternoon of 16 Aug. 44, the enemy's encirclement of our strong point [area command] was completed. Even the inner circle around the headquarters had been closed.

Then [late that night] in absolute darkness there was a sudden concentration of rifle, machine gun, sub-machine gun and artillery gun fire upon the strong point of FK, which caused panic among the occupying personnel. A relief party standing on the place in front of the staff building ran into the air raid shelter and some of the men who were committed followed. Having first driven out the scared men and distributed those I could get hold of in front of the tunnel, ordering them to occupy the space along the wall, the hedgerow and in places behind the trees, I hastened into the command post in order to report to the Corps by phone. Despite repeated ringing, there was no reply. Probably the wire was cut.

After a while, during a lull in the firing, I heard the loud voice of Lt. Pfannkuche, announcing: "The Americans are on the strong point. Cease fire! The entire occupation of the FK to assemble immediately, without rifles. Hurry up! In ten minutes the enemy will open fire again!"

These words of Lt. Pfannkuche, uttered with extreme excitement, I heard while I was trying to get a telephone connection. I stopped immediately and hurried out. In darkness I could see a number of men putting down their rifles on the place in front of the tunnel and marching away in a column behind Lt. Pfannkuche. After a short hesitation, together with my orderly who was the only man who remained with me, I joined my men into the American captivity.[24]

A postscript to the story of the trip to the prisoner of war camp by Bieringer is supplied by Robert Frederick who acted as his escort: "He told me he wanted to take his orderly and two suitcases full of clothing (at least I guess it was clothing), but I said, 'No, the orderly doesn't go with you,' and threw his suitcases over to the side and left them there. Then I put him in my jeep to take him down to [Lieutenant General Alexander] Patch's headquarters. Before we started the engine, I told him to take his German military cap off and pull a tarpaulin over his head and shoulders. He said no. So we drove away but when the French alongside the road started throwing things at him, that's when he took off his cap and wanted the tarpaulin. That's when he put it over his shoulders."[25]

« 5 »

And now came the bonus which, together with the heroics at Draguignan, permitted General Patch and his Seventh Army to move with unprecedented speed up the Rhone Valley toward eventual linkup with General Eisenhower's cross-Channel force. The pace of this movement, which has been described as one of the fastest deployments of a major American force ever executed, was substantially affected by the activities of Geoffrey Jones and his OSS detachment. Here is how Jones reconstructs his portion of the night of August 17:

"We had been getting these reports concerning active German movement . . . that they were shifting things and units around, making all kinds of deployments in various directions, but we could never get a serious clue as to what was actually going on. All the Germans were moving, but we didn't know if they were moving forward, backward or sideways.

"At this point, a group that I had behind the lines near Nice came back that night and told me that they had ambushed a German command car. With all due respect to them, I really think that they mostly shot up the car because they just wanted to shoot up any German group they could lay their hands on. But one of them had had the presence of mind to pick up a knapsack that was around one of the dead officers in the car and bring it back to me.

"We began to look through this thing, and by one of those great coincidences of life, we had an English officer with us who had just come from the beachhead where Patch had landed. He spoke fluent German and I didn't. He began to look over the knapsack's contents and he gasped, 'My God! This is a Field Order . . . it was written this afternoon!'

"So we began to translate this material. We put everyone on it who had any expertise at all in German documents. It was voluminous: maps, overlays, and all sorts of other pertinent combat material. The man killed had been obviously the G–3 [Operations Officer] of the commanding general's staff. He had had about four or five of these Field Orders in his knapsack and we soon realized that the Field Order under examination was one that showed the plan of retreat for the whole German Army in the South of France for the next three days!

"We really wouldn't have known what we had except for this Englishman. And he reacted as if he had spent his whole life

This is the actual map captured by Geoffrey Jones'
men which details all the German defensive positions in the Southern France Invasion area. The
blots in the upper left hand and lower right hand
corners are the bloodstains of the German officer
who was carrying the map when he was shot to death
by the Resistance fighters. (From the collection of
Geoffrey M. T. Jones)

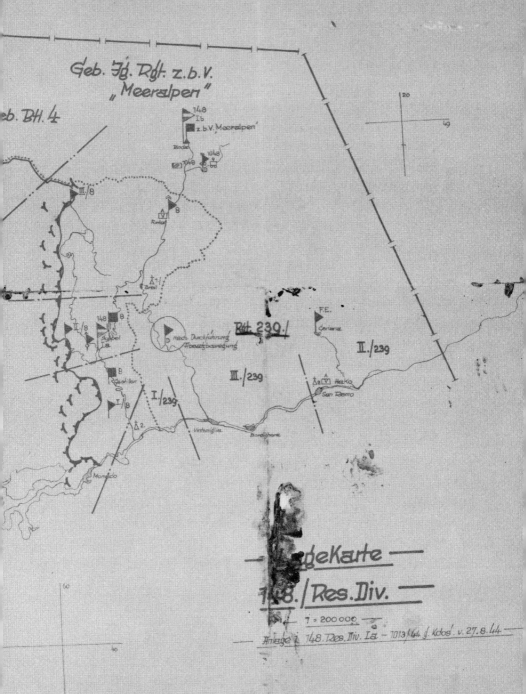

5. Geb. Div.

Geb. Jg. Rgt. z.b.V.
„Meeralpen"

Geb. BH. 4

LageKarte

148./Res.Div.

1 : 200 000

Anlage 7   148. Res. Div. Ia — 1013/44 g. Kdos. v. 27.8.44

waiting for this night. We had no lights, so we worked by candles.

"Of course it wasn't an easy job. Many of the papers were still wet with blood because, again with due respect to my boys, by the time they had decided to bring the knapsack back to me, they had probably finished taking off the wristwatches and looking for money, medals or anything else they could pull off the dead Germans. I wouldn't be surprised if they had just brought the knapsack back as an afterthought.

"Anyhow, about four or five o'clock in the morning, the captured orders began to fall into a pattern. We knew where the German units were going, where they wanted their headquarters moved . . . not only for that night but where it would be for the next three nights. They were obviously all set to fall back to prepared positions that the Italians had created to protect themselves in case of a French attack. In effect, they had prepared an orderly retreat to positions that they could occupy for the rest of the war.

"It was about an hour before daybreak when we finished translating the whole plan. We all felt the same way you do when you open an old drawer and unexpectedly find a pile of money . . . you don't believe it's there, you think it must be a mistake.

"General Frederick had left orders that he was not to be awakened by *anybody* because he hadn't gotten a night's sleep for quite a while, so they turned me away when I went over to his quarters. From there I went right over to Colonel Blythe and when I showed him what I had he agreed that orders or no orders, Frederick had to see these documents right away.

"Of course Frederick showed no annoyance at all at being awakened for this kind of reason. He quickly glanced through the file and then said, in a very quiet voice, for me to take his plane and fly down to the beach to show it to Sandy Patch.

"I took off in his little L–5 plane at dawn and by the time I got to the beach the sun was up. When I got there I refused to show the report to anyone but General [Alexander] Patch. I'm sure his staff thought I was a nut because I really looked like a bum in the first place. I don't remember if I was wearing any insignia or had anything else to identify me because I just hadn't been thinking about those things in the excitement of the night and the flight. You know, I had this leg wound with my left trouser leg cut away so as not to interfere with the dirty cloth I had been using as a bandage for it. Anyhow, I got in to see General Patch and handed over my papers.

"I've had other people tell me, and I'm convinced, too, that Patch's use of this file helped him go up the Rhone Valley a hell of a lot faster than he would have if he hadn't been so damned certain of what he needed to protect his right flank. You see, by knowing the German defense plan, he now knew exactly what force he had to use to keep them from interfering or slowing down his advance. He knew just what his opposition would be.

"Another thing: since the plan pinpointed the locations of German headquarters, troop movement schedules and bivouac areas, our headquarters was able to inform Vice Admiral [H. K.] Hewitt of the most advantageous targets for his fleet artillery, which was a great help since we didn't have very many big guns in the early stages. Hewitt had his gunners plastering every key enemy position in the area. The Germans couldn't move; no matter where they'd go, or how well camouflaged they were, the shells would come in on them within a few minutes after they got there. I guess they had no idea what was going on.

"I'm certain that when the First Airborne Task Force was finally committed to protect the Seventh Army's right flank, it was as a result of the information that came out of this captured Field Order."[26]

« 6 »

The military historians of ANVIL-DRAGOON generally consider that the airborne phase of the operation actually ended with the capture of Le Muy on August 16, but since the slashing attack of Frederick's troopers lost little of its impetus until after Draguignan fell, it seems more logical to pinpoint August 17 as the end of the mission.

First contact with the seaborne forces landing on the beaches had been made about an hour after Le Muy was taken when a tank named "The Anzio Express" rumbled into the town from the beachhead. By noon next day, substantial elements from the Seventh Army pushed on through the FABTF position, temporarily relieving the paratroopers from their combat assignment.

The mission had cost the First Airborne Task Force casualty figures of 434 killed, captured or missing and 294 wounded. In return, they had taken approximately 1,000 prisoners of war and had never stopped to count the wounded or dead Germans they had left lying in their path.

Added to this were the 283 casualties suffered in the drop, most of them in the glider landings since 357 of the 407 gliders involved were damaged to the point where they were considered unsalvageable.[27]

But the preliminary fight for a toehold in Southern France was over. It later became fashionable to describe the campaign as an easy one and this verdict has become so widely repeated that

even the men who fought there are almost convinced of its accuracy. After their capture, the German generals unanimously
insisted that they had only inferior troops and insufficient supplies to do the job and the Allied correspondents, conditioned
by the filthy inching-up fight in Italy, often communicated a feeling that victory had been handed out on a platter.

However, a tight examination of the campaign does not quite
confirm the impression that almost any show of force would have
won the day for the Allies. The enemy's initial reaction to the
airborne operation was one of complete surprise. Prisoner of war
sources revealed that the German LXII Corps command had
expected an airborne thrust within the Marseilles sector on D-Day.
The Le Muy effort completely disrupted enemy communications and the considerable professional abilities of the Task
Force made the Germans, for the first time in World War II,
appear disorganized and ineffectual.[28] Johannes Blaskowitz and
the other German generals had dispersed their divisions too far
to the west, reserve troops were committed in piecemeal fashion
and a major error was committed by underestimating the will of
the population to help the Resistance fighters in the area.[29]

The plain fact is that the German forces in Southern France
were demoralized[30] and although the discussion of whether they
were inferior troops to begin with will continue as long as World
War II campaigns are discussed, the words of Eric Sevareid,
one of the most perceptive of all the war correspondents present
at the time, ought to be at least introduced in evidence:

In battle the men's morale depends very little upon the supply of
little comforts; it is a thing of the heart and mind. Never had I seen
a greater contrast between opposed troops. The Germans, whose national cult was militarism, were behaving like a rabble of unwilling
amateurs. Only occasionally did they stand and fight with determina-

tion. They were strong and well fed, and their weapons as excellent as ever. But they felt they had been left in the south as a sacrificial offering. One sensed at once that most of them were already defeated in their minds. Our own men, whose cult was antimilitarism, whose habit it was to identify themselves merely as civilians in different clothes who detested soldiering, now subtly changed. There was a dash and a verve about them that I had rarely observed before, and young boys would frankly say: "In Italy all I used to think about was going home. Now I kind of hate to quit before we get to Berlin." It was as if they had suddenly realized they *were* soldiers by profession, with an honest desire to complete this masterpiece of their skill down to the last detail.[31]

There is only one more comment to add. Among the many official testaments to the ability displayed by Robert Frederick's men is this report made to the commanding general of the Army ground forces by his observer on the scene, Colonel Harvey Jablonski:

Characteristic of the fighting qualities displayed by members of the First Airborne Task Force was the enthusiastic manner in which they unhesitatingly attacked successive objectives, despite the numerous handicaps which prevailed. The hostile opposition encountered, however, was at no time sufficiently serious to test the full fighting capabilities of the Force. . . . The recently completed airborne operation DRAGOON was without doubt the most successful of its kind yet undertaken by Allied forces in this theater. The commanders of both the airborne and troop carrier units and their subordinates deserve full credit for the excellent manner in which they executed this mission.[32]

CHAPTER VI

GRASSE, CANNES, NICE

Other circumstances dictated that German forces on the eastern flank be pushed back to the Italian border. The entire French nation attached special importance to an early liberation of Cannes and Nice. The reasons were more psychological than military, although harbor facilities at Nice would no doubt be useful.

— History of the Seventh Army[1]

« 1 »

ITS initiative, fighting ability and guts would have entitled the First Airborne Task Force to consideration as an elite group in almost any army.

There were few soldiers who had been awarded more medals for bravery, few commanders who were more certain to take any assigned objective, and none who had been wounded in combat more often than the leader of the FABTF, Bob Frederick.

The only possible way they could have been strengthened in this particular theater at this particular time would have been to add that brutally efficient Canadian-American group, the First Special Service Force, to their roster of units. And this actually happened on August 18.

Then, in what appears to be the misuse of a remarkable weapon, Frederick and his men were detached from the main battle for France and Germany and sent east along the Riviera to the Italian-French border. This was the decision of General Jacob L. Devers who, in a postwar conversation, finally answered the question of why a first-class unit, in the thick of a hot campaign, was abruptly deployed to a relatively sedentary front.

"No one has ever made this particular point very clear, so I'd better straighten it out. You've got to remember that the commander was the British Sir Henry Maitland Wilson. I was the deputy commander to the Supreme Allied Commander [Wilson]. At that time it had been agreed that I was going to lead the

[*165*]

forces into Southern France. You must understand this, because it meant that I had to build a whole new staff, a whole new organization.

"So I made many decisions on my own . . . but with his authority. This has disturbed a lot of people because they didn't know where it [the decisions] were coming from. But we got results. Of course I'd always let him know what I was doing, but I didn't put everything down in writing.

"Now, when we got all this going, we were pretty successful . . . way ahead of schedule. And I had *nothing* on the right flank [of the Seventh Army as it advanced up the Rhone Valley].

"In the plan the First Special Service Force was to go over to that flank anyhow. But we thought they would be having some trouble on those islands [Cros, Levant] but they didn't. So we moved them [over to FABTF] immediately. Now remember that the landing was commanded by the corps commander, Truscott. Patch was the Army commander but he wasn't to take command until the French, whose job it was to go up the right flank, had landed . . . so we wouldn't have any mix-up in command.

"Patch came into the picture when the French landed. Then he was in command. I was representing Wilson and I'm the overall commander, but what I'm doing is getting the supplies in and getting the troops set, and generally straightening things out a little. I did it all orally. There are probably records of this, but I don't know where they are.

"At this point the French general, de Lattre, came in and said the job of guarding the right flank wasn't becoming to his successes and what he wanted to do was to go up the other side of the Rhone. I happened to come into the headquarters right then and I suggested to Patch, or his chief of staff, Doc White, 'Let him go. Let him go up the other side. I'll take care of that flank over there because we can keep the airborne in there and some others to protect it.'

"In other words . . . the airborne group under Frederick took over the job that had been originally assigned to the French. I didn't wire back for authority to do this. That's the way you lose battles. I got them to do what they did . . . Patch issued that order after I told him I'd take the full responsibility. I issued an order saying that I was eventually going to have to take command of this Sixth Army Group and therefore I am exerting certain influences.

"But that's the real reason that I took those people and kept them [the airborne] over there. The airborne force was spread all over the place but in the right spots . . . and they did an awful lot of fighting to help us get the drive going up that valley.

"We put them over there because Frederick was a commander I could trust, and he took it over, organized it with very little confusion. But there would have been [confusion] if I hadn't had the right people. It might have taken a whole division to do the job. One thing is certain, it would have seriously weakened us if a lesser group than Frederick and his men hadn't been on hand to do the job."[2]

« 2 »

After completing their mission of leading the entire Allied sea-borne Invasion into Southern France, the initial job assigned to the First Special Service Force by General Frederick was to capture the well-manned enemy bastion at Grasse. Reports from the FFI indicated that the Germans would make a strong stand here. Well-stocked ordnance supply dumps north of the town and the position of the city on the high terrain overlooking the approaches from the south indicated the prospects of a tough fight for a pivotal point.

Frederick had no doubt that the men he had trained and led until a few months past were equal to the job. Nor did they disappoint him. The 2nd Regiment, moving from St. Marc, encircled Grasse from the north and the 1st Regiment pushed up the highway from the east. By the morning of August 24 the two units met to create a vise which neatly cut off all resistance before it had started.

Geographically, Grasse appears as a small dot on the map of France, but it supplies most of the world's perfume oils and it seemed to the Forcemen to present an ideal place to relax for a few days, but there was no place in Frederick's plans for relaxing. The campaign that he visualized meant swallowing up great chunks of geography and Grasse would be only the first in a series of long hot marches. The men went on, betraying only a slight tendency to drag their feet as they marched out through the acres of flowers surrounding the city.

The only brake on the overall campaign plan that might occur to an objective military strategist would not result from the weariness of the men but rather from their lack of transport. The vehicles pouring in through the invasion ports were all earmarked for the main body of troops heading north. Little or no provision was made to ease the sixty-five-mile-wide path[3] to the Italian border for the men of the First Airborne Task Force. But this turned out to be only a minor problem. They simply stole as many Allied and French vehicles as they could find and as many German vehicles as they could "liberate."

In a letter home, Lieutenant Dick Spencer encapsuled a description of the way the men of the First Airborne Task Force added wheels to their trek:

Almost overnight the parachutists "mechanized" themselves. The column was cluttered with carts and bicycles, with and without tires. The Jerry convoys had taken a shellacking; it seemed that all their vehicles in Southern France had a white [Allied] star painted on the sides and top; and adorned with makeshift American flags and bright pieces of silk, nylon and rayon . . . and surmounted with 10 or 15 parachutists![4]

By the morning of the 24th, the Task Force had taken Fayence, Callian, La Napoule and was moving east in an array now sixty miles wide, reaching from the Mediterranean Sea up inland to the mountains. The bulk of these forces was within 15 miles of the coastline and was scheduled to attack the key seaports and cities while the others acted as a lid to make certain that no enemy elements could escape to the north.

At first the German artillery emplacements offered a strong resistance but the Navy provided the destroyer *Woolsey* and the light cruisers *Brooklyn* and *Le Terrible*[5] to supplement Frederick's fire power. In one ten-day period their big guns responded to eighty calls from the First Airborne Task Force.[6]

Nor did the Navy satisfy itself with simply lobbing in shells from the sea. The Riviera contains many beautiful valleys, all running perpendicular to the Mediterranean, in which the Germans had established fortified supply centers. With the consent of the naval commander, Rear Admiral Morton L. Deyo, air control parties were sent ashore to seek out enemy supply troops and relay the target information back to the ship. "Unfortunately," Colonel Bryant Evans adds, "one such party was captured in its entirety by the Germans, and even though they continued to give me support afterwards, they never did it as happily as they had previously."[7]

In the later afternoon of August 24, the 509th Parachute Battalion moving east under Colonel Bill Yarborough entered Cannes. Although the official reports say that the Germans evacuated the city without a fight, some of the men who were there testify that the flowers and the cheering and the wine bottles extended toward them from the French crowding the sidewalks along the line of entry didn't occur until after one last convulsion had cleared the way. Colonel Harry Pritchard recalls:

"A Company finally got up to the outskirts of Cannes. There's a little river there running by a hill which had some Germans on it who were surprised completely when we appeared. They just didn't have any idea that we were anyplace in the area because we had been moving pretty fast. So we took that.

"On the other side of the river there was another group of Germans, but our orders were to go to the river and stop. I tried to get permission to go on, because I could see the Germans; I could see them through my field glasses, they were walking around in undershirts, completely unaware of the fact that we had gotten there. But the orders from someplace were that we wouldn't cross the river, so we didn't.

"About an hour after we had occupied these German positions, the group on the other side found that we were there, and then we took the heaviest casualties I have ever been subject to throughout the war . . . even in the Bulge or in the Elbe River crossing.

"The Germans really gave us an unbearable shelling with their mortars and their heavy one hundred and fifty millimeters . . . whatever they had. This lasted for a little over an hour, during which time I lost all of my squad leaders, killed, and had about one third of the platoon wounded. We accomplished nothing. We just lay there and took casualties until it was over.

"The next day the Germans withdrew on the other side of

Cannes. We first became aware of this by the tremendous number of Frenchmen who approached our positions to tell us that the Germans had evacuated the city. We could see that this was the truth from the attitude of the crowd.

"We were going to move on but nothing would do but that we had to have a triumphant parade through Cannes. The French insisted on it. They finally got some bridges built and got some tank destroyers up there and we entered Cannes riding on the tank destroyers. I don't know where these other guys had been all during the 'exploitation,' but when it came time to pass out the wine they all showed up. I'll never forget that day as long as I live: the people were really joyful, tears were running down their faces, the girls were kissing everybody . . . even the johnny-come-latelies driving the tank destroyers . . . people were throwing flowers at us . . . just the way it's supposed to be."[8]

Another company officer, Lieutenant R. F. Ruyffelaere, after confirming that the artillery support had been diverted to "a more important mission on the left," adds a footnote to the description of the shelling the Americans took before Cannes: "At the height of it, I was down in my foxhole, and a lieutenant who had the section of machine guns attached to me started looking for a hole to jump into. They were all pretty well occupied so he finally jumped in on top of me, and he said, 'Gee, can I occupy this hole with you?' And I answered, 'Sure, stay here as long as you want.' He says, 'I sure appreciate your letting me stay in this hole with you.' We used to call this guy 'El Stupido' because he was so goddamned stupid he never really knew what was going on."[9]

Colonel Bill Yarborough continues: "While we were overlooking the city of Cannes, trying to figure out how to get in there from where we were on the high ground, Herbert Mathews of the New York *Times* joined me and said, 'You see that building down there? That's the Hotel Carlton. It's just not only the best hotel in France, it's the best hotel in the world and I would be much obliged if you don't do anything to wreck it.' So I promised not to, and when we finally got in there we found that the hotel was all sandbagged up but still had a big complement of waiters on hand. We had many and many a happy time thereafter at the Hotel Carlton."[10]

But the good times in Cannes did not occur until later. The next orders received by the 509th directed that they proceed to and cross the Var River. Terrell Stewart, the paratrooper who described the jump into France so graphically, takes over the narration:

"Shortly afterwards we all boarded vehicles and were driven down to the wide, flat bed of the Var River and across this between two white ribbons on short stakes marking a mine-free way across. The First Special Service Force, attired in OD's, walked across in two files at the same time — *while we rode!* Why did we enjoy the special treatment? I don't know.

"My group rode in a weapons carrier. It developed a flat tire about midway across. We troopers got out and stood around watching the First Special Service Force walk past us while the driver put the spare on. I knew this was the First Special Service Force by the patch on their shoulders. They followed one another silently at sling-arms. They looked just like any other infantry outfit. One would never have suspected, had it not been for their shoulder patch, that they were the rough-tough outfit that they were.

"The Var was very low at this point, hardly enough to get the tires of a vehicle or the soles of a soldier's boots good and wet. I had no doubt, however, that at other seasons of the year the Var probably contained much more water. At intervals throughout the wide, mostly dry river bed the Jerries had erected little pyramids of rocks cemented together. These were about two feet high and I surmised that they were meant to be obstacles against glider landings."[11]

Colonel Pritchard adds: "Being an airborne outfit, we had damned little transportation, but it's a good thing they assigned us the mission [to cross the Var] because a mechanized unit wouldn't have been any good at all in that area. Drainage along that part of the Mediterranean coast runs north and south and there's a bridge about every two or three miles over the river, which is really a very wide sand wash.

"The withdrawing Germans systematically blew those bridges so, being on foot and in damned good shape, we didn't have much trouble going across. As a matter of fact, most of the time we were without artillery because the heavy guns couldn't get across until the bridges were repaired.

"The resistance we encountered was relatively light when looked at from division level, but when you looked at it from the platoon and company viewpoint, it got pretty heavy because the Germans were leaving platoon and company detachments behind to guard the obstacles they had created out of the blown bridges. In the absence of artillery support, sometimes these rearguards presented pretty tough problems. We didn't actually get moving again with real speed until one of the offshore cruisers came in close enough to help out."[12]

In the last days of August, General Frederick had requested permission to take and occupy Nice, saying, "Conditions now existing in Nice make it urgent that the city be occupied by Allied Forces as soon as possible. Unless some show of Allied military strength is made within the city at this time, it is feared that riots and other civilian disturbances will reach such a scale as to seriously damage American prestige in this area."[13]

Frederick's chief of staff, Kenneth Wickham, later amplified this communication by saying: "The French Forces of the Interior in Nice rose up against the German Army elements there and it became necessary that we advance and take the city to preclude undue bloodshed. The French Army itself sent down a small contingent of perhaps a half dozen officers to the Nice area with the mission to assume control in the name of France of the FFI that were operating along the coast and inwards.

"Nice was a city of two hundred and fifty thousand people and, in our view, we could not afford to have those civilians ruinously defeated by the Germans in the city. [But even though we wanted to avoid civilian casualties] my recollection is that the VI Army Group headquarters was rather concerned over our continued liberation of territory. Actually there were approximately a million people along the Riviera coast [where we were operating] at the time. We were concerned because communications were rather poor during this period. The most reliable contact we had with headquarters was my liaison officer who took about two days coming and two days going . . . so we were not in current consultation with Army Group headquarters. Telephone communications had not been really established. We did have radio but we were not the most significant unit for the VI Army Group at the time."[14]

But there were some individual members of the Force who were not quite as concerned with military protocol as General Frederick and his staff. They simply refused to wait for official permission to go sight-seeing. For example, Henry Wenerzyno-wicz recalled with great relish: "That night [August 29], Privates Tony Marchese, Harry Sollis and I, after hearing so much about the Riviera, decided to see how the town looked. So when everyone went to sleep we snuck out of camp and went into the city. We found the Jerry, who must have loved Nice, had left it in one piece and took off. We met some girls at a bar and they told us that the kind of fun we were looking for was on the next block. We wasted no time finding the place, knocked on the door, and a Frenchman with a surprised look on his face at seeing American GI's opened up and let us in. Needless to say, there were about twenty or twenty-five other GI's inside there who had the same idea we did. We had a heck of a ball there that night."[15]

Lieutenant Dick Spencer, who had been separated from his battalion after being wounded, describes another moment before Nice: "There were three of us who were walking wounded so we got some weapons and ammunition together and started hitch-hiking back to the front. We didn't know where our outfit was. I'm not saying that I was trying to be a hero, I just wanted to catch up with my mail. You see, my wife was expecting and I wanted to find out if it was a boy or a girl.

"We spent one night in Cannes and the next morning we tried to find out where the paratroopers were. We were told that since Nice had already fallen, that's where we would probably find them.

"So we got to the edge of the Var River which is pretty wide right down there along the coast. But we could see people on the other side lying in the sand, . . . typical GI guys. We could see weapons and these guys lying around on the sand, not doing anything and who didn't seem too alert. So we hollered over to ask how we could get across. Naturally we were hollering in English.

"Boy, everybody jumped and we thought we had scared them.

They all jumped back to their weapons and the next thing you know they had opened fire on us and we were burrowing down in the ground as far as we could go, still hollering, 'Americans! Americans!'

"But they were Krauts. Nice hadn't fallen yet! In fact, the boys had taken a detour around the city and were coming in from another angle. Those bullets spit sand all around us, and we kept hollering 'Americans!' to get them to quit shooting. Then suddenly we realized that, by golly, they weren't Americans because although we couldn't tell anything from their rifles, we could hear the difference as soon as they opened their machine guns up on us. Nobody got hit and we beat it out of there and hitchhiked back to our outfit through a circuitous route."[16]

It fell to Lieutenant Ruyffelaere to bring in the final word concerning the situation in Nice: "I had been given the job of battalion Intelligence Officer because we were being deluged by information, but all of it in French which I spoke fairly well. Between a sergeant and myself we knew enough of that language to translate and evaluate the data coming in. We used to stay up late at night screening all of the information coming in, but almost all of it was too old to use. I feel it was given us, in many cases, in return for cigarettes, butter or whatever else we could scrounge up for the informants.

"One of our contacts in the Underground was a man by the name of Paul de Buisine who first came to us at about the same time the rumor started floating around that a column of five hundred Germans was coming back into Nice to defend the place . . . that they had changed their minds about evacuating it. He told me this and I said that there was only one way of finding out what was going on and that was by someone going there to check.

"He said that there would still be quite a few German squads and patrols in town and then added, 'I'll tell you what I will do; I will get you there in my car.' This meant going across the Var River. His car was parked on the other side of a bombed out bridge.

"So, after picking a noncom to go along with me, I made it clear to Monsieur de Buisine that if he was leading us into a trap, it was his last trap . . . if it was going to be ours, it would also be his.

"Then, of all places, he took us right into his house. There he dressed me up in his clothes, which was fairly funny because he is much taller and thinner than I am. The clothes certainly didn't look like mine, and the shoes he put on me proved that they weren't mine because they were so big on me that they squeaked with every step I took.

"So we set out to go into Nice as civilians. He was to do all the talking because we were afraid that my French might give us away. On this premise we went into town in search of the five-hundred-man column.

"And, winding through the streets, we finally discovered them! They turned out to be a column of very happy Polish soldiers in German uniforms who had thrown away their arms, led by two very drunken FFI's, all singing at the top of their lungs as they came down the street. They weren't going to defend Nice, they were going out to surrender!

"Since we were sure that it wouldn't be long before they found someone to surrender to, we didn't worry about getting the word back to headquarters. So when de Buisine said, 'Now that you're here, we might as well take advantage of the situation, let's take a look through the town. I know that the Germans are in Monaco, they've got machine guns there. I'll take you down there.' I agreed, saying, 'Let's take a chance, we've gotten away with it so far.'

"We went down to Monaco and actually got into the courtyard there where we saw groups of Germans behind machine guns. I wasn't worried for some reason about the Germans finding me out except through those damned shoes. My shoes had been squeaking like hell with every step I took and now my feet were beginning to hurt. But these Germans were not alert at all. I was able to look the place over; there really didn't seem to be more than a handful of Germans in all of Monaco. The rest had withdrawn beyond. Naturally this was interesting information to bring back."[17]

Meanwhile, the journal *Le Victorieux* provides a glance at what was happening in the city at the time:

These [communist-oriented, FTP] groups, apparently obeying an order of their own . . . had the ambition to impose upon the local powers named by Algiers [Free French Headquarters] their own officials and administrators, even using their armed groups as a threat.

The premature action towards liberation started by these FTP groups was immediately followed by the FFI groups, who did not hesitate to take part in the fight, afraid that their abstention might be interpreted unfavorably by the Communists and used against them by politicians.

This premature action for liberation might have had most unfortunate consequences for the different elements which took place in it, and also for the population, had the German forces started offensive operation against the FFI who were mostly armed with hunting rifles.[18]

Finally, Frederick received the permission of General Devers to take Nice. On August 30, the 509th Combat Team crossed the Var River and occupied the city. At the same time, Frederick

The First Airborne Task Force marches in a victory parade after the liberation of Nice. (From the collection of Robert T. Frederick)

sent one column of troops north to Saint-André to establish immediate contact with the First Special Service Force and another column proceeded east along the coast to Beaulieu.[19] The staff was established at the Alhambra Hotel in Nice, and this became the headquarters for the FABTF for the balance of the campaign.

The troops, filing into the city, were almost wide-eyed at their reception. One Forceman noted that "the welcoming was as if there was no war on. It was like a football team returning home."

But the clearest picture preserved of this preliminary entry upon the "Champagne Campaign" is to be found in an article in a local journal *Du Patriote* as it was translated and reprinted in the newspaper *The Thunderbolt* that the men of the 517th published for themselves with the help of Father Guenette:

THE FRENCH IMPRESSION OF THE AMERICAN ARMY

We can tell of the first Americans in Nice with more than enthusiasm and with an astonishment caused at the bottom of sensitive hearts by the most unexpected surprises.

When the rumor said that they were coming, we banked on the vision of sweating columns, on the sight of tired faces, on great roar of heavy trucks and tanks, but lo and behold! only two young and very calm faces on which a beard could hardly be distinguished appeared!

We were waiting for them. They laughed it off quite jokingly. "Where are they? — the Germans?", was their first question, and their smile made one think of the attitude of the "News Follies" admirers back home.

Yes, these first Americans were looking for the "Boches" who were expected to come back through the North of Nice. There were two paratroopers, proudly preceding the American strength which was penetrating Nice, two boys from Ohio and California with only one idea in mind: to get at a few more Germans! The rumor at the time was that the Germans were coming back in strength.

Kisses and ovations, and huggings were out of the question; they were coming to throw them out and massacre them in a modern way, a way taught by the spirit of liberty like the one they were bringing us.

That is the reason why the first Americans in Nice whom we have seen have told us only these words: "Where are they?"[20]

« 3 »

The march east was a long dusty trail for the Task Force. General Frederick, aware that an overnight stop in any of the villages or towns being liberated along the way would almost certainly result in a "morning-after" delay in getting his lusty young soldiers back on the schedule he had set for them, sent specific directions to all subordinate commanders that all bivouac areas be located well past any newly liberated town or village.

Naturally, the Forcemen grumbled at what they considered a denial of the fruits of victory. They looked at the cheering townspeople crowding the roads and streets and saw only an unalloyed gratitude that seemed easily translatable into highly personal concepts of relaxation.

But what many of the young men did not understand was that the happy faces of the French population were not a uniform expression of deep gratitude. Like a sunlit sea, in many cases the surface reflection was the only visible thing.

The histories, newspaper reports and personal accounts of the period indicate that much of this fervor was simply an emotional reaction to stirring military and political events. There were many who welcomed only the change and there were those who inwardly refrained from welcoming both the change and the Americans who had effected it. But both of these waved salutes just as enthusiastically as the men and women honestly express-ing unmixed prayers of thanks at the departure of the German occupation forces from their countryside.

Some of the Forcemen saw it. Eric E. Anderson, of the 517th, afterward noted: "In the towns the people seemed to welcome us with open arms, but when you attempted to become more friendly, you wondered whether the people trusted or wanted you, although wine and women were ours for the asking."[21]

It is a matter of record[22] that quite a few shopkeepers raised their prices in anticipation of the appearance of the American soldiers and several Forcemen report coming uneasily away from a visit with a French family. "They made you feel," said one of them, "that they admired the Germans for their efficiency and for the fact that, for the first time, Nice had received real guidance in the administration of its affairs. It seemed that they equated the Germans with progress and this, of course, made us feel like unwelcome transgressors. But these reactions rarely came to light until after several bottles of wine had been con-sumed."[23]

Captain Geoffrey Jones who had lived among the French be-fore the war and who had come to know them even better while hiding up in the mountains with the Resistance leaders before the Invasion, explains this by saying:

"You must remember that there were some very fine German career officers stationed in Southern France during the occupa-tion. They were aware that the best way to get along in occupied country was to make friends with the people. The German troops were more disciplined than ours; they were Nazi troops. So when their officers said, 'No one will go to town,' no one went into town. On the other hand, our troops were used to treating such a command almost as a game; they operated under more democratic conditions. A fellow saw no harm in sneaking off into town and getting loaded. Hell, even some of the junior officers would occasionally go with them!

"But the Germans were capable of literally stringing up such fellows. Admittedly, this extreme treatment might happen only rarely . . . but the point is, it *was* a possible punishment for breaking the rules. The discipline, the very nature of Nazi training, was different than ours. There was no fraternization between officers and men. Therefore, the German troopers, because of the discipline if nothing else, may have conducted themselves better as far as the townspeople were concerned. But I would question that this also meant that the Germans were better liked. It only meant that they were less annoying.

"It boiled down to this: the Germans said, in effect, 'If you people won't do *this*, we won't do *that*,' and to a great extent that's the way they were able to control the Resistance in Southern France, which numbered far less activists than in other parts of the country. Whenever the Underground did anything in this area, the Germans were able to isolate the event and immediately retaliate. As a matter of fact, they shot forty people in Nice just a few days before Frederick's men got in there. One of them was an operative that I had sent in.

"This, I think, is the answer to the way some of the American soldiers felt about the French. It wasn't that the French liked the Germans better, it's just that German control had kept unrealized some of the worst fears concerning an enemy occupation. If they disliked anyone, it might have been the Italians and this group

[*183*]

they viewed with something approaching disdain, not fear. They made jokes about Italian soldiers, saying that they were good singers and cookers of spaghetti but damned bad soldiers."[24]

The French seemed to save their strongest dislike for each other. An American advance into any town or village along the Riviera invariably served as a signal for the beginning of a storm of violent denunciations. Frenchmen deluged Frederick's head-quarters with accusations that other Frenchmen were Nazi sym-pathizers, Communists or were otherwise to be considered ene-mies of the Republic and deserving of immediate punishment by Allied officers. When it became apparent that General Frederick and his representatives had no intention of interfering in civilian affairs[25] they turned on each other in an internecine fury. The rancor which spurted from almost every quarter inevitably washed up against the presence of Allied troops and General Frederick recalled, long after the war, that "even the local French newspapers were disparaging to the Americans shortly after the Invasion."[26]

Joseph W. Welsh, the Civil Affairs officer for the First Air-borne Task Force, commented: "The French have always been a very difficult people. Perhaps they weren't as difficult then as they are now . . . but it's true that we had a number of de-nouncements. We were not the police, of course, so when we had people denounced to us who were not really Nazis, it was not our job to punish them. We turned them over to the French police at that point . . . [because] we had no right or no way in which we could take any action against the collaborationists."[27]

Unquestionably many of the patriots fitted into Eric Seva-reid's category, *maquis de dernière minute*[28] [Resistance fight-ers of the last minute], and one historian described them by reporting:

In this administration there was one qualified representative of the FFI. But, after [a] parade which followed the liberation, he collapsed over his desk, moaning: "Who the hell are all these people?" He had witnessed, parading before Monsabert, 1500 men wearing brassards, about three times the number there had been a week earlier.[29]

Blake Ehrlich adds:

And there were the lynch-minded idiots, filled with false patriotic frenzy, to whom every stranger was a spy or a fugitive collaborator. Yves Farge, De Gaulle's representative at Lyon, was arrested six times in one day by so-called *maquisards* who wanted to shoot him as an enemy because he did not carry a pass signed by himself. Other Resistance leaders who had outsmarted and outrun the Gestapo for four years, found themselves in the worst danger of their lives when arrested by such vigilante bands . . .

Tribunals of various sorts, most of them with no authority but that of their weapons, held court all over the country, mechanically sentencing suspects to die. Just how many nobody knows. Almost no one in France wanted to know, because what happened was beastly, stupid and painfully needless.[30]

There were members of the FABTF who had first-hand experience with these hate-filled days. Bob Morgan, an intelligence officer, found it necessary to go back to Draguignan in order to save a man whom he knew to be a loyal French patriot from a sentence of death. Morgan says, "Red-hunting was a big pastime; ordinarily I wouldn't have interfered but this man had helped us. He was innocent of every charge that had been made against him."[31]

Gabriel Rafael, the Frenchman who fought so valiantly, first in the Underground and then alongside the members of Yarborough's 509th, says: "All of these people claimed that they had always been in the Resistance. I don't know if Colonel Yarborough mentioned it, but one of them actually arrested me and Bill had to get me out.

"Cannes had already been liberated and on our way to Nice, Bill had given weapons to me and some friends of mine who came along for this duty. I had a pistol, carbine and then a tommy gun which I kept at home.

"Some people came one day and asked my mother if I had any arms there and my mother said I had this tommy gun up in my room. They said that they were members of the FFI. Actually, they were not . . . they were members of the FTP which was the Communist section of the Resistance who had never materialized before.

"You must remember that when the Germans were there, nobody moved; when the Germans left, then you had a good many members in the Resistance.

"Anyway, they seized this tommy gun and asked my mother where I was. My mother said that I was with the U.S. Army. So one of them, a Captain Barbier, left a note saying I should come see him. I knew this Barbier from before the war but I never knew him to be a member of the Resistance.

"A couple of days later when I had the chance I went to see Captain Barbier who told me, 'I arrest you.' I asked him why and he said, 'Because I am the Chief of the Resistance here and what right did you have to cross the line to go to the Americans?' I told him that I never knew that he had been a Resistance fighter and, what is more, that I had never heard of any organized Resistance activity in the area. Then he tried to make that sound as if I had done something very bad.

"But as soon as Bill heard that I was arrested I think that he got very angry. He sent a young lieutenant over to get me out. It was very funny because from my room in the hotel where they had put me I could see this jeep coming, and I started to laugh and tell my guards, 'Here comes trouble for my friend Barbier.'

"The young lieutenant, however, only got me out because he had with him a police order which said that I was assigned to the U.S. Army. But even so, this Captain Barbier insisted on striking a bargain and finally Bill gave him some weapons in exchange for my freedom."[32]

Father Guenette had a particularly intimate exposure to the violence of the period. He says: "In Nice, I had made contact with certain civilians, some of whom were in the FFI, some in the FTP. One night a doctor who was in with the Communists, the FTP, told me how they were getting rid of all these collaborators. I listened to him, horrified, and then broke in, not sure I had heard him correctly. 'You mean you are killing a hundred and fifty Frenchmen every morning without a trial?' In return he insisted, 'Well, a hundred and fifty is not enough . . . you'd be surprised how many collaborators there are.'

"I knew one family he mentioned. It consisted of a seventy-six-year-old man, his fourteen-year-old granddaughter and an uncle. From what the doctor said, I gathered that they were going to be shot next morning. I ran out, got my jeep and drove over to the jail where I got into a violent argument with the people who were there. But the man in charge kept saying, 'You don't understand what's going on.'

"I answered, 'I certainly do.' Then some woman gets up and says, 'You don't understand these things at all.' I turned on her and shouted, 'Wait a minute! I'm not speaking to you. You sit down! I want to speak to this man here.' Then I told him, 'Look, I studied in France in 1935 and 1939 and I've been following everything that's been going on with your Communists. All you want to do is to create a government along your own lines. You have no authority to condemn these people without a trial. You are making up your own authority right now. As far as I'm concerned, I've come to release these three people. What wrong has this seventy-six-year-old man done? And what has the fourteen-year-old granddaughter done? I want these three people released and if you don't, I'm considering you people as a bunch of criminals! It won't take me long to find out your names, and once we've mopped up a little bit around here we'll come back with these names and then we'll find out if we can't treat *real* criminals the way they deserve. You are all worse than Nazis. You make me ashamed of my French background!'

"Well, they released these three people, but the man said, 'You can have them . . . but you see this pile of papers over here? They represent all the people we are going to execute.' This made me angry all over again. I told him, 'You'd better watch out. I'm going to tell what I've seen here to my colonel and it won't surprise me if he makes the decision to come over here and destroy this place. We've got enough men and arms to do it!'

"I did go back and tell the Colonel about it. But he said, 'Chaplain, you mind your own damned business. We are not supposed to deal in the internal affairs of France; we've got a military mission and that's it. So you forget all about that pile of names!' "[33]

Perhaps a partial explanation for this bloodletting is found in the comments of the *Life* photographer who covered the campaign, Carl Mydans:

When the Germans retreated from Southern France, loosening the grip under which they held the French, there was a period before the laws of an established government could rule the people when each man's opinion, sparked by his long-pent emotions, counted as law. Frenchmen roamed the streets and broke down doors looking for other Frenchmen whom they thought deserved to die.[34]

Geoffrey Jones saw it as one of the manifestations of a power struggle: "To be brutally frank, there was very little Resistance. It was practically nonexistent in Southern France before the Invasion because of the independent French nature. It was a motley group that was down there and I don't think they ever got together. The only Resistance people that we really had were the FTP's, who were the Communist-organized groups as opposed to the FFI. These were organized and the FFI were not. And now the non-Communists were refusing to sit back and let the Communists grab power.

"There was a material side to this too. When the Germans were pushed out, we never filled the governmental vacuum that they left. They and their collaborators had been here for a number of years, some of them owned property and some of them had married and had children. When we came in, we never took over any of the property that had been abandoned by the Germans or their collaborators. Naturally, there was a scramble for it. Some of it was confiscated and put up at auction by the government, but there was quite a fight for the ownership of the bulk of it that was left. And this contributed to the frenzy of those days.

"Another thing causing confusion was that what real Resistance there had been was made up of quite a few small groups, very few of whom knew about each other. Even in my case where I had fourteen or fifteen such units working directly for me, there was rivalry. None of them wanted to cooperate with any of the others. Each group wanted to be assigned to its own specific task. Oh, they'd help each other out if they ran across one another's path, but rarely would they sit down to listen to a plan for a joint action.

"And that's all that the Resistance amounted to in Southern France, these small groups. It wasn't at all like up in the northern part of France where the Resistance forces were actually a small army. This is why it was so easy for anyone to claim that they had belonged to the Underground even though they never had, and why others would doubt the truth of some who claimed to be, and actually were, members of other groups."[35]

There is no question that much of the confusion was Communist-inspired. Evidently acting on orders from some central authority, the FTP did everything possible to increase the disorderly situation to the point where it would become possible for a coordinated minority to seize political control. Lieutenant Ruyffelaere saw one particularly blatant example of this opportunism. He said, "As Intelligence Officer of the battalion, and able to speak French, I stayed on fairly close terms with the local police. One of them told me that the Communists were putting up signs on a building which read: YOU ARE NOW ENJOYING THIS WHEAT THROUGH THE COURTESY OF THE U.S.S.R. In the building was a shipment of flour [which General Frederick had requested through General Devers] that we had sent in because the foodstocks of the city were down close to starvation level. And now, here were these very smart Communists in Nice putting up these signs claiming credit. I brought this to the attention of Colonel Yarborough who said, 'Tell them that if they don't take them down, we'll immediately declare martial law in the town.' Of course they did."[36]

When asked about the disorder, General Frederick responded,

"I was so busy fighting a campaign that I just didn't know who the hell was a Communist and who wasn't. I know that there were many false accusations and that some of these were made for personal reasons. If you didn't like someone, you'd call him a Communist. Some people ran up big bills at the grocery store and then when we came in they'd denounce the owner as a collaborator in order to take him out and get him hanged. Naturally this caused a tremendous amount of ill will."[37]

The Force's disenchantment with the French civilians extended, on many occasions, to the Maquis soldiers who attached themselves to the various units. Sergeant Major Planinshek, a member of the First Special Service Force, when asked about these men, replied, "On Mount Ours there were a few defensive positions that the Maquis held. When we were coming back with a prisoner we always made sure that one of our own men was in front of him and that one was behind if we wanted the prisoner for questioning. The Maquis used to shoot prisoners first and then ask questions later."[38]

Gene Frice, another Forceman, described many of the Maquis as "11th Hour Patriots." He said that some of them were "dedicated, quiet soldiers, but many more were the vocal braggadocio FFI wearing belts of hand grenades and carrying recently acquired Schmeissers [German machine guns] whose only contact with the Germans consisted of kicking, spitting, threatening and sometimes killing prisoners."[39]

Of course there were also American soldiers who found much to admire among the Maquis. John Hollowell said, "In Company B we had two of them who stayed with us just about the whole time we were in Southern France. They ate and slept with us and carried the doggonedest loads of water, munitions, or food. I have a great deal of respect for them because they helped us, especially in the scouting. They didn't seem to be afraid of anything."[40]

Jess Walls, the company commander who took Saint-Tropez, described the activities of Jacques Renault, who "was the FFI leader in the area. He contacted me within thirty minutes after the drop. While many of the FFI were celebrating the Invasion at some cafe, Jacques and another man joined the fight with a vengeance. He was shot through the neck, but after first aid was back in the thick of things."[41]

The disposition of many FFI members to swagger in warlike attitudes afforded considerable amusement to some of the Forcemen. Lieutenant Dick Spencer said, "They were a little bit like our teenagers today. They were carried away by the excitement of the whole thing. Sure, a bunch would show up when we came to the edge of a town, they'd go through the town with us, getting garlands of flowers and kissing all the girls. But at the other edge of the town they'd turn around and go back in while we went on."[42]

Lieutenant Colonel David Grange says, "We used to get a big kick out of them because when they were going out on a mission, they'd all assemble with a great deal of ceremony and much singing of the "Marseillaise" and everybody was crying and kissing each other and there were lots of flags flying. They'd get into a truck and off they would go towards where the Germans were last seen moving. But later on that evening we'd notice most of these same fellows back in town again. They had returned via the back way."[43]

But the indication that the Resistance movement in Southern France was not a thing of unblemished valor should in no way be extended to the activities of the civilians who had joined the

OSS detachment captained by Geoffrey Jones. Colonel William Blythe once commented: "Any information we received from the French came through Geoffrey Jones."[44]

« 4 »

If Blythe relied upon it, the information relayed by Geoffrey Jones must have been of value even though it started out with these two strikes against it: the Task Force members had come to distrust the information from the French; and the OSS was viewed in a jaundiced light by most members of regular army units. This was not an undeserved opinion. For much of the war, the OSS became a haven for quite a few incompetents and misfits. OSS members were generally regarded as overly prone to self-dramatization and the information they forwarded was rarely considered as a proper basis on which to risk the life of a man or a unit.

Jones inferentially admits this situation when he says: "Frederick never really accepted us until after the captured German defense plans were authenticated. Of course I never asked him if he was pleased with us because he was a formidable gentleman, but the very fact that he began to use us for something besides translating and running errands showed that he felt that we were a tool he could rely upon. But he never gave anyone a pat on the back. You knew you were doing your job if he continued to let you serve him.

"Just before we occupied Nice, I received what I considered to be final confirmation of his faith in us. He called me in late one afternoon and said, 'Admiral Hewitt [the naval commander] thinks our intelligence is very good. He's judging by what we have accomplished so far. Now he's asked us for what we can tell

[193]

him about the harbor facilities in Nice because he's been in some minor skirmishes and some of his ships need repairs. He wants to know if he can use the harbor in Nice for this purpose.' General Frederick then looked at his watch and added, 'It's now five o'clock. Can you get me this information by tomorrow morning? I'm having breakfast with the naval liaison officer and I want to show him just what we can do.'

"I went back to my tent and looked at the wall. I wasn't sure of quite what I was going to do because we had already that day had our radio contact with our operatives in Nice and we weren't due to have them reach us again until the next day. Just at that moment, as luck would have it, two of my men came in who were just returning from a mission behind the lines. And the uncle of one of them was the harbormaster at Nice!

"I told him my problem and he said of course he would go back in and what was it that I wanted to know. I started to explain about harbor depths, location of installations, the possible presence of submarines and whether there were any mines . . . but then, looking at him, I saw I had exceeded his capabilities. He was only a kid of twenty or so and all this naval talk about precise naval information was completely strange to him. So I shrugged my shoulders and said, 'The hell with it, I'll go with you.'

"So we got into my car and drove to the west bank of the Var and parked it in a clump of bushes. We got out, put on our blue suits and waded and swam across the river. It was about ten o'clock by the time we got to the other side and the night seemed to be going by at a terribly fast clip. We 'borrowed' a couple of bicycles from a farmyard and went on into Nice.

"Naturally there was a curfew in the city. No one was supposed to be on the streets at all. So it was fairly touchy while we were making our way to the house of the boy's uncle. Every so often we'd hear the hobnailed boots of the German patrols and we'd have to freeze in the shadows until they went by.

"But we finally got to where the uncle lived. The boy threw pebbles up against the bedroom window in order to wake him. Finally, he stuck his head out and I almost strangled keeping from roaring at the sight. It was too perfect. He was actually wearing one of those old-fashioned nightcaps!

"Anyway, between the boy hissing up to his uncle and the uncle yelling back down to identify ourselves and some of the other neighbors waking up and yelling out, 'What's going on?' and the like, it's a wonder we didn't rouse the whole German Army.

"But the uncle finally let us in. He turned out to be most cooperative. He had the maps of the port there and knew where everything was. He wrote it all down and even traced some over-lays on his maps. Then we started to bicycle back.

"Once we heard a German truck coming up behind us on the way out of Nice and, acting on a sudden flash of inspiration, I told the boy, 'Come on, turn your bike around and make believe we are heading for the city.' When the truck pulled up, one of the German soldiers sitting in the cab asked us where we were going. We told him we were heading for the city and he said, 'Don't you know there's a curfew in there? You can't get into the city now. Put the bicycles in the back of the truck and get in. We'll give you a lift back to where you came from.' So we rode with the Germans back to the Var River and we thanked them very po-litely and they let us off just across from where we had hidden the car.

"When we got back to headquarters we woke up a few of our girls who translated the French and typed up a clean copy for the

Admiral. At 7:30 next morning I went in to see the General who asked, 'Do you have anything for me?' I answered, 'I think so,' and handed him the complete report with all the information he wanted, including maps, overlays and so forth. Of course I wasn't at the breakfast but I understand that the Navy officer almost fell over when Frederick showed him where everything was, where the net was and where it could be pulled back to get in, the location of sentry towers, mines and the various depths.

"From here on in my relations with Bob Frederick became quite good. He trusted us with definite missions which had a place in his tactical planning.

"Naturally we had to have some pretty competent operatives to do the job that the General wanted . . . and I was lucky in this respect. I had people like *Josef Le Fou*, which freely translated means 'Joseph the Nut.' He got this name by killing with his bare hands some Germans he suspected of attacking his sister . . . and everyone felt you had to be crazy to kill a German during the occupation. He was a tremendously good agent.

"We had quite a few more like him. You see, most action people are individuals of a free stripe of some sort. They are either a little nuts or excessively independent, but one way or another they are nonconformists. These are the kind of people you get most often in this line of work.

"I also had Pierre Escot, a fanatically loyal and capable Frenchman who was the man to whom I most often turned for an evaluation of the capabilities of the civilian individuals and groups who wanted to affiliate with us.

"There were also quite a few women who acted as translators, typists and the like and quite a few businessmen. As a matter of fact, our chef had been a very prosperous lawyer. This isn't as frivolous as it might seem. Good food was important because we couldn't pay these people for the work they did, nor would they have accepted it. So when they would come back through the lines or would work around the clock, it was awfully important to have a good meal waiting for them. This was a major job; I had as many as a hundred and twenty people like this working for me at a time. Only two of them were Americans; one was a radio operator and the other was an intelligence sergeant who was a map specialist.

"Our headquarters was apart from Frederick's. We had our own place for security reasons and because we wanted to work in our own fashion, which was something that characterized everyone in the section from myself on down. You see, I was practically independent. When I had jumped in, I was under Alexander's headquarters in Algiers, but after the Invasion the Task Force came under the Seventh Army. I had never been transferred over to it so they didn't even know that I was alive. I was left pretty much to my own devices which, later, led to trouble with Bill Yarborough.

"His outfit, the 509th, was always up in the thick of things and they would invariably seize and detain my operatives as they came back through the lines. They had no way of making a fast identification, but I almost always needed the information they were carrying in a hurry. So Bill and I locked horns on military procedures but, finally, Frederick got it straightened out and from then on Bill also came to trust our outfit . . . even though our uniforms were sewn (under Josef Le Fou's direction) out of sheets and blankets by some of our ladies.

"So we never really had any serious trouble. Our outfit was made up of a wonderful group of people for whom, I guess, I was the catalyst. These were the Frenchmen who honestly produced results for their country. These were the kind of people that are worth respecting and the hell with the ones who were busy denouncing each other in order to get political power or the possessions that the Germans and the collaborators left behind."[45]

« 5 »

Although Geoffrey Jones's headquarters seemed populated exclusively by colorful characters, some of the women attracted especial notice simply because they would have drawn the spotlight in almost any situation. There was Solange de Ganay, of one of the most aristocratic families in France, who before the war specialized in museum reports on the wildlife of Africa. Liliane Grunewald, the sculptress, and Lucy Fould, daughter-in-law of the steel baron who built such great French ships as the *Normandie,* saw nothing strange in working alongside the cooks, typists and chambermaids assigned to working behind German lines as spies.

The Marquise de Forbin, born Claire Charles-Roux, whose father was the French Ambassador to Russia before the war, had worked in the Resistance since 1943, becoming an area leader in the vicinity of Puget-Théniers. Shortly after the D-Day drop, Madame de Forbin received word that nine American paratroopers and their twelve German prisoners were lost and wanted to return to their unit. In an official dispatch it was noted:

Madame de Forbin left at once, taking with her a guide who knew the mountain passes. She knew that there were many German soldiers in that district and that a large number of heavily armed Germans were coming up a certain road which passed through Tanneron where the Americans were. Thinking nothing of her own safety, she went at once, getting out with the guide all of the paratroopers and their prisoners.

She has always shown great courage in all of her work. At the risk of her own life she has protected many people.[46]

The closest friend of the Marquise was Isabel Pell, who joined the First Airborne Task Force when it reached Grasse. General Frederick said, "I think she came up there because she wanted a uniform. Well, we told her we didn't have any women's uniforms and that she would just have to go about in civilian clothes. She was very good in Southern France and I understand that she finally did get hold of either a Wac or a nurse's uniform because, for some reason, they sent us two American nurses when we were in Nice."[47]

Although Isabel Pell rarely worked directly for Jones, she was largely responsible for getting together the effective female cadre he had working as operatives for him. Because there was a friendship between their families, Jones felt he could trust the woman's judgment in a matter as sensitive as personnel selection. This trust was never found to be misplaced.

Jones saw that having lived in the area, Pell knew "who were the good people and who were the bad." In effect, Jones saw her as a one-woman Civil Affairs task force, a condition which remained in effect until Captain Joseph W. Welsh's detachment caught up with FABTF after a misdirected D-Day glider landing. "She was the one American expatriate in Southern France who was honestly trying to help the Resistance people to do some good," he said.

Captain Welsh says, "When we got to Grasse, I found that Isabel Pell had sent in a note to General Frederick offering her services. He, having no idea who Isabel Pell was, sent her to me.

Our families had known each other in New York so her name was known to me. Isabel was sort of a black sheep in the family, had been living in France for many years because that's where she found it easier to pursue the kind of life that appealed to her. At any rate, she told me that she could be of great help to us and that she spoke beautiful French (I found out later that she didn't at all) and that she had a lot of contacts and friends in the area. So I brought her in to General Frederick, who seemed to take an instinctive liking to her. When I asked him about employing her he answered, 'Sure.'

"After the meeting I checked her out and discovered that she had done quite a bit for the French Resistance, in hiding American soldiers who were lost, had escaped capture, or had been dropped in by airplane behind the lines.

"She was a great help to us even though she was a stubborn woman. She wanted her own way, wanted to do things in her own fashion, so every once in a while we had a little trouble with Isabel. But nothing ever really serious. She deferred to Frederick because he was the boss and she liked and respected him very much. But he was just about the only one. Her unorthodox approach to life didn't bother me at all and it certainly didn't bother General Frederick who, in addition to his own brand of sophistication, doesn't give a damn about personalities. All that ever counted with him was whether or not a person could do the job he assigned him.

"Isabel was quite a heavy drinker, although I never saw her drunk or unruly in public. I don't think she was an alcoholic. However, I must admit I've seen her act quite obstreperously on a few private occasions.

"Everyone loved Isabel. The men at headquarters thought she was crazy, but they all liked her immensely. She was outspoken, didn't really care about authority. Even though she respected and liked Frederick, she disagreed with him quite often.

"It's hard to define her specific duties. She was a great help in telling me what had gone on in the area before we got there, who were the French who had actually sided with the Germans and the Italians during the occupation, and who were the ones who had remained loyal. In other words, she helped us pick the real people from among the fakes. I used to check with her about the people who came in to see me as Civil Affairs Officer. Princes, princesses and the like were a dime a dozen along the Riviera. All these people with title from all over Europe were down there, all starving to death and wanting handouts. Sometimes they even wanted jobs. Isabel would tell me things like, 'This guy has two servants still in the house, he's not that hungry.'

"There were a number of churches, convents and monasteries in the area and some of them sometimes came to me for food and clothing for the nuns and monks in these places. Once I went to visit the Mother Superior of a convent and found that conditions were quite pathetic. They had no food at all. This was the kind of a situation that Isabel could straighten out beautifully. She got a truck, loaded it with canned meat rations, and took it to the nuns. Later they sent me a lovely bouquet of flowers in thanks for my help.

"Incidentally, to go back to the fact that she didn't speak French very well . . . it was extraordinary; having lived in France for as long as she had, she really spoke *atrocious* French! She knew enough words to get along, maybe using four or five pet phrases over and over again, and everyone seemed to understand. She made the French speak English and those that didn't loved her so much that they were on her wavelength — they all seemed to understand what she was telling them."[48]

November 28, 1944. Joseph W. Welsh reads the proclamation renaming the plaza in Puget-Théniers in honor of Isabel Pell as Miss Pell looks on. (From the collection of Joseph W. Welsh)

In November 1944, the French recognized Isabel Pell's service to their country by naming a plaza in the town of Puget-Théniers *Isabel-Pell*. Colonel Graves recalls: "The day we arrived at Puget-Théniers, Miss Pell could have taken over the town if she desired. All the kids followed her around, singing whenever she went down the plaza named in her honor."[49]

There are some people who seem peculiarly out of step during uneventful times but whose lives achieve sharp meaning during extraordinary periods. Isabel Pell was one of these. After the war she returned to America and, in 1958, toppled over dead in New York, the victim of a sudden heart attack.

« 6 »

These were the days when, more than ever, the activities of Robert Frederick became the narrative thread of the American occupation of the Riviera during World War II. The major engagements in this particular campaign had taken place and now there came a change of emphasis from military to civilian affairs. Because the First Airborne Task Force was moving in a milieu remote from the titanic struggles zigzagging across France and Germany, Frederick was now an unnoticed and almost self-sufficient power.

He was in a position to make serious mistakes. The complicated people and politics of these Mediterranean communities were literally begging for a scapegoat upon whom to blame the violent public disorder, the low foodstocks and the almost complete lack of new clothing, fuel and transportation. The Germans were gone so the Americans could have easily filled this role. They could have kept the residents of the Riviera from an uncomfortable self-scrutiny.

His men had fought too long and marched too many sweaty miles. The slightest evidence that Robert Frederick was sampling any of the fleshly delights still available in a few of the more notorious playgrounds would have sent his stock as a leader tumbling down to zero.[50]

Like most generals, Frederick was a remote presence to the majority of the men in the ranks. Some of the answered questionnaires accumulated during the research for this book indicate that there were evidently quite a few men who did not even know him by name. But, as in the other groups which he commanded in World War II, this did not extend to the men around him. A 517th trooper named Webb, who had been detailed to headquarters duty during the first few days of the fight after the drop, described Frederick's meeting with a captured German general: "The general, who had hurt his leg on the jump, was treating it when some intelligence unit brought in this Heinie General who was all sharped up, Iron Cross and all. Frederick wouldn't even look at him. This general kept squawking about how he was due better treatment and finally Frederick told the interpreter, 'Tell that son of a bitch that when he tells me what I want to know then we'll talk about protocol.' "[51]

Colonel Bryant Evans, in a postwar conversation, referred to Bob Frederick as the most fearless man he had ever known, fearless almost to the point of insanity. He said that Frederick would go out on patrols for "kicks" and that on a number of occasions Evans had to remonstrate with him, arguing that a wounded general officer was no good for anything.[52]

Colonel William Blythe described him as a "very brave and aggressive leader. I never fully understood his thinking. Many times patrols that were sent out from forward units would often arrive at an intelligence objective and find that the General and his driver were waiting for them there. In fact, he operated very much in the forward areas when he wanted to — which was not infrequent."[53]

Richard Seitz, who was promoted to major general in command of the 82nd Airborne Division, is not, on the basis of his record, given to offering inflated evaluations of either bravery or military ability. When asked his impression of Frederick in Southern France he replied: "Dynamic individual. The man was fearless as a leader, absolutely fearless. Maybe he shouldn't have gotten one or two of all the Purple Hearts he was awarded . . . I understand that some of them were just scratches . . . but he was a tremendous man. Really competent. And he was interested in his troops."[54]

Another soldier with Frederick during the night of the drop remembered that Frederick seemed very relaxed, smoking, making jokes (which was not typical of him) but giving no appearance of being particularly concerned. "Once," the soldier recalled, "the General said, almost to himself, 'It's all but over, fellows. These guys are really running away.' "[55]

Since civil affairs were now demanding a larger share of command attention, it is not surprising that Frederick began to find himself in closer contact with the two men who were used as his liaison with the residents and civilian administrators of the area. Both Captain Jones and Captain Welsh had increasing opportunities to judge General Frederick at close quarters. Jones says: "I think that one of the most interesting facets of this operation was that it ran so smoothly that very few people even heard of it . . . and that makes it a safe assumption that the General did not make any bad major decisions. He held a very sensitive area very well. It would have been easy for him to make the mistake of throwing his weight around in local politics. I know that in some other campaigns, the commanding generals did commit this error and it hurt us later on.

"I don't really know what the answer is as to whether Frederick had other options, because it was all such a mess down there; you have everybody from all over Europe hiding out down there. We had refugees from the Germans and then, later, refugees from the Allies. Obviously Frederick could have made mistakes if he had been less than the man he was. He was very circumspect; he didn't go out, or use his position to be wined and dined. If he had done that to excess, he certainly would have come in for very serious criticism . . . the kind that plays real havoc with a campaign because it seeps through to higher headquarters. But he was against that kind of display."[56]

When asked the same question Captain Joseph Welsh answered: "Well, I think that Bob Frederick was strictly a military man. He protected his staff from getting involved in the problems of French government, local government and the Underground people. He may have been naive in some respects, but this was to be expected; after all, he had no civil affairs experience in his background. He realized this and that's why he gave us such a free hand.

"But even so, he handled things beautifully. Although it might not be generally noticed, he has quite a sense of humor and this got him through some fairly sticky spots. I remember once he received an invitation to visit the Prime Minister of Monaco. He went but took me along. When we got there we were presented with the request that, on behalf of the United States, we annex Monaco as American territory. We couldn't believe he was serious. We thought he was making a joke!

"But he wasn't. The Prime Minister went on to say that it made good sense to have the Principality become a part of the

United States. You see, they had been wanting to disassociate themselves from the French for some time and since we were now in the vicinity, they thought it to be a very practical thing to offer themselves to the ranking American.

"We told them as diplomatically as we could that this was no function of ours and that such a representation could be made more properly through State Department channels. I don't know how we kept straight faces until we got out of there, but we did. When we got back to headquarters we just exploded. Somebody on the staff, it might even have been Frederick, suggested that we cable Washington to tell them that if they wanted a forty-ninth state, we were ready to supply it!

"Frederick actually shunned socializing, preferring to get on with the war. He relied on Isabel Pell to act as a sort of social secretary for him. I remember he had her arrange whatever functions and parties that we advised him were absolutely necessary. But by and large, he steered completely clear of any show of ostentation or pomp. I'll say it again: he was all business. He rarely thought of anything but getting on with the war in the most efficient way possible.

"Although he had no interest in the Riviera social life, he did not offend anyone in a key civilian position because we all did everything we could to properly advise him. We must have done a good job in this respect because I've never heard of his being criticized by the French who are fantastically sensitive in social matters.

"I would say that everyone on the staff was wholeheartedly behind General Frederick. We respected him because we knew that his only concern was to do a soldierlike job and that he had little or no personal vanity. I've heard that he was extravagantly respected and admired by his men in Italy and this also applied one hundred percent in Southern France. As a matter of fact, there were quite a few of us who felt that General Frederick was wasted down there. We suspected that he had been sidetracked and that he should have been given command of any of the divisions that were in the thick of things up north. At the very least, he could have been used in a high-ranking staff position dealing with combat operations. We believed he was capable of doing a first-class job in almost any military position."[57]

In 1967, after these comments had been correlated, General Frederick was asked whether he, too, felt that his military career was foundering in the continuation of the Southern France campaign. He answered, "No, we had an important job to do. There were roughly sixty miles of Italian border to defend and I did want to go back down [to Italy] and clean up the rest of the Germans there."[58]

CHAPTER VII

FIGHTING THE
CHAMPAGNE CAMPAIGN

They called it the "Champagne Campaign," this war in the Maritime Alps, because of the way the champagne flowed in the celebrations of the liberated people at Antibes and Cannes and Nice during the pursuit of the Germans.

True, the men of the Airborne Task Force that liberated the Côte d'Azur could still get 48-hour rest periods in Nice, an hour's drive away, and those who wanted to risk the MPs and a stiff fine could still filter into Monaco to walk with the girls of Monte Carlo in the royal gardens of Prince Louis II.

But when they went back into the mountains, to their fox-holes on the terraced hillsides under the shelter of the OD olive trees, they returned to a full-fledged war — an infantryman's war.

— HOWARD KATZANDER,
Yank *Staff Correspondent*[1]

« 1 »

FOR the bulk of the Invasion forces the war in Southern France
had become a series of lightning-like moves. On September 12,
some left-flank elements of General Patch's Seventh Army had
made contact (at Châtillon-sur-Seine) with the Allied army
brought in by General Patton over the Normandy beaches. Two
days later a more solid contact was established farther to the
northeast at Chaumont. Although the major battles for France
and Germany were still ahead, the war was over within a few
days for several hundred thousand German troops cut off in
south and southwest France.[2]

But strangely enough, this did not make it an easier campaign
for Frederick and his Force. On September 12, one of General
Sir Henry Maitland Wilson's staff officers visited the First Airborne Task Force headquarters at Nice to discuss the balance of
the battle. At this time, the Force was still assigned to the Seventh
Army in order to protect its right flank as it went up the Rhone
Valley. After Frederick pointed out his shortage in special units
and service troops due to the peculiar nature of his forces and his
lack of reserve due to his extended front, it was agreed that he
would "take command of the entire sector . . . not only the
Riviera coastline but also all activities along the French and
Italian border."[3]

To ease his supply problems he was detached from Seventh
Army and placed directly under the commanding general of the

VI Army Group. So, although he still had less than a division of men, he was, in effect, being treated as an independent force . . . almost as if he were commanding an army off by itself.

He considered that his job was to seal off enemy escape routes from this section of the country. By cutting off and isolating the German troops between his positions and the French-Italian border, he could keep them from pouring down to Italy. But a physical law intervened and made his job more difficult each day: as his forces advanced, they compressed more Germans into a tighter concentration and this had the effect of reinforcing each of the strongholds he had marked for capture. Since he was given no more men and only a slight trickle of supplies, he soon became faced with the toughest resistance he and his men had encountered since parachuting into Southern France. These German troops and their officers had recovered from the initial shock of the landing and were now functioning with something approaching the professionalism that had marked their movements in the past.

As the Americans crossed the Var River, the German 148th Reserve Division withdrew in orderly fashion to prepared strongpoints flanked by outposts and roadblocks. Along the Menton-Sospel-Breil road, the Nice-Ventimiglia highway and at Turini Pass, the enemy had skillfully camouflaged artillery positions covering crossroads and narrow defilades.

A group of American military historians noted that:

Rear guards were left behind to yield only when pressure became great, since the main object of this delaying action was to prevent any quick Allied thrust which might be followed by the movement of artillery and heavy weapons. The Germans destroyed or damaged several fords, a highway bridge, and a railroad bridge, as they withdrew from the Var. By the end of the period the 148th Reserve Division had ceased to be a part of the German Nineteenth Army. It was subsequently incorporated into the newly formed LXXV Corps, which had the mission of defending northwest Italy against any Allied threat to the rear of German forces.

The enemy made skillful use of mines throughout this phase of withdrawal by placing them in all possible by-passes after blowing craters in the roads.

The crossing of the Var River and the establishment of a defensive line to the east of the Var Valley marked the opening of a new phase in the protection of the Seventh Army's eastern flank. Difficult terrain restricted maneuver and made supply problems acute [for the First Airborne Task Force].[4]

It was not simply Teutonic stubbornness that dictated the strong defense attempts in this area. A division commander, Generalleutnant Karl Pflaum, said after the war:

The protection of the passes at the France-Italian mountain frontier was especially important for the German troops in Italy. An advance by American troops over the passes into Italy in the rear of the German front could mean its destruction. Apparently they [the German High Command] preferred weakening the Nineteenth Army to paralyzing the Italian front.

General Pflaum, in the same statement, then succinctly underlined:

From the very beginning it could be supposed that the American forces would attempt an advance into Italy from Southern France over the Alpine passes. It was very tempting, indeed, highly possible and promising.[5]

« 2 »

Although the Germans' skill in extricating themselves from a tight position proved as exasperating to the men of the Task Force as it had been to Mark Clark's Fifth Army as it inched up the Italian boot, there was one important difference: here everyone scented the unmistakable odor of victory. Colonel Hensleigh inferentially acknowledged it when he permitted himself this comment:

"I remember one time sitting on a hill and watching one of our ambulances take a wrong turn and go blaring right out into German territory. When it got to a place where you could expect a roadblock, a German came out in the middle of the road and stopped it. He pulled out a map and laid it on the flat Dodge hood and showed the American where he had made his mistake. The meat wagon turned around to go back and as it did, it hit a 'Schuh Mine' and blew out a tire. The Germans and the Americans changed the tire and the Americans eventually came back to our lines. Stories like these are probably surprising to many Americans who didn't actually take part in the war . . . that a lot of times a good, straight old-line outfit of Germans would do something like this. They weren't all storm troopers and SS types who were real stinkers who would not stop at anything."[6]

Not many members of the Devil's Brigade would have been capable of the same objectivity. These men of the First Special Service Force had been molded by Frederick into faithful reflectors of his own personality. An enthusiastic eagerness to destroy as many of the enemy as possible was an essential part of their mystique and it would have been a rare Forceman who would concede that the Germans were more than faceless targets.

In a postwar questionnaire sent to all surviving members of the Brigade, there were less than a half dozen answers which indicated anything but hatred (and this was after the passing of two decades) for the enemy. One reply, selected almost at random, is typical of their dominant recollections:

Frederick Molson, a 2nd Regiment man, wrote, "I was wounded on the march east in France and I'll never forget the women and children that I saw who were shot by the Germans. I remember returning in an ambulance with two other GIs and a wounded woman to Nice. The woman was pregnant. The Germans shot her through the stomach. We drove to several civilian hospitals to get her aid, but none wanted to take her because they had no more room. This was an awful thing to have to witness (and up until that time I had seen plenty) but when poor women were shot it made me glad to know that I had gotten my own quota of the enemy."[7]

Under orders dated September 3[8] the First Special Service Force had been ordered to relieve the 509th on the right flank of the defense line. Colonel Yarborough's first meeting with Frederick and the First Special Service Force had been back in Italy, at Anzio. "At that time," he says, "I took a dim view of anything that wasn't a ranger or a paratrooper. And these Forcemen, well, I didn't like the cut of their jackets or their jibs or anything else. I thought they were interlopers in a necessary business in which they had no real concern. But I learned to change my views."[9]

By September 8, the 2nd Regiment of the First Special Service Force advancing along the coastal road, had entered Menton and reached the Italian border. Here the advance was stopped and defensive positions established because it was anticipated that the northward push in Italy of the Allied Fifth and Eighth Armies across the Po Valley might cause the German armies in northern Italy to hack an escape route through the Franco-Italian frontier.

Meanwhile, the 1st Regiment of the FSSF had moved up to the high ground west of the Castillon-Menton road and the 3rd Regiment, having been against only isolated enemy resistance, established roadblocks to the east and north of Castillon. Task Force headquarters then ordered this line to be held by the three regiments without any further advance.[10]

The men of the Devil's Brigade now began to experience their first real taste of Riviera living. Their rear installations were set up outside Nice in Madame Coty's *Villa Fabron,* which was a fabulous assortment of mansions and guest cottages. The forward echelon of the Force first occupied a small villa in La Turbie and then later moved to the Princess Hotel in Menton. The 2nd Regiment used the Imperial Hotel in Menton as a rest camp and a nearby villa as headquarters. The 1st Regiment chose the Winter Palace north of Menton as headquarters. Other attached elements bedded down in the Harriman Villa east of Menton near the border.

However, good luck didn't smile equally on all of the Forcemen: one regimental battalion was headquartered in a collection of shepherds' huts up in the mountains, while the entire 3rd Regiment headquarters detachment found themselves directing operations from a flea-infested stable.[11]

When the FSSF halted, the Germans immediately launched a series of counterattacks. On September 12 they mounted one of the most bizarre operations of the war in an attempt to destroy the Allied ships cannonading them from offshore positions. They assembled a fleet of between thirty and forty one-man submarines with a rabid Nazi diehard at each wheel and, since these ultra-secret vessels, each carrying a single torpedo, could not be submerged, it was obvious that they had been engineered for last-gap suicide forays.

The mission was a complete failure, resulting in the death or capture of every one of the participants. The prisoners later identified their unit as the *Kamptverbande* (Marine Battle Group) located in San Remo. Of the ten "Water Huns" (as the Navy quickly described them) actually launched, three of the operators were captured and turned over to the First Special Service Force, three were kept by the Navy and the remainder were killed. No damage was suffered by the Allied ships.[12]

This type of effort indicated that there was still a solid determination among the Germans to hold on. Although some of the reports of the period characterize the German 148th Reserve Division as "bewildered," "disorganized," and "composed of a majority of non-Germanic soldiers," the observation of John Gilbert Bourne, a Canadian member of the FSSF, serves as an accurate summary of the reaction of most Forcemen: "The Germans were withdrawing and, as usual, they fought a series of brilliant rearguard actions. Very few determined men with a minimum of weapons were able to delay us sufficiently to allow their main body to withdraw [to prepared Alpine positions]. As far as we were concerned, it meant long forced marches, short bitter engagements and then on with the pursuit."[13]

Every personal account of the campaign echoes the remembrance of the hard march to the east. For example, another member of the Devil's Brigade said: "We did quite a bit of tough fighting during the eastward push. However, the big thing was the walk. And, man, did we walk! The idea I suppose was to keep the enemy pulling back, not giving him a chance to stop and dig in. I saw men so tired that they fell off their feet into a sleep while marching. One night we were hiking along and had to crawl under an abandoned roadblock. The man walking in front of me went smack into the roadblock, apparently walking along in a half-sleep."

Sholto Watt, a Canadian newspaperman attached to the FSSF, sent home one dispatch which began with this awed observation:

I have seen them [the FSSF] marching with full packs under a broiling sun, trudging all afternoon along a dirty, dusty road, or through the forests of Southern France, in order to reach a starting line at nightfall so that they could fight.

I have seen them fight for sixty hours straight to capture a town, and then still have enough energy left to help the townspeople celebrate their liberation in an all-day party before they moved forward again at night.[14]

Another Forceman, Sergeant Major John A. Planinshek, said: "Of course it wasn't all fighting and marching. We managed to have a lot of fun, too, because after our battles in Italy we almost considered Southern France as a sort of a vacation. I remember one time that the gendarmes put one of our men in a local jail. We went to visit him and then decided that it wasn't fair that they had thrown our lad in there, just because he had beaten up a Frenchman. We didn't feel that anyone had the right to do this to a member of the Brigade, so we got a bit hostile. So we took their weapons away from the gendarmes that were there, locked them up in their own jail and released our own man and all the rest of the prisoners as well.

"We all went over to a local cafe to celebrate and the pro-prietor, who didn't seem to be in sympathy with us, decided in the middle of the party to close the place up for the night. We didn't think that this was a proper thing to do so we pulled the front door off its hinges. The owner called our Provost Marshal but we got away before the MP's arrived.

"Another time while we were up on Mount Ours, I was sent back to Nice for a minor operation. They operated on me about four in the afternoon and at six I ducked out of the hospital and went into a local cafe for a few beers. Later when I tried to sneak back into the hospital that night, I was caught and put on report. Next morning the Medical Officer came around and said, 'If you're fit enough to go downtown, you're fit enough to go back to your outfit.' I was back there by the afternoon and that night I was sent out on a patrol in which, incidentally, we captured twelve Germans."[15]

Although the Forcemen were unquestionably a brutal lot in battle, they entered into or reported almost every off-duty event in a spirit of wry humor. For example, John Dawson, another Canadian, recalled that "while the Force was gathering at Sylvabelle, on the coast near Cavalaire, preparing for the march east, the French Army was also moving through the same area, mostly North Africans and coal-black Senegalese, who made our quartermaster truck drivers look practically Nordic by comparison. They also had the novel, by our standards, custom of trailing their women and goats behind them, and the lack of glamor of the former led some wags to speculate that perhaps the officers got the goats and the enlisted men had to make do with the women. There was at least one public accommodations establishment (of French girls I'm told) that had two queues of prospective customers, one French and one Force. Race-conscious Yanks and Canadians wouldn't allow coloreds in our line, but the extra-black Senegalese were readily admitted to the French line, and both lines converged to the same waiting (and bed) rooms.

"The trip across the Riviera was more like an extended route march than a battle to our brigade, who were used to a rougher grade of competition. Our biggest scrap was at Villeneuve-Loubet. We forded the river and as we came into town in the early morning it looked like another of those occasions when the Germans had pulled out on us. We started down a street which had houses on one side and an open park on the other. Frenchmen came out of their houses in considerable numbers to see the Americans or relieve their bladders, the second seeming to preoccupy them most, for there was a solid rank of peeing Frenchmen. About that time some fire started coming from some cleverly camouflaged foxholes. They were designed to cover the river, and the Jerries were as surprised as we were, and though we had two or three wounded they had let too many of us get too close. They were grenaded out fast. But this was only the first of many engagements that day.

"The town's M.D., Dr. Lefebvre, was very active as the day wore on in patching up our wounded. I don't recall where our medics were, but he was with our company, and I imagine the townspeople acted as stretcher bearers to get casualties back. Anyhow, as dusk approached and we expected a counterattack, my platoon was holed up in and around the Doc's house. He and his wife were giving us wine and brandy, the full V.I.P. treatment. A bit later they turned sour and sullen, scarcely speaking. I had quite a time getting the story from them, but they finally told me their house had been looted. I was embarrassed. It seemed too dirty after the events of the afternoon, and besides, with a probable counterattack coming up, it is best to be on good terms with your sawbones.

"I called the guys together, told them what had happened, and said no charges would be made if the stuff reappeared in a certain room in ten minutes. It did, and the doc and his wife were pleased.

"All Southern France was full of partisans, generally quite helpful, sometimes flighty, sometimes querulous. Two or three of us Forcemen were sent along with a large patrol of partisans to probe the defenses of Mount Agel. At that time they were pretty good. We were downhill from them and a deadly small-arms fire and some mortar came down on us. The Frogs fought back quite well, inflicting some casualties, but less than they received. I remember seeing one partisan hit, and to illustrate how steep the slope was, every time this fellow was about to stop rolling, he would tumble over another ledge. He must have fallen halfway to Monte Carlo.

"Our battalion came out of the hills above Menton and approached it via the coastal road. We became the extreme right flank and 1st Platoon, 6th Company was literally touching the water. We lived in a millionaire's mansion, which did depreciate a bit with artillery fire over the months. We settled down to patrolling, laying mines, and an occasional pass back to Nice."[16]

Another Forceman, Lieutenant Pat Harrison, added emphasis to Dawson's reminder that the war, although containing less concentrated bursts of the misery and fury that characterized the Italian campaign, still contained an abundant quota of danger:

"I thought that our positions [in the mountains] were risky enough, but then one night I was just getting into my sack when the field phone rang — it was the colonel — he gave me a map coordinate and told me I was to be there next morning by first light. When I located it I just about sh– myself — it would put us out forward on the next ridge, a good eight hours farther out in front. He further said we would have to take supplies and be prepared to hold three days, so he had sent a five-man fighting patrol up to lead the way as my men would be loaded down. After hanging up the phone I really told him off, but of course we had to go, scared or not.

"We pushed off down the mountain and about 2:00 A.M. we had started up the next ridge. There was just a single mountain path and we were strung out in single file, the patrol, then me and my platoon. Everything was very quiet, too damn quiet — it scares the hell out of you. Suddenly there was an explosion up forward, I spread the men out, then ran up and sure enough, one of the patrol had stepped on a shoe mine and lost a foot. I went back to the platoon and got Hal Sibley, our first aid expert.

"Then a soldier named Mac and I were back and forth from the patrol to the platoon a dozen times. Mac said, 'I'm going to see how they're doing.' He only got halfway when there was another explosion. I dashed over and there was Mac, pitched off the trail, one foot shattered and bleeding badly from the eye. (He subsequently lost an eye and a leg.)

"We found out later that there had been two mines on the trail that he and I had been over those many times; this last time up he wasn't so lucky.

"But Jeez, what a spot, so far out on a limb and then I lose my right-hand man, truly my right arm. We got Mac patched up, gave him a shot, got he and the other wounded guy together, then I told him, 'Mac, I've sent someone back to base to get you two out. You know my orders, I have to be out there in position by first light, I gotta go, good luck fellow.' He said, 'Sure sir, and good luck to you too.'

"This was getting pretty late in the game, most of us had been wounded at least once and every once in a while we lost some more of our good old pals. I thought, 'How long can it go on, how much can a person stand?'

"As I said good-by to Mac that night, I actually envied him — at least he was going to go home.

"I told the men to stay off the trail the rest of the way as there probably would be more mines. It was really rough going when we got off the trail but at least we were out of the mines then. Three days later when they sent supplies out to me (as I had to hold that spot indefinitely) they brought along an engineer with a mine detector — he picked up twenty-three more mines along the way, one right beside the one that got Mac."[17]

Getty Page, the Red Cross man assigned to the First Special Service Force, demonstrated on many occasions that he had enough guts and stamina to entitle him to the Force's respect, but he never permitted himself a loss of objectivity. His reports of some of the Forcemen's activities along the Riviera add touches to the profile of the Force that would never appear from reading their histories or listening to their stories. He says:

"We went over to Nice where I set up my G.I. Hangout in the drawing room of King Carol's [of Rumania] Riviera home. In this room were two grand pianos and quite a bit of statuary. Apparently one of the rules of war is that the invading or conquering army can take over the same villas that the retreating army abandons. The Germans had been in King Carol's home, so when we went in we took it over too. It was nice when we first went there, it wasn't quite so nice when we left.

"My jeep driver developed quite a business of getting watches for the men. Since my jeep was the only one that could carry civilians (supposedly when I was in it) it had quite a bit of freedom and my driver used this freedom to go into business for himself.

"It was fall, now, along the Riviera and this we somehow construed to mean that it was basketball season. We developed an enlisted man's team which was known as 'Getty's Go Getters' and the officers formed a team called 'Page's Punks.' Some French promoter got the idea of having my enlisted man's team play various French teams and the area became plastered with French and English signs announcing that *Les Getty's Go Getters* was going to meet such-and-such a local outfit. This began to stir up quite a bit of interest among the local population and in some of the cafes it became the chief topic of conversation. Then, one day, I received a call from Colonel Wickham who wanted to know whether the First Special Service Force was still a group of fighting men. I told him that, to the best of my knowledge it certainly was, and he answered, 'Well, General Frederick is starting to wonder. He doesn't think much of your sporting events and he certainly doesn't want to see so many men engaged in sports and games while there are still German Army units left in France.' So I had to run all over Nice pulling posters down.

"Of course I didn't win friends for the Red Cross all the time. I remember one fellow came in and asked me for a pack of cigarettes which I gave him. Then he asked, 'Can I have two packs?' I said, 'No, I've got a limited supply that I'm trying to stretch as far as I can because I can't get any more right now. If you come back tomorrow I'll give you another pack.' Then he announced his point of view: 'Why, God damn the Red Cross, it never did anything for anybody!' I am sure he still holds that point of view today.

"Across the gardens from King Carol's home was Madame Coty's mansion which was quite beautiful. Our headquarters company put its mess hall in there. I remember, particularly, the bathroom; you had to go up four steps to get into the black marble tub. It was a real fine thing for the men to enjoy the luxury of getting washed in Madame Coty's bathtub.

"When we first went to Nice the civilians seemed glad to see us. After about three days or so, I am sure they were asking, 'Why don't you go home?' The American soldiers were evidently quite different than their German predecessors who remained under strict officer control and who always tried to impress upon the French that they were concerned about the well-being of the civilian population. The Germans seemed to have had a better sense of public relations because they refused to let any incidents crop up between the soldiers and the civilians. But the Americans came in with a far different attitude. They said, in effect, 'See, aren't we wonderful? We have liberated you. Don't you owe us something?' This attitude certainly was difficult for the Frenchmen to bear.

"We had a stockade on Madame Coty's grounds. Every now and then we would hear gunshots and that would mean that one of the American soldiers was escaping from the stockade. One fellow had talked a guard into letting him out so that he could see his sweetheart in town. The guard let him go and, of course, the fellow never came back so they put the guard in the stockade to take his place. Wherever we went we carried our own stockade of prisoners along with us."[18]

The Army Civil Affairs records for the period confirm that Getty Page's estimate of some of the Forcemen's off-duty conduct was not overly severe. One letter, sent to the commanding general and signed by Captain Welsh, contained a file which listed a cross section[19] of the serious crimes "committed by paratroopers which have come to the attention of the editor of the local newspaper." This editor had refrained from publicizing these offenses in his journal, *L'Espoire de Nice*, but had sent in the following letter after a conversation with Welsh:

My Dear Captain [Welsh],

Referring to our conversation the other day, I do not consider it inconvenient to write, black on white, the things that I told you personally, concerning the stay of the paratroopers in Nice.

You know yourself how the American troops were received in the South of France. Never have any foreign soldiers been received in the same way. Everything was open to them: the homes and the hearts.

Nice, that has wept with joy when the first Americans entered the town, has unfortunately given shelter to a corps of parachutists who have committed the most unimaginable follies.

Because of them, because of their fights, thefts, window pane breaking, their armed attacks, because of the well-known story of the woman who died after having been puffed up and God knows what other stories, the Niçois who adored the Americans now detest and even hate them.

And when, one month ago, the paratroopers left Nice, there was a great sigh of relief all over the town.

The Nice population did not make any difference between American paratroopers and Americans in general. Since then, however, their feelings have changed. The town, since the departure of the ABTF has become calm again; one may go about the streets at night without fearing the worst. And the Niçois have learned that the small and big troubles they had to suffer were solely due to these paratroopers, admirable, brave soldiers, but bad "civilians."

I have to tell you that Nice now wishes the return of Americans and is waiting impatiently and with pleasure for the arrival of those soldiers who are said to come and take a rest on the Riviera.

Sincerely,

Georges Cravenne[20]

But, fortunately, most of the infractions of discipline for the First Special Service Force and the rest of the Airborne Task

Force, as well, rarely went past the level of spirited high jinks. Colonel Wickham once sent a bulletin to all of the Task Force units which bore the title, "Interference With Civil Police," and read, in part:

Civilian authorities have reported that in numerous instances the duties of the civil police have been very difficult to perform because of the interference of American military personnel. The civilian authorities are constantly checking the identification of French civilians found in night clubs and bars. These checks are made for security reasons and are a legal, proper and necessary duty of the civilian government. American military personnel have frequently shown objection to these routine checks when the personnel being checked are their guests.[21]

The bulletin was sent out because Wickham wanted to make certain that the civilian authorities resumed control of their area as soon as possible. In effect, he was telling the paratroopers that the day when they constituted the law in the towns and villages they had captured was over.

Colonel Isenberg, the Provost Marshal, obviously had his hands full during this period, but he admits that he often found it difficult to keep the straight face of duty intact in some of the situations he was asked to correct. "One time," he remembers, "I was called over to my headquarters in the early hours of the morning where two civilians were raising bloody hell. They had come to lodge a complaint which, as my interpreter told me, consisted of an offense of a most serious matter. It seems that two of our soldiers had grabbed them and stuffed them into a baby carriage they had stolen somewhere and then ran down the street with them in it, screaming like hell at the top of their lungs. I couldn't help it. I just doubled up with helpless laughter. This is the kind of thing you get when a hell-raising bunch of young soldiers are pulled out of the lines and put in a place where there is plenty of liquor and other opportunities!"[22]

« 3 »

It was unavoidable. The combination of pretty girls, glamorous places and momentary lulls in the fighting, all interacted to produce the period which most veterans of the First Airborne Task Force still fondly recall as the high spot of their war. You could almost hear him cluck in wonderment when the usually subdued Colonel Graves, writing about the 517th after the war, said: "This was the beginning of the so-called 'Champagne Campaign' where a soldier was reported to have dashed out of a cafe in Nice remarking that he had to get back in order to go out on a patrol."[23]

The story is not apocryphal. Terrell Stewart once described how a patrol, sent from his unit up in the mountains, made a wrong turn and found itself in Nice. One of the members later told him, "When we found ourselves in the city, we simply boarded a street car exactly as we had come down from the mountains; all in combat gear, rifles, grenades, etc., and rode the street car to the other side of Nice where the 509th's rear echelon was located. We were, of course, the object of many curious eyes on our passage through the town. When we got to rear echelon headquarters, they put us aboard a truck and we were driven back to Peïra-Cava."[24]

And among the historical records of the First Airborne Task Force this sentence stood out like a rosebush in a factory parking lot: "They [the soldiers] walked with the belles of Côte d'Azur along the broad promenades by the sea to return the next day to the fighting among the trees and white shale of the Maritime Alps."[25]

Philip DiStanislao begins the description of what it was like to be a young soldier taking a Riviera vacation during World War II:

"We'd get a three-day pass and come back to Nice. Another fellow and I had a room at the Hotel Negresco so we lived it up pretty well. You know, it was so incongruous; we'd carry in our musette bag with food (mostly Ten-in-One) rations with butter and bacon and we'd give it to them, then go up to the room to take about five baths to get clean. When the water was clear, we knew we had finally succeeded in this job. Then we'd rinse ourselves two or three times more and by that time they'd call us to say that our dinner was ready. We'd go down to the dining room and there would be all these characters in livery arranging the finest silverware at our places. The Negresco was a very elegant hotel and when you would see the crystal chandeliers and all these servants standing around to wait on you it was quite overwhelming.

"Then a team of them, after you were seated, would begin the service. They'd bring up this tremendous covered silver platter, lift the lid, and there inside you'd see an olive-drab G.I. can full of G.I. butter or whatever else we had brought. They seldom took it out of the cans because, I guess, they didn't want us to think they had kept any for themselves.

"One time while we were there another fellow and I got so carried away with the atmosphere that we just got tired of being in uniform. So we went out to a haberdashery shop and bought the loudest ties we could find. They were yellow with white polka dots. We put these on our O.D. shirts and started strolling along the boulevard. We really felt dressed up. Of course we were also half drunk and that helped.

"While we were walking, an American woman (there were a lot of American and English people living along the Riviera) who was about fifty years old came over to us and asked, 'Pardon me, but what kind of a tie is it that you are wearing?' We told her that they were our old school ties and at this she burst out laughing and invited us up to her place where she served us ice cream and cake while she played old Rudy Vallee and Sophie Tucker records on her phonograph. It turned out to be one of the nicest afternoons I've ever spent."[26]

Colonel Graves remembers: "We had taken over the Hotel Negresco but they [the management] kept the entire staff on duty. They were willing to work if we would supply the food; you see, there was plenty of money around but no food. It was amazing; you could be up in the hills in a foxhole being shelled, living the doughboy's life with C-Rations, grenades and all the rest of it, then get into a truck and drive thirty miles to a completely different world. You'd walk into the main dining room of the Hotel Negresco in dirty fatigues and your old jump boots and the waiters would flock around to serve you."[27]

Sergeant West explains how some of the American soldiers kept up their version of Riviera living standards: "I was in the hospital which overlooked Nice. I wasn't confined to bed, all that was required of me was that I be there at eight o'clock in the morning for the doctor when he made his examination, which usually consisted of asking me how I felt. After I replied 'okay,' he'd go on and I wouldn't have anything else to do until the following morning.

"So, generally, around ten in the morning I would take off for town. I had been away from my unit for a long time and hadn't received any pay, but about a block away from the hospital, walking down the hill into town, was the quartermaster supply depot which fed all of the Task Force in the area. I used to stop there and pick up a can of Spam and a carton or two of cigarettes, which if you watched it, could carry you for a week. It seems to me that when I first started doing this a carton of cigarettes was worth about forty dollars and Spam was equally expensive on the black market. After getting my supplies I'd never go further than another block before being approached by three or four people who wanted to buy the items I had in my hand. This would equip me for a big day and night.

"Nice was an exciting place for youngsters like ourselves. It was full of entertainment of all kinds. Some of the finest hotels and restaurants in the world are there and every one of them seemed to be willing to put themselves at our service in exchange for the supplies we carried.

"There was also excitement in the fact that we could go out on patrol during the day, maybe getting into a little fire fight, perhaps getting all bloody and muddy in the process, then five hours later be sitting in one of the biggest night clubs in the world with a babe and a bottle of champagne."[28]

Captain Joseph Welsh describes a refinement on the high life available to the American soldiers during that period: "The officers and men assigned to the Task Force had a delightful time; plenty of girls around and plenty of champagne and cognac to go with them. The girls were quite receptive. We used to go skiing. We'd take a jeep and go up the mountains to a little resort about an hour and twenty minutes away. You could ski in the morning with your girl friend, come back in the afternoon . . . a bunch of guys and girls together . . . go to a first-class hotel and then go swimming in the ocean. It was quite a life!"[29]

Of course this kind of living presents a few pitfalls which are not, perhaps, as drastic as a battle wound, but are certainly as real. They fall into two well-defined groups and Colonel Graves mentioned one of them in the periodic column he wrote for the 517th Combat Team's newspaper, *The Thunderbolt:*

Venereal cases were on the upswing for a while but apparently most men are getting smart and taking care of themselves. As Major Velia remarked the other day, "You can't take a couple of sulpha pills and escape a virulent case of syphilis if you are exposed to it."

Even gonorrhea is not prevented by these sulpha pills in a majority of cases. And don't think Nice isn't full of the above-mentioned maladies.[30]

The second common non-combat casualty is most clearly illustrated by this plaintive letter received by the commanding officer of the First Airborne Task Force:

Vive la France.

Vive America, my second fatherland.

You will excuse, General, that I take the liberty to write you. God, our Supreme Master, has permitted that I know and love one of your soldiers, Fred M——, sergeant, US Army, who left last Saturday for Sospel. I write you without his knowing it.

You will not allow, General, you who are commanding the Mediterranean Forces, that he be perhaps killed by our mutual enemies, you are said to be very kind, you will certainly not refuse the sincere request which a humble but good little French girl addresses to you: that you post in Nice, for the duration of the war, him whom I consider my betrothed before God. He has already paid his tribute to his fatherland. If you consent to have him affected in Nice or, if preferable, in the immediate neighbourhood where he would continue to serve with his total devotion.

As a sign of gratitude, I make you the gift of all my liberty and

I offer to serve you, I too, as best as I can, in Nice, at the place that you will assign me to, until our final victory.

When you were twenty years old, you have loved too, General? I implore you to soften your heart, in remembrance of these first happy days. Get softhearted, General, I implore you, do not refuse my ardent request, allow us to bless you all our life, so that, thanks to you, we may be reborn in a new hope, live and be happy.

I end my letter, my heart full of hope, and send you, with confidence, all my gratitude, and my absolute and respectful devotion.

HELENE M——

P.S. General, I send you this message quite confidentially, if you consider my request inacceptable, I beg you to destroy this letter so that nobody else but you ever knows its contents. But if you judge me worthy of an answer, be good enough to let me have it through the same channel.[31]

However, it would be a mistake to accept the definition of one of the troopers that "these were the days of wine and roses." The tough and grueling campaign continued and, at best, the days of strolling with the girls along Riviera boulevards were only brief interludes for most of the Force. Colonel Yarborough recognized this ambivalence when he said: "The overwhelming thing was the strange character of the combat there. It was hard, it was tough, and we lost a lot of men killed and wounded. And yet the fleshpots were close by. We didn't destroy the beautiful Riviera, so we would go back and have a bottle of wine and a bath and then go up into the mountains for another battle. It was like being in the ring where you get the sponge and the towel between rounds.

"But the fight was anything but easy. The terrain was tough and the rearguard action in this type of territory is a difficult thing to cope with. There, for the first time, we saw the little *Goliath* tanks that the Germans ran out on a wire at us. In fact, when I went back to visit the South of France, I remembered every turn in the road where there was a machine gun and where the little tanks came out, and all of the delaying roadblock positions."[32]

Colonel Hensleigh agreed: "It was a long, hard siege of combat with hardly any real relief at all. I think that there were only about two days out of over a hundred that we weren't actually in the lines as a unit.

"There's quite a bit of talk about the Southern France campaign being a Champagne Campaign, but being in combat that long with huge stretched-out lines so thin that many times the Germans could have driven a regiment between our columns without anyone knowing about it, added quite a bit of nervous strain. It was a rugged, physical campaign, going up and down those mountains.

"I remember once that I was showing a new outfit which had joined us where our outposts were. I went up one mountain at my usual clip and none of these men could even begin to keep up with me. This isn't because I was extraordinary, all of us in hiking up and down the mountains had gotten in very good shape.

"They say we took light casualties, but I knew that on occasion a whole platoon would be wiped out. It's hard to tell an outfit hit that hard that casualties are light. They look around and think they were damned heavy. It's only in the big picture that you can call losing a platoon 'light casualties.' "[33]

General Zais feels the same way: "They talk about the Champagne Campaign, but it wasn't that to people like us who did the fighting. Our regimental combat team had no more than approximately twenty-five hundred men on the flank. Out of these, we suffered a hundred killed and perhaps seven hundred wounded during the time we were involved in this action. So it wasn't a Champagne Campaign while we were on the lines, although I'll have to admit that it was delightful to be able to stop every once in a while and go down and enjoy a day or two's rest and recreation in Nice."[34]

There were quite a few men as well as the leaders who felt this way. Douglas W. Jones, a 517th paratrooper, said: "The guy who named it the Champagne Campaign got to Nice more often than I did. We were on the line from the middle of August to the end of November, and to say that we were a bit 'gamey' would be an understatement. We were strafed, attacked by tanks, railroad guns, 88's, etc. For a while, personal cleanliness became such a problem that we began to shave our heads. A day later we heard Axis Sally describe us in her broadcast as 'those baldheaded gangsters from Chicago.' "[35]

Perhaps Ralph G. Martin put it most succinctly in his book, *The GI War*, when he wrote:

What the paratroopers said was, "If this is war, we want more." They said it softly, though, because up in the cold snow of the foggy mountains, patrols had a way of going out and never coming back. It was an eerie war, too.

But what they were talking about was Nice itself, sitting within shell-fire range of the front, with its neon lights blazing, its modern little nightclubs filled with real Scotch whiskey and beautiful women dressed in soft silk, and hot pianos beating out boogie-woogie just like it was Cafe Society Downtown in Greenwich Village.

Occasionally the glass in the windows shivered from the nearby naval shelling but the beautiful babes weren't paying any attention and neither was the pianist, and neither was the bartender. But then one of the paratroopers looked at his watch and said, "Well, this has to be the last drink because I have to go on patrol pretty soon."[36]

« 4 »

"The Hair-Lined Streets" made almost as strong an impression on the members of the First Airborne Task Force as did the more agreeable attractions of the Riviera. This was the name that some of them used to describe the post-liberation head-shavings of the girls who had been denounced as having fraternized with the German soldiers during the Nazi occupation.

A Chicago *Tribune* dispatch of the period relayed the picture that many of the young soldiers carried away as an enduring memory. It said in part:

> While jeering townspeople and embarrassed American soldiers crowded about, the girls were plunked one by one into the chair. They had been sentenced by a seven-man committee of liberation.
>
> An old woman hit one of the girls on the head with a bucket as she was made to go through a lane of people after the hair-cutting, but otherwise the crowd did not touch the girls. One woman with golden blond tresses crossed her knees and tilted her head coyly as the clippers slid over her skull, but the others wept and buried their heads in their hands.[37]

Percy Crichlow, a member of the First Special Service Force, said: "I watched them turn a girl collaborator out of a street. She was shaved bald and ran sobbing into a side street where a friend gave her a scarf to cover her head. In another place the French drove a girl in a jeep with her head shaved and two swastikas painted on her naked breasts."[38]

There were some Forcemen who could not resist treating the matter with their customary lightness. One company officer recalled, "At the time it just seemed odd with all this hair laying on the streets and the walks, but we soon learned from some FFI guys that any girl or woman who 'collaborated' was shorn of her locks. Girls wearing scarves around their heads were then sought out by some of our men for a little further 'collaborating.' "[39]

Henry Wenerzynowicz whose sense of humor easily stretched to fit situations like these, recalled:

"After a while we were sent back to a rest area from where we were camped about four miles from Nice. One day when I was walking in to Nice I noticed a house off the main road. I asked a Frenchman if someone lived there. He told me a very wicked woman lived there. Being a normal soldier, I wanted to know what a wicked woman looked like. Well, when I knocked on the door, a very pretty girl opened the door and I asked her for a drink of water. After about a forty-five minute conversation, she let me in and then she told me her story about her boyfriend who was a Kraut and how they shaved her head and marched her through town. She told me their accusations were false. After I cuddled up to her on the couch with her head on my shoulder, I told her I agreed with her. We settled down to be very good friends. After about a week of her friendship, one day I asked a friend of mine named Frank to meet my very nice girl friend. We got there in the early evening, and after a few drinks, I kind of took a walk into the next room. While sipping a drink of booze, I watched Frank cuddle up to her on the couch and then he started to smooch and when things got a little heated up and they paid me no mind, I snuck up behind the couch. The room had only a soft light, and when he started to kiss her again, I pulled her wig off.

"Frank jumped back in disbelief and I don't think I will ever forget the look he had on his face. She begged me to give her back her wig which I did. Then Frank tried to continue where he had left off and after a few minutes I snuck back and pulled her wig off again. Well, this was more than the Moose, which was his nickname in camp, could take so he said let's go, he had enough."[40]

Charles Keen and Doyle Gray, the pair whose feat of talking three hundred Germans into surrender, almost earned them a medal before they spoiled their chances by taking off (without official permission) on a premature victory celebration, figured in one particularly colorful episode. Keen says: "We heard that in the Hotel DuPont in, I think, Sospel, the FFI were holding about five or six girls as prisoners waiting for trial. Doyle and I made a beeline for the place where we succeeded in talking the guards into letting us in to see the girls. Everyone seemed quite agreeable in there, so we also convinced the guards into letting us stay in the room overnight.

"Next morning, one by one, they took each girl out to this little plaza in the center of the town. They sat each girl down and cut off all of her hair. Then everybody in the town who had crowded into the plaza would applaud.

"Gray and I didn't join in the cheering. He said to me, 'The only ones they are shaving are the girls without brothers in the FFI, but I'll bet that just about every girl in this town did their share of collaborating. These girls here just don't have any influence.' "[41]

John Hollowell, another 517th enlisted man, was also there in the plaza and adds: "After the head shavings they led the girls out. Some of the people in the crowd would run up and kick the girls, knocking them down to the cobblestoned street. The girls headed for the little bridge that led out of town, but it was a rough time with the men slugging them as they went. The girls had been stripped but this didn't even stop the women who would try to push the running girls into the walls and knock them to the street again."[42]

Predictably, some of the men were revolted by what they saw. Sergeant Major Planinshek said: "We were sitting above a village one day and we could hear the women in the town screaming as their heads were being shaved. Our officers wouldn't let us go in to see it because they were all very hostile towards it."[43]

There were other reactions in the same vein. John W. Holt of the 517th observed: "Hungry women will do anything."[44] Another man, Joe Broudy, said, "Most of these girls had sex for sale and they sold it to whoever was there: Germans, French, Americans or English. The fact that some of them sold their bodies to Germans did not necessarily make them collaborators."[45] John Alicki, the 517th original recruiter, asked, "A woman is a woman and so long as she just fraternized, what was the beef? When the hunger pangs get to you and your little ones, maybe you have no recourse except to give yourself for food."[46]

Perhaps the most reasoned judgment is relayed by Eric Sevareid who was in a small village when it was swept by this kind of fury. The de Gaullist lieutenant who had been placed in charge of the area by the French Army said to him:

I suppose this looks terrible to some of you people — our letting them do it. But we've got to let them [go on with the head shavings]. We can't suppress all of this — we can only let them blow off steam and try to keep it under control. You don't know how these people feel. If we clamp the lid on everything, there would be an explosion and we would lose our power to keep order here before we gained it. Some of these girls probably would have been murdered if they hadn't paid the price this way.[47]

« 5 »

The mass frenzy of those seeking revenge, political or economic power, followed the First Airborne Task Force along the Riviera in a violently churning wake. General Frederick had been told by higher headquarters to steer clear of political affairs, but invariably, the competing factions among the population turned to him as a court of last resort. And, to compound the confusion, he also frequently found himself being drawn into conflict with the Riviera mentality which, in its most unattractive form is flamboyant selfishness.

Quite a bit of his trouble came from the expatriates who had left their native countries in order to nestle down along the Riviera. Colonel Yarborough admitted that he looked upon them without sympathy because, "for example, the American expatriates in Monaco felt they were having a rough time since they were down to their last bottle of champagne. I had very unchristian feelings towards these Monte Carlo types."[48]

These feelings were even shared by some of the French at one time. General de Lattre de Tassigny met at a coastal resort with some of his brother generals in order to plan the advance of their troops. Although they had taken over the hotel in which they were meeting, it had nevertheless retained many of its civilian customers. "When the generals arrived to discuss the war, they saw a pretty terrace with chairs and sunshades where idle civilians in summer clothes accompanied by beautiful blondes were nonchalantly drinking apéritifs. The girls were scantily clothed and the drinks were iced. As for the men, they seemed indifferent to the soldiers fighting and dying a few kilometers away."[49]

Even a random dip into the Civil Affairs files for the period presents the ready conclusion that the expatriates represented an unmitigated pain in the neck. In exasperation, General Frederick finally delegated most of these matters to Captain Welsh and a sampling of his correspondence furnishes an insight into just how tough the job must have been:

In a letter sent to the Swiss vice consul, Welsh authorized him to tell the Americans who were demanding of him that they be supplied with food that (a) the American military authorities expressly forbade supplying Army foodstocks to the civilian population; (b) all food supplies were presently desperately needed by the American fighting forces; and (c) if the Americans were outraged by the prices they were being charged on the black market, it was because they, the American expatriates, had aided and abetted it in the first place. Welsh closed his letter by telling the consul that he should remind the expatriates that they had been repeatedly urged to come home before the war had broken out.[50]

In another letter Captain Welsh warned the commanding general not to give in to the pleas of an influential American woman whose car had been requisitioned by the French, saying, "My policy has always been one of 'hands off' in cases like this, despite any personal connection that might exist . . . [The French administration] is very touchy . . . and [in a previous matter like this] I have had my ears pinned back!"[51]

When an Englishwoman claimed that the American officers were drinking, hell-raising and bringing loose women into the house they had requisitioned from her, Welsh, after a personal investigation of the matter, informed his superior that "with respect to the loose women who allegedly frequented the building and who also were supposed to have stolen furnishings and clothes, Lieutenant S—— states that since his occupancy he has invited a lady visitor for cocktails one evening and that she is definitely not to be classified as loose."[52]

Admittedly, these are all minor incidents. But after multiplying them by the scores of such situations that arose each week, it becomes evident that Frederick, functioning in the partial vacuum caused by the conviction of his superiors that he required very little supervision, was being forced into taking on a large, annoying and distinctly non-military load.

It wasn't only the Americans. Everyone turned to him. A wealthy Italian named Bianchi sent a stream of complaints concerning the activities of the artillery battery located on his farmlands. It seems that they were causing too much damage to his home and livestock whenever they opened fire on the enemy. He considered this to be a thoughtless procedure.[53]

The Italian Committee of Liberation wrote protesting the treatment they were receiving from other political groups in Nice, demanding that General Frederick look into "the campaign of Italian phobia that has started in the region, based on the pretense of our slight inevitable mistakes."[54] Conscientiously pursued, an investigation like this could have taken a staff of men many months to complete. Frederick and Welsh, who had begun to learn their way around corners like these, smothered the complaint under a flow of bland double-talk.

Before landing with the glider troops on D-Day, Joseph Welsh had been a Seventh Army liaison officer who assisted in the planning of the Invasion of Southern France. There, his job had been to work in coordination with some of the French officers attached to headquarters. He remembers his first meeting with General Frederick:

"About ten days prior to the Invasion, I was asked (in very

strong terms) if I would like to 'volunteer' to work with Frederick's Task Force. The officer who made the suggestion was General Patch's G–5 [Civil Affairs Officer] and, naturally, I told him I would be delighted and he immediately sent me to Rome to meet General Frederick.

"Frankly, I was quite impressed with the General. I had heard that he was a very dynamic young fellow, the youngest two-star general in the Army, and was a determined and rugged individual. And that's the way he struck me when I met him. He wasn't a grandstander like, for example, Patton, because he was quite soft-spoken and was far from flashy in his dress. But there was no mistaking that he was a tough man who knew how to command.

"After we had landed in France, our Civil Affairs job turned out to be maintaining smooth relations between the French civilians and government on one hand and our military authorities on the other. Our biggest problem was to get food and supplies to the native population. We brought in several ships carrying thousands of tons of wheat because they had no flour at all with which to make bread.

"You must remember that this little area in the South of France has a dry climate where they have never grown very many vegetables because they have been concentrating on growing flowers for perfume. These people were perfectly delighted whenever we succeeded in bringing in truckloads of canned vegetables, meat and other Army rations. One of the things that Isabel Pell did was to take trucks like these and drive them herself to the outlying areas where she would distribute food to the people who needed it.

"The biggest frustration was to get our own government to supply us with enough wheat for these purposes. After all, foodstocks in the area were damned near down to starvation levels and these people didn't know which way to turn. They couldn't get anything from other areas in France because each section was having its own problems.

"Eventually we succeeded in bringing in quite a bit of food and this, along with the habit of the American soldiers of sharing soap, cigarettes and rations with whatever civilians were in the neighborhood, helped us lick the problem.

"But apart from allocating and dispensing food, I didn't exercise much real authority over the civilian population. I wasn't supposed to. Our [the Civil Affairs Detachment] job was to smooth out relations for the American presence in the area and help the French as best we could to re-establish their own government. The way I saw it, our function was to keep the American image polished and make sure that we got credit for whatever we did. There was always the danger that Russians, or some of our other Allies, would attempt to claim credit for the wheat and other food supplies we were bringing in. We all realized that this would become an important consideration in the postwar world."[55]

« 6 »

But Monaco stood alone.

Since it furnishes the setting for a majority of the stories of eccentrics and eccentricities along the Riviera, any narration of General Frederick's tenure in Southern France must contain at least an indication of the complications that sometimes threatened to swamp him in this tiny patch of glamorous Mediterranean soil.

The roulette wheels in the Monte Carlo Casino never stopped spinning in World War II. During the early stages of the war, the flight of many of the American and English expatriates caused the tempo to slacken a bit but this picked up and even increased once the German Army became aware of the virtues of preserving the enclave as a recreation center for their men and a listening post for their spies.

Officially, Monaco remained neutral, a status that was only briefly threatened when elements of the Italian Army marched out of their garrison at nearby Menton and into the tiny principality. The Italian residents, in what turned out to be an excess of optimism, broke out their green, red and white flags, and then abruptly resheathed them when Mussolini in one of his more intelligent situation summaries declared that he had not entered the war to conquer Monte Carlo.

This was not an undiluted gesture of nobility on the part of Il Duce. In effect, it preserved Monaco as a playground for the French collaborators, German and Italian businessmen, Nazi officers on leave, and that anonymous school of sharks who always seem to hover at hand to make a profit out of any war. Between 1940 and 1942 more than a hundred new holding companies were registered in Monaco. Many of these were thinly veiled fronts for Nazi leaders like Goering and Himmler who used the companies to smuggle the treasures they had been looting into various caches in Switzerland and other neutral countries.

After the Seventh Army had landed on August 15, and the First Airborne Task Force began moving east along the coast, the businessmen, collaborators and Axis officers paid their bills and hastily headed for Italy, leaving behind a garrison of three hundred soldiers in the fortress of Mount Agel above Monaco. On September 3 a jeepful of American soldiers rolled up to and stopped at the Place d'Armes. The first words on this historic moment were addressed to the doorman in front of the luxurious hotel. They were: "Hey, bud, where are we?"

Frederick's first inclination was to set up canteens, clubs and PX's, turning the principality into a leave center for his ten thousand men, but Prince Louis prevailed on him to preserve his mini-country's neutrality. After briefly reviewing the impact that the exuberance of his men had had on some of the other Riviera showplaces, the General agreed. He announced that Monte Carlo would be off-limits to all Allied personnel, regardless of rank, an order that was respected by General Eisenhower when, in the summer of 1945, he arrived on the Riviera for a few days' rest. The Supreme Commander stayed at the Eden Roc, which is on French soil near Monte Carlo.[56]

However, it is no surprise that a flourishing black market began blooming almost at the moment that the Americans arrived on the outskirts of Monaco. Allied soldiers had supplies to swap, the principality contained an abundant number of adventurers used to living by their wits and these two groups were propelled into each other's arms by the twin facts that Monaco grew none of its own food or manufactured any of its supplies and there was no immediate way to bring these items in from other areas.

The situation was almost completely mirrored in a then current report to the commanding general issued by Captain Welsh:

During this period, the Principality also got its hands upon as much food as it could from other sources, including MARSEILLES and PARIS. At one time the Prince sent a personal representative to both these cities to pick up whatever might be available to the Principality. During the stay of the 1st ABTF in this sector, the Prince also sent representatives several times to General Frederick's headquarters complaining of the lack of food available in Monaco

[*246*]

and requesting assistance from the Airborne Troops. The undersigned as Civil Affairs Officer of the Task Force contacted both the Food Commission of Nice and Marseilles on several occasions upon the orders of General Frederick in an endeavor to work out a more equitable basis of supply for the Principality. During all these negotiations at no time was it ever possible to place any confidence in statements made by representatives of the Prince. One of the greatest difficulties to surmount was the continued jealousy and suspicion existing between the Monaco and Nice Food Commissions. Neither trusted the other.

As a result of the black market the people with average or little means in the Principality are practically starving. Almost all the food received is channeled through the Monte Carlo Casino to the fantastically high priced black market available only to the very wealthy. There is practically no food of any description in the market places, or so little that only a small percentage receive their share.[57]

Frederick, faced with the unmistakable unrest of the citizens of Monaco, finally decided that in order to check the spread of open resentment along the Riviera, he would first have to be certain of its roots. A group of intelligence officers were sent out to collect and evaluate information and the report of one of them seems to describe most accurately the prevailing conditions. This officer told General Frederick:

Behind the general unrest seems to be the resentment of large numbers of persons, mostly Communists, to the tight control exercised by the monied interests of the Casino over the Prince and the Monacan government of the Principality. The food situation is almost desperate, the people existing to a certain extent only through the black market which is flourishing. It is even claimed that medical supplies are obtained through purchases from American soldiers.

It is believed by these people that the black market operations are carried out in Monte Carlo by the same persons who handled them under the Germans. They consider that under Russian occupation such a situation would never be permitted to exist. Many feel their only chance to wage a winning battle against the financial interests is now while many of the financiers are tainted with collaborationism and while the United States forces are in the vicinity. Should these forces be removed, they feel their opportunity would have been lost.[58]

With this report as a beginning point, Frederick finally began to isolate the chief causes of the situation. A quickly thickening file[59] on the Minister of State, Emile Roblot, indicated that he was a primary thorn. According to the information received, Roblot had been a collaborator with the Germans, had hobbled the Resistance movement along the Riviera, and had been a key factor in more than one black market ring. Much of this information may have been inaccurate and, perhaps, politically inspired, but nevertheless it seemed solid enough to Frederick to use as a basis for a dramatic move. By personally firing Roblot, he would, in effect, be telling the residents of the Riviera that all the old game rules were being swept away.

Accompanied by two jeeploads of military police, his aide, Captain McCall, and Pat O'Neill, the ex-Shanghai policeman he had used as the instructor in unarmed combat during the training days of the Devil's Brigade and whom he had just made a Provost Marshal in Monaco, General Frederick headed one night for the residence of Monsieur Roblot. He describes the errand: "We all drove up there and I arranged the MP's on either side of the front door. Then McCall and I went up and rang the bell. When the butler came to the door, we told him we wanted to see Roblot and were informed that the Minister of State was resting upstairs. I said, 'Get him down here. Now!' and the butler said he would.

"Well, as soon as Roblot heard we were there, he must have known why we had come, so he left by way of the back door. I understand that he headed for Marseilles, because that's the way his car was headed as he drove away. At least that's what the MP's told me whom I had stationed outside for observation purposes. It suited my plans to have him run away because I didn't particularly want to waste time locking him up and seeing that he was brought to trial.

"Then the butler came downstairs and very formally announced, 'Monsieur Roblot doesn't seem to be here,' which wasn't exactly news to me.

"We got rid of him because he had worked for the Germans in Monaco and had been making money on the black market by issuing all kinds of phony building permits. And I know that my doing this had made Prince Rainier and his sister very happy. They had been visiting me in Nice, complaining about him for some time before I moved."[60]

Two other groups hampered General Frederick's effort to get on with his campaign during this period: the spies and the expatriates. Captain Geoffrey Jones describes the first: "The really major political decision that we made was to seal off Monaco. This turned out to be very helpful to me because, as I explained to the General at the time, many of the secret agents, turncoats and informants stationed along the Riviera had shrunk back into the principality as the Task Force advanced toward them. So we had them all in one place, and although I didn't have enough people to go in and identify all the agents we wanted to lay our hands on, I did manage to get quite a few CIC [Counter-Intelligence] boys in there. Unfortunately, most of them eventually succumbed to the lure of the Monte Carlo fleshpots, but that's another story."[61]

Colonel William Blythe restates the other subject of concern: "There were many Americans living there at the time we came in. These people were very wealthy and most of them had refused to return to the United States when the war broke out. General Frederick didn't look with favor on them, and as a matter of fact, gave them minimum assistance after we arrived on the scene, no matter how much influence they tried to bring to bear on him. He had utter contempt for these people."[62]

Evidently Frederick tried to stay as far away as he could from what passed as the Riviera "elite." On one occasion this resulted in his receiving one of the most expensive decorations that Europe has to offer. He had been invited by Prince Louis (grandfather of the present Prince Rainier) to be his guest at a benefit performance which starred the entertainer, Josephine Baker. When Frederick arrived, he saw a Vichy Frenchman and an American expatriate sitting in two of the seats that had been reserved for the General's group. Frederick excused himself and said that he would prefer to sit elsewhere. Next day, as an apology the Prince invited Robert Frederick to become a member of the Order of Saint Charles, an honor which carries with it a decoration which features a large pigeon's blood ruby.

« 7 »

Frederick's order had been blunt: No Allied Personnel In Monaco! It was generally obeyed, but the Force would have been incapable of achieving their combat record if they had not also been incapable of regarding this as a challenge. The recollections of some of the soldiers and officers positively glow with accounts of how they talked their way into Monte Carlo. One man said that "some of the wheels that wouldn't turn for less than a thousand dollar bet in peacetime were now spinning for cans of our C-Rations."

Even Chaplains Brown and Guenette went in but, being men of the cloth, they were evidently incapable of the duplicity that would have enabled them to get away with it. Lieutenant Dick Spencer, on a mission of his own, drove by while they were standing in custody of the MP's who had caught them.

"I've found you can go a long way on gall," he said, "so I got out of my jeep and went over to where they were all standing. I winked to the Chaplains (they were both good guys — one of them had married me) not to let on they knew me, and I turned to the MP and said, 'Soldier, are these the two prisoners I'm supposed to pick up?' That kind of slowed him up a little bit and he answered, 'No, I just caught these two men,' and I answered, 'Well, somebody called us down in Nice this morning and they said that they had two prisoners that we were supposed to come up here and pick up. Dammit, let's get on the ball. Let's get this straightened out because we made a whole trip up here to get these prisoners!'

"The MP thought for a while and said, 'No, we sent two prisoners down last night.' And I asked indignantly, 'Well, why didn't they notify us? How about these two men here — you want me to take them down?' He said, 'You can't, they haven't been booked yet,' and at this I acted like I had gotten real sore and I yelled, 'Well, can't you get all that information from them right now, so while we're going back we can take them with us. That'll save us from another damned long trip!'

"By this time the MP was standing at attention and saying, 'yessir, yessir,' . . . but we still couldn't get them out. But he was probably more afraid of the Provost Marshal than he was of us because we just couldn't get them out and I figured I'd better get out of there before I got caught too."[63]

Father Guenette confirms the story, but explains: "I had been out to see the Fathers at Menton and our path back took us through Monaco. The Colonel, when he heard about it, was ripping mad. He told us, 'You're not taking enough precautions. You'd better watch out!' "[64]

CHAPTER VIII

THE FORGOTTEN FRONT

Airborne troops are equipped for only four or five days of lightning fighting. The transportation and artillery which normally accompanies them is insignificant. Thus, when General Frederick's men began marching eastward, they had to carry almost everything on their backs. They lived for days on what French peasants would give or sell. They packed heavy mortars on long marches and 75 mm. howitzers were pulled and shoved by hand. Boots wore out and men were nearly barefoot.

Supply was more of a problem than hastily organized German defensive maneuvers, even with every manner of captured enemy vehicle pressed into convoy work. And as the mountains became rougher and higher, mules had to be found to carry food, water and ammunition up to platoons fighting on nearly inaccessible peaks. Yet Seventh Army officers could only listen sympathetically and shake their heads when FABTF men asked for trucks and guns; the need of the divisions hurling the Germans into the Belfort Gap was greater.

This was the forgotten front — and it still is. The soldiers down here, suffering their losses, taking here a town and there a mountain pass don't make the headlines. They know this and they'll tell you so. Some say it with a touch of bitterness, thinking of their scanty transportation and not-too-warm clothing. Others, looking forward to a pass to glorious Nice next weekend, grin and say, "Hope we stay forgotten."[1]

— SERGEANT GEORGE DORSEY, *staff reporter,* Stars and Stripes, *November 5, 1944*

ALTHOUGH the "Champagne Campaign" was rapidly drawing
to a close, the hardest time still lay ahead for the men of the First
Airborne Task Force. The enemy had retreated to positions in
the Maritime Alps atop mountains beyond the range of the small
spotter planes used by Allied artillery units. The remnants of the
German infantry elements in the area had been gathered into
disciplined fighting forces supplemented by substantial numbers
of seasoned Alpine troops. Their mountain-artillery batteries
were well emplaced and manned by fresh troops who had been
waiting for the war to come their way and who seemed to know
every path and trail in the area.

Further, evidence was continually being uncovered that the
Germans had made extensive plans for sabotage in the wash of
the Allied advance. A school for saboteurs, operated by a Waffen
SS unit, the *Sonderkommando,* was discovered in Avignon. Spies
for the *Abwehr* and the *Sicherheitsdienst* (German Intelligence
Services) formed a stay-behind net for operational information
and, among them, the Allied counter-intelligence groups found
many agents who were to be part of the German system, even
after the war.

Fortunately, this elaborate and well-planned operation showed
little results. Allied armies moved so rapidly in all directions
that the German high command found the information virtually
useless during the hasty retreat back into Germany.[2]

But General Frederick's biggest problem was supply. The hundreds of thousands of men in the Allied army under General Alexander Patch were sweeping north at such a rate that the overworked supply depots in the invasion ports gave no evidence of having ever heard of Frederick and his ten thousand men off by themselves in the east. As a result, one observer who was briefly with the Task Force during the period said, "The biggest story here is the ability of American troops to improvise. They have none of the things you expect a division to have: organic transportation, heavy artillery or a flow of food and clothing; and yet these people are driving the German Army up into the Alps. I think it's a great lesson in how you can improvise and conduct a campaign without having any of the things that are really necessary for such an operation."[3]

It is an accurate summary. The men achieved a sort of fame for themselves as entrepreneurs. The 517th, for example, became known to many rear echelon supply officers as "Colonel Graves and his Five Thousand Thieves." They stole everything they came across that wasn't under lock and key. One time a raiding party sent back to see what could be done about looting a quartermaster depot at Marseilles, returned with among other things six cases of Good Conduct Medals. When it was explained to Colonel Graves that they had been stolen by mistake, he suggested, "Well, what the hell, give one to everybody who hasn't gotten a venereal disease."

Colonel Yarborough said: "We were very light on transportation in those days . . . so we began to 'requisition' everything we could find. We took some bicycles to push our fifty caliber machine guns and we took a few civilian cars too. As a matter of fact, I ended up with a Cord front-wheel drive that had belonged to Charlie Chaplin and I put jeep wheels on it and this became quite a sight up and down the Riviera."[4]

Lieutenant Alicki also traveled in style. After he and his men knocked out an antiaircraft battery they found an almost new Mercedes-Benz sedan parked behind it. Alicki proudly drove all over Southern France in it until an MP officer finally convinced him that eventually one of the Allied aircraft overhead was sure to identify him as a target of opportunity.

The Frenchman, Gabriel Rafael, who had attached himself to Colonel Yarborough's 509th said, "The Germans abandoned cars and trucks, many in good condition. But after a while we learned that if a vehicle looked untouched, it was probably booby-trapped."[5]

"We picked up everything we possibly could," said Colonel Hensleigh. "We had oxcarts, mules, bicycles, some motorcycles and quite a few civilian automobiles. Actually we looked more like a tribe of gypsies than we did an army outfit."[6]

Food was equally hard to come by in the early days in the mountains. Even the C-Rations so generally treated with scorn by most American soldiers became sought-after delicacies. The men learned to strip the vegetable gardens in the villages they passed in the line of march. It became a common sight to see a unit going down a road, its members chewing on fresh onions, grapes, carrots, peppers and tomatoes. One 517th scrounging expert on a trip back to the beaches shanghaied one of the small army supply boats, which proved to be crammed with five-gallon tins of fruit cocktail and nothing else. "I'm telling you, we sure got a bellyful of pears, peaches and other fruits," said John Hollowell. "When we moved off to the attack every man had loaded fruit cocktail into his canteen, helmet and every other container he could lay his hands on. I haven't eaten fruit cocktail to this day."[7]

General Devers eventually offered a very judicious comment concerning these activities: "They [the Task Force] were invaluable. Anything they did, I would say was in the name of the Lord. They were on their own, but they knew how to think."[8]

« 2 »

At this point the First Airborne Task Force resembled nothing so much as a thin knife blade separating the concentration of German units in North Italy from those in the Maritime Alps. A sufficiently strong attack from either direction would have cracked and fragmented them, but the Germans never felt that they had the strength to take the offensive in this area and the Force, needless to say, simply did not have enough of anything to continue its drive. So a stalemate evolved.

Colonel Graves explains the situation: "We had now come as far east as consistent with our mission of protecting the right flank of the Seventh Army. We were certainly also in contact with the Germans and from our positions on the Tête de Lavina, Plan Constant and the hills surrounding Peïra-Cava we could observe their every movement during daylight and place artillery fire whenever that movement appeared. The enemy posts at Agaisen and Barbinette bothered us somewhat and we were taking a few casualties daily. However, to push on against the posts would not only put us in a disadvantageous position but would have lengthened our already long supply lines back to Fréjus, and would have put us in plain view of the enemy from the still higher mountains towards the Italian border. So we settled down to hold, at the same time keeping a steady pressure against the Germans by means of patrols and artillery fire."[9]

The stalemate suddenly came to an end in the middle of October with a vicious outbreak of defensive fighting. The ridge from Col de Braus south was nicknamed "Bloody Stump" because of the never-ending flow of casualties being evacuated from it. The trees had once been part of a heavy forest. Now they were jagged and splintered stumps and the ground became torn and pitted from constant shelling. Any movement during the day brought a concentration of high-velocity shells from the forts on Mount Agaisen behind Sospel. Continuous and destructive patrolling was carried on by both sides, keeping everyone on the alert.[10]

These patrols were carried on under curious circumstances. Sometimes the fighting would come in tough, concentrated doses and then there would be periods in the early morning when the sounds of shells would be completely absent. The thin plumes of smoke that could be seen curling upwards through the valley from both positions would mean that coffee was being brewed over German and American campfires.

It became apparent as enemy mortar and artillery fire grew in intensity that this was a cover for the general withdrawal of German troops to the east. At the end of October, the 517th became aware that Sospel had been evacuated and they filed into this key stronghold without opposition. Then, except for intermittent long-range shelling, the sector became quiet.

The 517th remained in this position until the 13th of November when it was relieved by the 19th Armored Division. It had been in the lines continuously for three months and the men, with weary pleasure, looked forward to an extended period of rest and recreation back in Nice. But their stay there was shorter than anyone had expected. The German Army broke through in the

Ardennes and Nice became only a short way-stop in the 517th's trip to the Battle of the Bulge.

<< 3 >>

In contrast to its brief and exciting career, the First Airborne Task Force was not deactivated in any dramatic fashion.

With the exception of the First Special Service Force which was pulled back to Villeneuve-Lobet and formally disbanded on December 5, 1944, in a sentiment-saturated atmosphere, the remaining units were soberly and methodically withdrawn and sent on to other jobs. By Thanksgiving Day, the 550th Airborne Infantry Battalion was relieved by elements of the 14th Armored Division and was in a rest camp near Nice. The 442nd Regimental Combat Team, composed of Americans of Japanese descent and troops of the French Army, were assigned as replacement units and, by the year's end, the Force's history was complete.

It had accomplished much. Later, the Seventh Army was to issue a description of its activities, and although quite brief, the concluding paragraph can stand as an absolutely accurate summary of its four months of life:

These successes, in driving a strong enemy from a large section of France in which he had every advantage of observation, terrain and organized defense, were won at a high cost to the First Airborne Task Force. Virtually one-third of its personnel were either killed or wounded. However, the damage inflicted on the enemy far exceeded our losses. Approximately 4,000 of the enemy were captured and unknown numbers were killed and wounded. The German 148th Infantry Division was completely decimated and the 34th Division, which was rushed to its rescue, was badly mauled. The aggressive spirit manifested by the officers and men of the First Airborne Task Force has added another glorious page to the history of the American army.[11]

« 4 »

Naturally, there was no possibility that higher headquarters would not avail themselves of the further services of Robert Frederick. During the last week in November he received the news that he had been promoted to the command of the highly respected 45th Division. One of his last official acts in the Task Force was to address the following letter to the men who had served so creditably with him:

22 November 1944

To the Officers and Men of the First Airborne Task Force:

As I am leaving the First Airborne Task Force for another assignment I want to say good-bye and congratulate each of you on your fine performance of combat duties.

The Task Force came into being with many handicaps. There was little time to prepare for the operation for which it was formed. Few of the units knew the other units with whom they would work. Some units had to be converted for an entirely new manner of employment, and others had to be formed, trained and equipped. That the Task Force was ready on time for its difficult mission is evidence that the officers and men of the force worked well and hard.

Your accomplishments in the initial phases of the invasion of Southern France are well known. While the airborne units were landing in the rear of the enemy and disrupting his defense, the First Special Service Force was capturing Levant and Port Cros Islands. Each of these operations was accomplished with outstanding success and materially assisted the main invasion operations.

After the beachhead had been secured the Task Force was assigned the mission of protecting the right flank of the advancing Army. It was in the accomplishment of this mission that you showed your versatility, aggressiveness, and superior combat ability. You were at a disadvantage from the start. We had barely any motor transport; our weapons were light and we did not have the supporting arms normally furnished; and the terrain over which you fought was of the most difficult type. The enemy had the advantages of adequate supply, prepared fortifications and superior terrain. In spite of your disadvantages, the enemy's advantages, and the hardships you endured, you attacked with vigor and determination day after day until you destroyed an enemy division and forced back other enemy forces that were superior in numbers and especially trained and equipped for the terrain.

You may take pride in your accomplishments knowing that you performed difficult missions well. I am proud of having commanded a force of superior combat soldiers whose aggressive, offensive spirit brought defeat to the enemy throughout a long series of engagements.

I wish each of you good luck and hope that in all of your future assignments you achieve the same success that has marked your operations in Southern France.

> ROBERT T. FREDERICK,
> *Major General, U.S. Army*[12]

« 5 »

Obviously, so exuberant a soul as Geoffrey Jones would feel quite keenly the absence of a fitting recognition ceremony of the disbandment. As a captain, he was without enough rank to order a major military display, so he decided to stage a private affair that would be equal to the occasion. He describes the farewell party in these terms:

"When it became certain that Frederick was leaving and it seemed fairly sure that I would leave too, it seemed quite logical to me to have this party. One of the hotels had a large ballroom which we took over for the night and decorated with flowers. We also got an orchestra from somewhere.

"Marcel Giraud, my mess officer after a certain mission to Grasse, outdid himself by trading off all of our K-Rations for some really fantastic food.

"It was while the Christmas season was starting and we all felt very sentimental. Even Josef Le Fou, who showed up with some of the fellows he had been going out with on ski patrols, seemed to be impressed by the generally bittersweet feeling.

"The party started out to be very sedate. Quite nice. Everyone was getting together for the first time . . . sort of all coming out from under the rocks because we had, up till then, been working under tight security precautions. Very few of my group had ever known what the others were up to. But then all of the fellows began to really get into the spirit of things. As a matter of fact, most of them got pretty drunk. Even the women dancing around the floor weren't exactly what you might call decorous.

"Naturally, General Frederick was the guest of honor. All of my people like him, he was what they called 'correct.' So when he showed up around midnight they made a beeline for him. Suddenly I saw Josef Le Fou and three of his boys run at the General, grab him and put him up on their shoulders. Then they marched all around the hall that way, singing and cheering. I thought to myself, 'Oh my God!' but the General took it very well. Being the kind of leader he was, he understood what they were feeling even though he couldn't understand a word of their songs or cheers.

"After a while (and quite a few more drinks) they finally put the General down and he was able to escape. But it was a very moving moment to all of us.

"The First Airborne Task Force left shortly after this but I continued on. I had been hoping that I'd spent enough time in the bush to get a short leave but it didn't work out that way. So I continued doing pretty much the same kind of work for the rest of the war."[13]

« 6 »

After the war, General Frederick was asked for his personal evaluation of the men and the achievements of the First Airborne Task Force. He answered, "Did you see the letter I sent them when I left? I meant every damned word of it."[14]

CHAPTER NOTES

CHAPTER I

1. "Gen. Bowen Shows He Knows Men of 517 Very Well," *The Thunderbolt,* Sept. 1964.
2. Colonel Howard E. Hensleigh, interview, Mar. 22, 1967, at Arlington, Va.
3. From completed questionnaires of 517th Parachute Regiment in possession of authors.
4. From completed questionnaires of 517th Parachute Regiment in possession of authors.
5. From completed questionnaires of 517th Parachute Regiment in possession of authors.
6. Dr. Philip T. DiStanislao, interview, Mar. 27, 1967, at Petersburg, Va.
7. From completed questionnaires of 517th Parachute Regiment in possession of authors.
8. Richard Spencer, interview, June 6, 1967, at Colorado Springs, Colo.
9. Chaplain Charles L. Brown, interview, Aug. 12, 1967, at Blowing Rock, N.C.
10. Hensleigh, interview, *op. cit.*
11. Spencer, interview, *op. cit.*
12. The officer does not wish to be identified.
13. Colonel Rupert D. Graves, interview, Oct. 2, 1967, at Stuart, Fla.
14. Brown, interview, *op. cit.*
15. John Hollowell, interview, Apr. 11, 1967, at Alexandria, Va.
16. Father Alfred J. Guenette, interview, Apr. 12, 1967, at Alexandria, Va.
17. From completed questionnaires of 517th Parachute Regiment in possession of authors.
18. Graves, interview, *op. cit.*
19. Charles M. Keen, Jr., interview, Mar. 27, 1967, at Petersburg, Va.
20. Frank K. James, interview, July 21, 1967, at Fayetteville, N.C.
21. DiStanislao, interview, *op. cit.*
22. Hensleigh, interview, *op. cit.*
23. From completed questionnaires of 517th Parachute Regiment in possession of authors.
24. Major General William P. Yarborough, interview, Mar. 10, 1967, at Washington, D.C.
25. Gabriel Rafael, interview, Mar. 18, 1967, at Middletown, N.Y.
26. Major General John S. Guthrie, interview, May 27, 1967, at Wayzata, Minn.
27. Major General Kenneth G. Wickham, interview, Mar. 20, 1967, at Washington, D.C.
28. Major General Robert T. Frederick, interview, June 4, 1967, at Palo Alto, California.
29. Correspondence, Patrick Harrison with authors, 1965.
30. Much of the material on General Frederick and the members of the First Special Service Force was documented by the authors in their earlier book *The Devil's Brigade*; also from selected interviews conducted by authors with officers and men of the First Special Service Force and completed questionnaires in possession of authors.

31. The authors have spent much time in an attempt to authenticate this description. It occurs in several histories of the period but no date is given. When General Frederick was queried in a 1966 conversation with the authors, he answered, "My hunch would be that it occurred right after we took Mount La Defensa in Italy at the end of 1943. From what I understand, it occurred in a conversation between the Prime Minister and General Eisenhower."

CHAPTER II

1. Conversation Captain Geoffrey M. T. Jones with authors, New York, N.Y., Dec. 1967.
2. Captain Geoffrey M. T. Jones, interview, Mar. 19, 1967, at New York, N.Y.
3. A document, issued on Mar. 22, 1943, by the Vichy collaborationists, carries an interesting description of the organization of the United Resistance Movements and the Secret Army. In part, it says: "The Secret Army is a recent element of the Resistance. It was organized during 1942 when some active and reserve elements of the French Army, noting the development of the war, felt it would be imperative for them to identify themselves with any formations eventually aiding an Allied landing. . . . The aims of the Secret Army are identical with those of the Resistance: to co-operate in the expulsion of the occupation troops by force of arms, and the overthrow of the political regime of the Armistice. The immediate aims are to prepare a vast program of action in case of landings, a program to be undertaken jointly by the Resistance and the Secret Army. The short-range aims are to create a pre-revolutionary state of unrest, to counter measures taken by the Government or ordered by the Germans (requisitioning of manpower for the German war machine), and the mobilization of men and materiel for military or guerrilla operations at the moment of Allied landings. . . .

"Although a newcomer among the active elements of the Resistance, the Secret Army has nevertheless been built by political and military groups having already done considerable work. It has understood that for efficient preparation and execution of its aims, it must co-operate with all other elements working separately or together for the same ends. This is why the Secret Army has made contact with the Resistance groups and certain formations controlled by British and American intelligence services, as well as with high-ranking officers working for the regrouping of soldiers of the Army of the Armistice. . . .

"The Secret Army has been in contact with an unnamed agency of British and American intelligence with a view to disorganizing the enemy's rear at the proper moment. . . ."
4. A. J. Liebling, *The Road Back to Paris*, p. 216.
5. General Jacob L. Devers, interview, Mar. 11, 1967, at Georgetown, Washington, D.C.
6. See Paul-Marie de La Gorce's *The French Army: A Military-Political History*, in which he comments (pp. 334, 335) : "Nothing more was involved, until the end of 1942, than personal attitudes, individual commitments, deliberately adopted by officers who went against the general tide of opinion among the military. Obviously, those eager to fight at once and unwilling to content themselves with preparing a fictitious resumption of the struggle by the Army as a whole, did their best to join Free France. Most of them had succeeded in this by 1940 or at the latest, by 1941. They were undoubtedly in the minority. The Anglophobe propaganda of Vichy discouraged most of them. Of

the 20,000 men in the Levant, only 2,000 chose to join the Free French when, hostilities having ceased, they were offered the choice of returning to France or getting back into the war. In France itself, only the dissolution of the armistice army provided all with the opportunity to make a definite return to combat." But de La Gorce qualifies this almost blanket condemnation by observing (pp. 347, 348): "De Lattre was passionately convinced that the injection into his army of the new blood represented by the F.F.I. could be of enormous value. He was fascinated by the adventurous and nonconformist but dynamic and youthful aspects of underground warfare. He had, too, absolutely no respect for the traditional forms of military bureaucracy. Of all the officers of the old Army, he was best fitted to bring about the fusion of the F.F.I. with the regular Army. He was entrusted with this task. The First French Army under his command comprised 250,000 men, at the moment of the Allied landing. He incorporated 137,000 men of the F.F.I. into it. Quite apart from the additional strength that this represented, de Lattre looked on the operation as a fascinating psychological problem. 'Nothing more colorful and more ardent can be imagined,' he wrote, 'than the long, exciting effort to get a grip on this force, vibrating and tumultuous, without deforming it so that — though backed by puny resources — it might be induced to transcend itself without being annihilated. It was a struggle. A struggle against the routine outlook, against prejudice and intransigence. A struggle against indigence, anarchy and the easy way out. And it was a victory — perhaps no other has given me greater joy, because it was a victory for the spirit of synthesis and for French brotherliness.'" This last amalgam seems to be primarily responsible for the overwhelming victories won by the French Forces in Italy and in the campaign for Southern France.

7. Letter from Capitaine François to Isabel Pell, c. Nov. 1944. (Civil Affairs Documents, File #2.)
8. Colonel Bryant Evans, interview, Mar. 14, 1967, at Olney, Md.
9. Jones, interview, *op. cit.*
10. William B. Goddard and members of the Seventh Army Historical Section, *The Seventh United States Army in France and Germany 1944–1945, Report of Operations*, p. 32.
11. From completed questionnaires of 509th Parachute Infantry Battalion in possession of authors.
12. Combat reports and features, Chicago *Tribune*, Aug. 15–19, 1944; see also "Woman Says Laval, Pétain, Must Die," New York *Times*, Aug. 16, 1944. In a letter to the authors dated May 6, 1968, General Frederick added, "and there was the time when I learned that the French members of the Waffen SS had jammed meat hooks into the chins of a group of Frenchmen and left them so hanging until they died . . . the young Frenchwoman who would not answer German questions and had her breast cut off and then two days later when she still refused to answer their questions, the Germans took her out and shot her."
13. Pierre Galante, interview, Mar. 19, 1967, at New York, N.Y.
14. Jones, interview, *op. cit.*

CHAPTER III

1. Lucian K. Truscott, Jr., *Command Missions.*
2. Chicago *Tribune*, Aug. 16, 1944; see also, "Latest Invasion Called War's Most Open Secret," New York *Times*, Aug. 16, 1944.

3. The memoirs of General Alexander, the Army Group Commander and Mark Clark, commanding general of the Fifth Army, fairly bristle at General Eisenhower for withdrawing from them a substantial part of their forces after the fall of Rome. But in a conversation with the authors, General Eisenhower pointed out that the fight in Italy in 1943–1944 was necessary only because the Germans had to be engaged somewhere. After D-Day in Normandy, however, Italy assumed the aspects of a secondary arena, important only to keep the Germans from reinforcing their troops in France. See Robert H. Adleman and George Walton, *Rome Fell Today.*

4. It was General Eisenhower's deep conviction that the capitulation of Germany could be secured only by defeating them in their own country, and that the shortest route to Germany did not lie through Italy or the Balkans, but through France.

5. In the period prior to June 6, 1944, England had taken on the aspect of a tightly packed armed camp. Observers who were there during this period (including one of the authors of this book) can testify that it seemed impossible to find the physical space that even one more division would require. It must be remembered that the bulk of the Allied supplies was being shipped from America and this would have imposed an almost unmanageable extra strain on the ports receiving the supplies needed for the troops already on hand. Also see "South France Seen as Reich Back Door" and "Many in Algiers Saw Blow Coming," New York *Times,* Aug. 16, 1944.

6. For some time prior to June 6, 1944, it had been contemplated that the Allied Invasion of Southern France would take place at the same time as the cross-Channel invasion of Normandy. When, for logistical and other reasons, this secondary thrust could not be mounted in time, there was great pressure put on General Eisenhower by the English to abandon the project. He refused, saying that he needed the southern ports for additional avenues of supply and to broaden the front which an already overstrained German force would have to maintain. The picture can be simplified if it is remembered that while the Allied troops were pouring through the Normandy beachheads in the west, the Russians were rolling in one vast wave from the east, so to bring another major force up from the south could not help but intensify the crunch.

7. From the unpublished report Invasion of Southern France in the Saint-Raphaël-Le Muy-La Motte-Saint-Tropez Area from 15, 16 Aug. 1944 as Seen from the Point of View of the 800 District Commander at Draguignan by Ludwig Bieringer and The 19th Army in Southern France (1 July to 15 Sept. 1944), Remarks and Opinions of the OB of the 19th Army by Friedrich Wiese.

8. *The AAF in the Invasion of Southern France — An Interim Report,* Wings at War Series, No. 1, pp. 1–3.

9. From the unpublished report "Battles of Southern France" (to mid-Sept. 44) by Horst Wilnetzky, p. 8.

10. From the unpublished report "German (OB Southwest) Estimate of Situation Prior to Allied Invasion of Southern France" by Johannes Blaskowitz, p. 1.

11. Wiese, *op. cit.,* p. 2.

12. Major General Robert T. Frederick, interview, June 4, 1967, at Palo Alto, California.

13. General Jacob L. Devers, interview, Mar. 11, 1967, at Georgetown, Washington, D.C.

14. At the time of this writing, Brigadier General Wickham is the Adjutant General of the United States Army.

15. Major General John S. Guthrie, interview, May 27, 1967, at Wayzata, Minn.

16. Colonel Michael M. Isenberg, interview, Oct. 1, 1967, at Miami Springs, Fla.

17. Wings at War Series, *op. cit.*, pp. 26, 27.

18. *Ibid.*, pp. 28, 29.

19. Captain Harris W. Hollis, The Operation of the First Airborne Task Force in the Invasion of Southern France 15–20 August 1944 (Personal Experience of an Assistant G–2), an unpublished monograph, p. 7; William B. Goddard and members of the Seventh Army Historical Section, *The Seventh United States Army in France and Germany 1944–1945, Report of Operations*, p. 110.

20. Many histories of the era refer to this operation as ANVIL but this name was abandoned before the Invasion because it was felt that the widespread familiarity with the name made it useless as a cover. But no evidence exists that DRAGOON ever misled anyone, either.

21. Colonel Bryant Evans, interview, Mar. 14, 1967, at Olney, Md.

22. Guthrie, interview, *op. cit.*

23. Captain Albert C. Reinert, Operations of the First Airborne Task Force in the Landing in Southern France 15 August–17 August, 1944 (Southern France Campaign), an unpublished monograph, p. 6.

24. Frederick, interview, *op. cit.*

25. Isenberg, interview, *op. cit.*

26. Sergeant Major Virgil L. West, interview, July 21, 1967, at Fort Bragg, N.C.

27. Richard Spencer, interview, June 6, 1967, at Colorado Springs, Colo.

28. Letter in possession of authors.

29. Duffield W. Matson, Jr., interviews, May 31, 1967, at San Francisco, Calif., and Oct. 1, 1967, at Miami, Fla.

CHAPTER IV

1. Richard Spencer, interview, June 6, 1967, at Colorado Springs, Colo.

2. From the unpublished report The 19th Army in Southern France (1 July to 15 Sept. 1944), Remarks and Opinions of the OB of the 19th Army by Friedrich Wiese, p. 11.

3. Headquarters Allied Force G–3 Section Report on Airborne Operations in "Dragoon," Sept. 16, 1944 (unpublished), p. 11.

4. Chicago *Tribune*, Aug. 16, 1944; Berlin Radio, Aug. 16, 1944.

5. The documents dealing specifically with these estimates are listed in the Bibliography under section E.

6. From the unpublished report Invasion of Southern France in the Saint-Raphaël-Le Muy-La Motte-Saint-Tropez Area from 15, 16 Aug. 1944 as Seen from the Point of View of the 800 District Commander at Draguignan by Ludwig Bieringer, p. 23.

7. *Ibid.*, p. 20; Wiese, *op. cit.*, p. 14.

8. Bieringer, *op. cit.*

9. William B. Goddard and members of the Seventh Army Historical Section, *The Seventh United States Army in France and Germany 1944–1945, Report of Operations*, Vol. I, p. 68. In this volume, the estimate of available French Forces of the Interior was listed as 15,000 to 20,000 armed men and between 30,000 and 40,000 unarmed but mobilized.

10. Samuel Eliot Morison, *The Invasion of France and Germany 1944–1945* (History of United States Naval Operations in World War II, Vol. XI), p. 234.
11. Although the questionnaires received and the interviews conducted by the authors would leave an impression that the Force was dropped helter-skelter all over France, Colonel William Blythe, Intelligence Officer for the unit, ascertained after a lengthy investigation that approximately 85 per cent of the troops landed in their Drop Zone or in its immediate vicinity. This is a much higher percentage than had been attained in any major Allied drop in the war so far. See Hq. Allied Force G-3 Section Report on Airborne Operations in "Dragoon," Sept. 16, 1944, p. 13. In this report to the commanding general the excessive drop pattern was described as having been caused by a faulty light mechanism (the "drop" signal) in one of the leading aircraft. Also, see *The AAF in the Invasion of Southern France — An Interim Report*, Wings at War Series, No. 1, p. 34.
12. Correspondence, Terrell E. Stewart with authors, 1967.
13. C. Donald Wire, "Southern France Landing," *Blue Book*, Apr. 1948.
14. Major General Robert T. Frederick, interview, June 4, 1967, at Palo Alto, California.
15. Colonel William J. Blythe, interview, June 8, 1967, at Austin, Texas.
16. Edward Sakai, interview, June 3, 1967 at Palo Alto, Calif.; taped conversation of the meeting, Oct. 27, 1967.
17. Edward Sakai, interview, *op. cit.*
18. Blythe, interview, *op. cit.*
19. Major General John S. Guthrie, interview, May 27, 1967, at Wayzata, Minn.
20. Frederick, interview, *op. cit.*
21. Colonel Michael M. Isenberg, interview, Oct. 1, 1967, at Miami Springs, Fla.
22. Duffield W. Matson, Jr., interviews, May 31, 1967, at San Francisco, Calif., and Oct. 1, 1967, at Miami, Fla.
23. Frederick, interview, *op. cit.*
24. Major General Kenneth G. Wickham, interview, Mar. 20, 1967, at Washington, D.C.
25. Brigadier General Melvin Zais, interview, Mar. 20, 1967, at Washington, D.C.
26. Jacques Robichon, *Le Debarquement de Provence*, pp. 175, 176.
27. *Ibid.*, p. 178.
28. Colonel Rupert D. Graves, interview, Oct. 2, 1967, at Stuart, Fla.
29. Father Alfred J. Guenette, interview, Apr. 12, 1967, at Alexandria, Va.
30. Chaplain Charles L. Brown, interview, Aug. 12, 1967, at Blowing Rock, N.C.
31. From completed questionnaires of 550th Infantry Battalion in possession of authors.
32. Frank K. James, interview, July 21, 1967, at Fayetteville, N.C.
33. Dr. Philip T. DiStanislao, interview, Mar. 27, 1967, at Petersburg, Va.
34. Major General William P. Yarborough, interview, Mar. 10, 1967, at Washington, D.C.
35. Headquarters Allied Force G-3 Section Report on Airborne Operations in "Dragoon," Sept. 16, 1944.
36. Colonel R. F. Ruyffelaere, interview, Apr. 14, 1967, at Arlington, Va.
37. Colonel Bryant Evans, interview, Mar. 14, 1967, at Olney, Md.
38. Captain Harris W. Hollis, The Operation of the First Airborne Task Force in the Invasion of Southern France 15–20 August 1944 (Personal Experience of an Assistant G-2), an unpublished monograph, p. 22.

CHAPTER V

1. General Jacob L. Devers, interview, Mar. 11, 1967, at Georgetown, Washington, D.C.
2. Captain Harris W. Hollis, The Operation of the First Airborne Task Force in the Invasion of Southern France 15–20 August 1944 (Personal Experience of an Assistant G–2), an unpublished monograph, p. 25.
3. *Ibid.*
4. Colonel William J. Blythe, interview, June 8, 1967, at Austin, Texas.
5. Captain Geoffrey M. T. Jones, interview, Mar. 19, 1967, at New York, N.Y.
6. From the unpublished report The 19th Army in Southern France (1 July to 15 Sept. 1944), Remarks and Opinions of the OB of the 19th Army by Friedrich Wiese, p. 14.
7. Major General Robert T. Frederick, interview, June 4, 1967, at Palo Alto, California.
8. Richard Spencer, interview, June 6, 1967, at Colorado Springs, Colo.
9. Blythe, interview, *op. cit.*
10. Colonel Bryant Evans, interview, Mar. 14, 1967, at Olney, Md.
11. Major General John S. Guthrie, interview, May 27, 1967, at Wayzata, Minn.
12. Frederick, interview, *op. cit.*
13. For a detailed description of the tactics used in the capture of Le Muy, see p. 15 *et seq.* of the unpublished monograph, The Operations of the 550th Infantry Airborne Battalion (First Airborne Task Force) in the Airborne Invasion of Southern France 13–16 August 1944 (Southern France Campaign) — (Personal Experience of a Battalion Executive Officer). Also Richard Mower's account, "Nazis Run as Glider Men Take Town," in Chicago *Daily News*, Aug. 17, 1944.
14. Blythe, interview, *op. cit.*
15. Colonel William J. Blythe, journals, personal records and correspondence.
16. Charles M. Keen, Jr., interview, Mar. 27, 1967, at Petersburg, Va.
17. Major General Richard J. Seitz, interview, July 21, 1967, at Fort Bragg, N.C.
18. Brigadier General Melvin Zais, interview, Mar. 20, 1967, at Washington, D.C.
19. Edward Sakai, interview, June 3, 1967, at Palo Alto, Calif.
20. Colonel Howard E. Hensleigh, interview, Mar. 22, 1967, at Arlington, Va.
21. Spencer, interview, *op. cit.*
22. 551st Parachute Infantry Battalion, "Letters to the Home Front" (personal collection of Colonel William J. Blythe).
23. Blythe, interview, *op. cit.*
24. From the unpublished report Invasion of Southern France in the Saint-Raphaël-Le Muy-La Motte-Saint-Tropez Area from 15, 16 Aug. 1944 as Seen from the Point of View of the 800 District Commander at Draguignan by Ludwig Bieringer.
25. Frederick, interview, *op. cit.*
26. Jones, interview, *op. cit.*
27. The authority for the figures in this and the preceding paragraph is found on p. 29 of Captain Hollis's unpublished monograph, *op. cit.*
28. First Airborne Task Force German Intelligence Reports, July–Nov. 1944.
29. *United States Army in World War II, Historical Record, the War Against Germany and Italy: Mediterranean and Adjacent Areas.*

30. Combat reports and features, New York *Times*, Aug. 1–Dec. 1, 1944.
31. Eric Sevareid, *Not So Wild a Dream*, pp. 440, 441.
32. Quoted in Captain Hollis's unpublished monograph, *op. cit.*, p. 33.

CHAPTER VI

1. William B. Goddard and members of the Seventh Army Historical Section, *The Seventh United States Army in France and Germany 1944–1945, Report of Operations*, p. 230.
2. General Jacob L. Devers, interview, Mar. 11, 1967, at Georgetown, Washington, D.C. Confirmation of the French desire to be relieved of duties on the right flank will be found in Charles de Gaulle, *The Complete War Memoirs of Charles de Gaulle*, p. 695; confirmation of General Devers's role is found in First Airborne Task Force Operations Summaries (July 15–Sept. 30, 1944), par. 38.
3. *The AAF in the Invasion of Southern France — An Interim Report*, Wings at War Series, No. 1, p. 40.
4. "Iowa Graduate Describes SUI Reunion before 'Take-Off Hour,'" *Daily Iowan*, 1944 (undated).
5. Samuel Eliot Morison, *The Invasion of France and Germany 1944–1945* (History of United States Naval Operations in World War II, Vol. XI), p. 277.
6. *Ibid.*, p. 278.
7. Colonel Bryant Evans, interview, Mar. 14, 1967, at Olney, Md.
8. Colonel Harry H. Pritchard, interview, Apr. 14, 1967, at Arlington, Va.
9. Colonel R. F. Ruyffelaere, interview, Apr. 14, 1967, at Arlington, Va.
10. Major General William P. Yarborough, interview, Mar. 10, 1967, at Washington, D.C.
11. Correspondence, Terrell E. Stewart with authors, 1967.
12. Pritchard, interview, *op. cit.*
13. Goddard, *op. cit.*, p. 234.
14. Major General Kenneth C. Wickham, interview, Mar. 20, 1967, at Washington, D.C.
15. From completed questionnaires of 517th Parachute Regiment in possession of authors.
16. Richard Spencer, interview, June 6, 1967, at Colorado Springs, Colo.
17. Ruyffelaere, interview, *op. cit.*
18. Military Government Records, Misc. (Nice), as translated by General Frederick's Civil Affairs staff. (Personal files of General Frederick.)
19. Goddard, *op. cit.*
20. Military Government Records, Misc. (Nice). (Personal files of General Frederick.)
21. From completed questionnaires of 517th Parachute Regiment in possession of authors.
22. Memorandum, Captain Joseph Welsh to CG, Feb. 17, 1945 (Civil Affairs Documents, File #4).
23. From completed questionnaires of 517th Parachute Regiment in possession of authors.
24. Captain Geoffrey M. T. Jones, interview, Mar. 19, 1967, at New York, N.Y.
25. This decision had been made on higher levels. See New York *Times*, Aug. 19, 1944.

26. Gabriel Rafael, interview, Mar. 18, 1967, at Middletown, N.Y. Letter to the authors, Dec. 12, 1967.
27. Joseph W. Welsh, interview, Dec. 18, 1967, at New York, N.Y.
28. Eric Sevareid, *Not So Wild a Dream*, p. 443.
29. Robert Aron, *France Reborn*, p. 339.
30. Blake Ehrlich, *Resistance: France 1940–1945*, pp. 266, 267.
31. Robert Morgan, "Unpublished Recollections of the 517th [Parachute Regt.]," Mar. 1967.
32. Rafael, interview, *op. cit.*
33. Father Alfred J. Guenette, interview, Apr. 12, 1967, at Alexandria, Va.
34. Carl Mydans, *More Than Meets the Eye*, p. 173.
35. Jones, interview, *op. cit.*
36. Ruyffelaere, interview, *op. cit.*
37. Major General Robert T. Frederick, interview, June 4, 1967, at Palo Alto, California.
38. Sergeant Major John A. Planinshek, interview, May 30, 1967, at Salt Lake City, Utah.
39. From completed questionnaires of the 517th Parachute Regiment in possession of authors.
40. John Hollowell, interview, Apr. 11, 1967, at Alexandria, Va.
41. From completed questionnaires of 509th Parachute Infantry Battalion in possession of authors.
42. Spencer, interview, *op. cit.*
43. Lieutenant Colonel David E. Grange, Jr., interview, July 31, 1967, at Fort Bragg, N.C.
44. Colonel William J. Blythe, interview, June 8, 1967, at Austin, Texas.
45. Jones, interview, *op. cit.*
46. Biography of Marquise de Forbin born Claire Charles-Roux (undated) (Civil Affairs Documents, File #3).
47. Frederick, interview, *op. cit.*
48. Welsh, interview, *op. cit.*
49. Rupert D. Graves, "Combat Team," *Blue Book*, Feb., Mar. 1948.
50. "In Command of Forces in Our Region — Robert T. Frederick," *L'Espoire de Nice*, Sept. 6, 1944.
51. From completed questionnaires of 517th Parachute Regiment in possession of authors.
52. Evans, interview, *op. cit.*
53. Blythe, interview, *op. cit.*
54. Major General Richard J. Seitz, interview, July 21, 1967, at Fort Bragg, N.C.
55. From completed questionnaires of 517th Parachute Regiment in possession of authors.
56. Jones, interview, *op. cit.*
57. Welsh, interview, *op. cit.*
58. Conversations, Major General Robert T. Frederick with authors, Feb. 5, 1968.

CHAPTER VII

1. "Champagne Campaign," *Yank*, Mediterranean Edition, Aug. 1944.
2. Address by General Jacob L. Devers to a meeting of the American Military Institute, Washington, D.C., May 27, 1946, "Operation Dragoon: The Invasion of Southern France," *Military Affairs*, Vol. X, No. 2, Summer 1946, p. 41.

3. FABTF Operations Summaries, July 15–Sept. 30, 1944, pars. 40, 41.

4. William B. Goddard and members of the Seventh Army Historical Section, *The Seventh United States Army in France and Germany 1944–1945, Report of Operations*, p. 239.

5. Unpublished report Activities of the 157th Reserve Division in Southern France by Karl Pflaum, pp. 4, 5. Also, General Frederick's letter to the authors, dated May 6, 1968, in which he comments: "Just about the time that the FABTF reached the Franco-Italian border and I could see the Germans in Italy, I sent word to Gen. Devers that the Task Force was going into Italy. Gen. Devers said not to go into Italy because if we did we would then be in Maitland Wilson's Theatre of Operations instead of Gen. Devers'."

6. Colonel Howard E. Hensleigh, interview, Mar. 22, 1967, at Arlington, Va.

7. From selected interviews conducted by authors with officers and men of the First Special Service Force and completed questionnaires in possession of authors.

8. Field Order No. 8, First Airborne Task Force.

9. Major General William P. Yarborough, interview, Mar. 10, 1967, at Washington, D.C.

10. Goddard, *op. cit.*, p. 240.

11. Robert D. Burhans, *The First Special Service Force*, p. 289.

12. Hans Speidel, *Invasion 1944*, p. 1.

13. From selected interviews conducted by authors with officers and men of the First Special Service Force and completed questionnaires in possession of authors.

14. More detailed descriptions of the activities of the First Special Service Force during the long march to the Italian border will be found in an earlier book by the authors, *The Devil's Brigade*.

15. Sergeant Major John A. Planinshek, interview, May 30, 1967, at Salt Lake City, Utah.

16. Adleman and Walton, *op. cit.*

17. *Ibid.*

18. From selected interviews conducted by authors with officers and men of the First Special Service Force and completed questionnaires in possession of authors.

19. Memorandum, Captain Joseph Welsh to CG, Feb. 7, 1945 (Civil Affairs Documents, File #4).

20. *Ibid.*

21. "Interference with Civil Police," Hq. FABTF Memorandum #9, Oct. 12, 1944.

22. Colonel Michael M. Isenberg, interview, Oct. 1. 1967, at Miami Springs, Fla.

23. Rupert D. Graves, "Combat Team," *Blue Book*, Feb., Mar. 1948.

24. Correspondence, Terrell E. Stewart with authors, 1967.

25. Colonel William J. Blythe, journals, personal records and correspondence.

26. Dr. Philip T. DiStanislao, interview, Mar. 27, 1967, at Petersburg, Va.

27. Lieutenant Colonel David E. Grange, Jr., interview, July 31, 1967, at Fort Bragg, N.C.

28. Sergeant Major Virgil L. West, interview, July 21, 1967, at Fort Bragg, N.C.

29. Joseph W. Welsh, interview, Dec. 18, 1967, at New York, N.Y.

30. *The Thunderbolt*, published for the men of the 517th Parachute Infantry Combat Team, Sept.–Nov. 1944 (personal files of Don Murphy).

31. Letter to Brigadier General Tobin, Dec. 4, 1944 (personal files of Joseph W. Welsh).
32. Yarborough, interview, *op. cit.*
33. Hensleigh, interview, *op. cit.*
34. Brigadier General Melvin Zais, interview, Mar. 20, 1967, at Washington, D.C.
35. From completed questionnaires of 517th Parachute Regiment in possession of authors.
36. Ralph G. Martin, *The GI War*, p. 182.
37. Chicago *Tribune*, Aug. 19, 1944.
38. Adleman and Walton, *op. cit.*
39. *Ibid.*
40. From completed questionnaires of 517th Parachute Regiment in possession of authors.
41. Charles M. Keen, Jr., interview, Mar. 27, 1967, at Petersburg, Va.
42. John Hollowell, interview, Apr. 11, 1967, at Alexandria, Va.
43. Planinshek, interview, *op. cit.*
44. From completed questionnaires of 517th Parachute Regiment in possession of authors.
45. From completed questionnaires of 517th Parachute Regiment in possession of authors.
46. From completed questionnaires of 517th Parachute Regiment in possession of authors.
47. Eric Sevareid, *Not So Wild a Dream*, pp. 440, 441.
48. Yarborough, interview, *op. cit.*
49. Robert Aron, *France Reborn*, p. 335.
50. Letter to Brigadier General Tobin, Feb. 28, 1945 (Civil Affairs Documents, File #4).
51. Memorandum to CG, Jan. 6, 1945 (Civil Affairs Documents, File #3).
52. Letters from Felix Blanchi to Civil Affairs Section, 44th AAA Brigade, Feb. 5, 1945 (Civil Affairs Documents, File #4).
53. Statement and investigation of Lieutenant H. W. Chipman and Captain Fukuda, Jan. 21, 1945 (Civil Affairs Documents, File #4).
54. Military Government Records, Misc. (Nice). (Personal files of Major General Robert T. Frederick.)
55. Welsh, interview, *op. cit.*
56. Much of the material in this section is expanded upon in George W. Herald and Edward D. Radin, *The Big Wheel*, pp. 139–150. See also David Dodge, *The Rich Man's Guide to the Riviera*, pp. 147, 148.
57. Memorandum from Captain Welsh to CG, Feb. 17, 1945 (Civil Affairs Documents, File #4).
58. Letters from Civil Affairs Section, Hq. 44th AAA Brigade to Chief Civil Affairs Officer, Delta Base Hq., "Monaco Food Situation," Feb. 9, 1945.
59. See complete Military Government Records, Misc. (Monaco) file on M. Roblot. (Personal files of Major General Robert T. Frederick.)
60. Major General Robert T. Frederick, interview, June 4, 1967, at Palo Alto, California.
61. Captain Geoffrey M. T. Jones, interview, Mar. 19, 1967, at New York, N.Y.
62. Colonel William J. Blythe, interview, June 8, 1967, at Austin, Texas.
63. Richard Spencer, interview, June 6, 1967, at Colorado Springs, Colo.
64. Father Alfred J. Guenette, interview, Apr. 12, 1967, at Alexandria, Va.

CHAPTER VIII

1. George Dorsey, "Beyond Riviera–Roaring Death," *Stars and Striples,* Mediterranean Edition, Nov. 6, 1944.
2. Headquarters FABTF, Annex IV, Counter-Intelligence Summary, Aug. 15–31, 1944.
3. Reported to Colonel George Walton.
4. Major General William P. Yarborough, interview, Mar. 10, 1967, at Washington, D.C.
5. Gabriel Rafael, interview, Mar. 18, 1967, at Middletown, N.Y.
6. Colonel Howard E. Hensleigh, interview, Mar. 22, 1967, at Arlington, Va.
7. John Hollowell, interview, Apr. 11, 1967, at Alexandria, Va.
8. General Jacob L. Devers, interview, Mar. 11, 1967, at Georgetown, Washington, D.C.
9. Rupert D. Graves, "Combat Team," *Blue Book,* Feb., Mar. 1948.
10. Colonel William J. Blythe, journals, personal records and correspondence.
11. *Ibid.*
12. Letter of farewell from Major General Frederick to officers and men of FABTF, Nov. 22, 1944.
13. Captain Geoffrey M. T. Jones, interview, Mar. 19, 1967, at New York, N.Y.
14. Conversation with authors, Dec. 1967.

BIBLIOGRAPHY

UNPUBLISHED SOURCES

A. UNPUBLISHED MATERIAL IN POSSESSION OF AUTHORS

"Attack," Published by the 517th Parachute Combat Team (Germany: Privately printed, 1945).

Blythe, Col. William J.: "A Brief History of the First Airborne Task Force," n.d.; correspondence with authors, 1967.

Bower, Conrad C.: Letters to authors, Dec. 28, 1944.

First Special Service Force Officers and Men: Selected interviews and question-naires conducted by authors, 1962–1965.

463rd Parachute F. A. Bn.: Questionnaires completed and returned to authors, 1967.

509th Parachute Inf. Bn.: Questionnaires completed and returned to authors, 1967.

517th Parachute Regt.: Questionnaires completed and returned to authors, 1967.

550th Airborne Inf. Bn.: Questionnaires completed and returned to authors, 1967.

Frederick, Maj. Gen. Robert T.: Correspondence with authors, 1967–1968; con-versations with authors, New York, N.Y., Feb. 5, 1968.

Goerler, Albert T.: "War Poems," 1944.

Guenette, Alfred J.: Correspondence with authors, 1967.

Headquarters First Airborne Task Force: Annex IV, Counter-Intelligence Sum-mary, Aug. 15–31, 1944.

Headquarters Seventh Army: Report on Mission to Airborne Task Force, Sept 4, 1944; The Department of the Alpes-Maritimes: Committee of Liberation and Public Order, Sept. 9, 1944.

Hollis, Capt. Harris W.: "The Operation of the First Airborne Task Force in the Invasion of Southern France 15–20 August 1944 (Personal Experience of an Assistant G–2)," Monograph in the Library of the Advanced Infantry Officers' Training Course, Fort Benning, Ga., n.d.

Isenberg, Col. Michael M.: Correspondence with authors, 1967.

Johnson, Edwin P.: "A Record of Company 'C', 517th Parachute Infantry, in the War Against Germany" (unpublished recollections of the campaign), n.d.

"Letters to the Home Front," from 551st Parachute Inf. Bn. (Personal collection of Col. Wm. J. Blythe).

McAvoy, Thomas A.: "Company H, 3rd Battalion, 517th Parachute Regiment," 1967.

Matson, Duffield W., Jr.: Correspondence with authors and others, 1967.

Miscellaneous Commendations, 1944. Copies in possession of authors.

Morgan, Robert: "Unpublished Recollections of the 517th [Parachute Regiment]," Mar. 1967.

"The Operations of the 550th Infantry Airborne Battalion (First Airborne Task Force) in the Airborne Invasion of Southern France 13–16 August 1944 (Southern France Campaign), (Personal Experience of a Battalion Executive Officer)," Monograph in the Library of the Advanced Infantry Officers' Training Course, Fort Benning, Ga., n.d.

Reinert, Capt. Albert C.: "Operations of the First Airborne Task Force in the Landing in Southern France 15 August–17 August 1944 (Southern France Campaign)," Monograph in the Library of the Advanced Infantry Officers' Training Course, Fort Benning, Ga., 1949–1950.

Stewart, Terrell E.: Correspondence with authors, 1967.

B. PERSONAL PAPERS AND DIARIES

Blythe, Col. William J.: Journals, personal records and correspondence; Hq. FABTF G–2 Reports, Aug. 1–31, 1944, Sept. 1–30, 1944, Oct. 1–31, 1944, Nov. 1–30, 1944; Hq. Provisional Troop Carrier, Air Division, USAAF Report for Operation DRAGOON, Aug. 22, 1944; Hq. Airborne Training Center, "Notes on the Operation of RUGBY FORCE, in Operation DRAGOON," Sept. 9, 1944; 602nd F. A. Bn. (Pack) History, July 20, 1942–Dec. 31, 1944.

Frederick, Maj. Gen. Robert T.: Hq. Provisional Troop Carrier, Air Division, USAAF Field Order No. 1 for Operation DRAGOON, Aug. 7, 1944; Military Government Records, Misc. (Alpes-Maritimes, Cannes, Monaco, Nice); address by Gen. Jacob L. Devers to a meeting of the American Military Institute, Washington, "Operation DRAGOON: The Invasion of Southern France," May 27, 1946 (also reported in *Military Affairs*, Vol. X, No. 2, Summer 1946).

Guthrie, Maj. Gen. John: *Rouge-Midi* (Quotidien Régional Du Parti Communiste Français), Aug. 24, 1944.

Murphy, Don: *Thunderbolt, The*, published for the men of the 517th Parachute Inf. Combat Team, Sept.–Nov. 1944.

Ovenden, A. W., 2nd Regt. First Special Service Force: Diary, 1944.

Welsh, Joseph W.: Military record, n.d.; Reuters dispatch, c. Sept. 1944; letter to his mother, Sept. 1, 1944; uncredited file of French newspapers dealing with the ceremonies surrounding the dedication of the Rue Isabel-Pell, Nov. 28, 1944; letter to Brig. Gen. Tobin, Dec. 4, 1944; letter from Mastoianni Antonio to American Military Command, Jan. 29, 1945; letter to CG, 44th AAA Brigade, "Civilian Personnel, Civil Affairs Section," Mar. 22, 1945. Confidential Reports on Nice-Cannes-Monte Carlo: "Report to Col. Parkman on General Conditions in Nice," Sept. 2, 1944; memorandum to A. C. of Staff G–5 7th Army, Sept. 3, 1944; Civil Affairs Hq. FABTF Civil Affairs Report

#2, c. Sept. 10, 1944; Lt. Col. Hivett-Carnac, "Report on Conditions in the Area Nice-Cannes with Special Reference to Public Safety," Sept. 14, 1944; Capt. Routledge, "The Ten Little Nigge-Boys of Antibes," Sept. 27, 1944. Civil Affairs Area Reports, Nice-Cannes: "Newspaper Survey — Nice, France," Nov. 8, 1944; Area Reports — Nice, Nov. 17, Nov. 30, Dec. 16, 1944. Civil Affairs Documents (File #1): Letter to Swiss Vice-Consul, Sept. 28, 1944; Civil Affairs memorandum to CG, Oct. 4, 1944; Ministry of Agriculture to Capt. Welsh, "Stock of Oats and Barley in the Slaughter House of Nice," Oct. 18, 1944. Civil Affairs Documents (File #2): Letter from Paul Latzke to Capt. Welsh, Oct. 12, 1944; letter from M. Honore Castely to CG, Oct. 17, 1944; letter from Societe Nationale Des Chemins De Fer Français to Capt. Welsh, Oct. 28, 1944; letter from Captaine François to Isabel Pell, c. Nov. 1944; Hq. 44th AAA Brigade, memorandum to CG re Civil Government, Department of Alpes-Maritimes, Nov. 28, 1944; letter to Col. Henry Parkman, Jr., Dec. 1, 1944. Civil Affairs Documents (File #3): Letter to Supply Officer 6839th Civil Affairs Regt., "Press Comments on the American Food Shipments to Nice," Nov. 25, 1944; letter from Capt. Welsh to CG, Dec. 28, 1944; memorandum to CG, Jan. 6, 1945; Biography of Marquise de Forbin born Claire Charles-Roux, n.d. Civil Affairs Documents (File #4): Statement and investigation of Lt. H. W. Chipman and Capt. Fukuda, Jan. 21, 1945; letter from Felix Blanchi to Civil Affairs Section 44th AAA Brigade, Feb. 5, 1945; memoranda from Capt. Welsh to CG, Feb. 7, Feb. 17, 1945; "The Principality of Monaco," Feb. 28, 1945; letter to Brig. Gen. Tobin, Feb. 28, 1945.

C. TAPED INTERVIEWS

Interviewee	Date of Interview	Place of Interview
Col. William J. Blythe, Sr.	6/8/67	Austin, Texas
Chaplain Charles L. Brown	8/12/67	Blowing Rock, N.C.
R. Leonard Cheek	10/5/67	Columbus, Ga.
Brig. Gen. Chester B. DeGarve	4/27/67	Onancock, Va.
Gen. Jacob L. Devers	3/11/67	Georgetown, Wash., D.C.
Dr. Philip T. DiStanislao	3/27/67	Petersburg, Va.
Col. Bryant Evans	3/14/67	Olney, Md.
Maj. Gen. Robert T. Frederick	6/4/67	Palo Alto, California
Pierre Galante	3/19/67	New York, N.Y.
Lt. Col. David E. Grange, Jr.	7/31/67	Fort Bragg, N.C.
Col. Rupert D. Graves	10/2/67	Stuart, Fla.
Father Alfred J. Guenette	4/12/67	Alexandria, Va.
Maj. Gen. John S. Guthrie	5/27/67	Wayzata, Minn.
Col. Howard E. Hensleigh	3/22/67	Arlington, Va.
John Hollowell	4/11/67	Alexandria, Va.
Col. Michael M. Isenberg	10/1/67	Miami Springs, Fla.
Frank K. James	7/21/67	Fayetteville, N.C.
Capt. Geoffrey M. T. Jones	3/19/67	New York, N.Y.
Charles M. Keen, Jr.	3/27/67	Petersburg, Va.
Duffield W. Matson, Jr.	5/31/67	San Francisco, Calif.

C. TAPED INTERVIEWS

Interviewee	Date of Interview	Place of Interview
Duffield W. Matson, Jr.	10/1/67	Miami, Fla.
Col. John W. Pierce	7/21/67	Fort Bragg, N.C.
Sgt. Maj. John A. Planinshek	5/30/67	Salt Lake City, Utah
Col. Harry H. Pritchard	4/14/67	Arlington, Va.
Gabriel Rafael	3/18/67	Middletown, N.Y.
Col. R. F. Ruyffelaere	4/14/67	Arlington, Va.
Edward Sakai	6/3/67	Palo Alto, Calif.
Maj. Gen. Richard J. Seitz	7/21/67	Fort Bragg, N.C.
Richard Spencer	6/6/67	Colorado Springs, Colo.
Col. George Walton	8/26/67	Wrightsville Beach, N.C.
Joseph W. Welsh	12/18/67	New York, N.Y.
Sgt. Maj. Virgil L. West	7/21/67	Fort Bragg, N.C.
Maj. Gen. Kenneth G. Wickham	3/20/67	Washington, D.C.
Maj. Gen. William P. Yarborough	3/10/67	Washington, D.C.
Brig. Gen. Melvin Zais	3/20/67	Washington, D.C.

D. UNIT REPORTS AND HISTORIES
IN THE NATIONAL ARCHIVES, WORLD WAR II DIVISION, ALEXANDRIA, VA.

Allied Force Hq. G–3 Section Report on Airborne Operations in "Dragoon," Sept. 16, 1944.

Headquarters Seventh Army, "The Communists and the Committee of Liberation in Marseilles," Sept. 1944.

Headquarters Seventh Army Report on the Political Situation in Nice, Sept. 1, 1944.

Headquarters VI Army Group General Policy Concerning F.F.I., Oct. 10, 1944.

First Airborne Task Force German Intelligence Reports, July–Nov. 1944.

First Airborne Task Force Operations Summaries, July 15–Sept. 30, 1944.

Headquarters First Airborne Task Force, "Nourishment of Children, Dept. of Alpes-Maritimes," Oct. 3, 1944.

Headquarters First Airborne Task Force G–5 Civil Affairs Report on Nice, Oct. 5, 1944.

Headquarters First Task Force Memorandum #9, "Interference with Civil Police," Oct. 12, 1944.

Headquarters First Airborne Task Force Ground Operations of FABTF in DRAGOON, Nov. 20, 1944.

Headquarters First Airborne Task Force General Orders #41 (Award of Silver Star to Col. Edwin A. Walker), Nov. 21, 1944.

First Airborne Task Force Letter of Farewell to Officers and Men from Maj. Gen. Frederick, Nov. 22, 1944.

First Special Service Force Misc. Operations and Intelligence Reports, Aug.–Nov. 1944.

Headquarters First Special Service Force Misc. Official Records, 1944–1945.

Headquarters 44th AAA Brigade Civil Affairs Section Letter to Chief Civil Affairs Officer, Delta Base Hq., "Monaco Food Situation," Feb. 9, 1945.

Headquarters 44th AAA Brigade Commendation Miss Isabel T. Pell, Mar. 20, 1945.

517th Regimental Combat Team Operational Summaries, Aug. 15–Sept. 30, 1944.

442nd Inf. Regt. Narrative of Events, Dec. 1–31, 1944.

Headquarters 1st Bn. 551st Parachute Inf. Regt. (Reinforced) Unit History, Aug. 1–31, 1944 (Dated Oct. 4, 1944).

463rd Parachute F. A. Bn. Historical Narratives, Aug. 15–Sept. 30, 1944.

550th Airborne Inf. Bn. Operations Reports, Aug. 1–Oct. 31, 1944.

63rd Senegalese Co. (attached to 550th Airborne Inf. Bn.) Report for Day of Sept. 28 and the Night from Sept. 28 to Sept. 29 Morning.

Civil Affairs Office, Cannes, First Report, Sept. 9, 1944.

Headquarters Riviera District Delta Base Section, "Investigation by CIC of Miss Isabel Pell," Mar. 9, 1945.

Shirey, Orville C., "Americans — The Story of the 442nd Combat Team," Washington *Infantry Journal Press*, Dec. 1946.

Stars and Stripes, Mediterranean Edition, "Allied Units Six Miles of Toulon," Aug. 19, 1944; "Allies Invading South France!" Aug. 15, 1944; "Beginning of Landings Caught Nazis Off-Guard," Aug. 17, 1944; "Bombers Support Landings," Aug. 15, 1944; "Churchill Reported on French Beaches," Aug. 17, 1944; "Crews of Carrier Group Decorated," Aug. 15, 1944; "Devers Commanding Invasion Operations," Aug. 17, 1944; "15th Fortresses Blast Targets Near Invaders," Aug. 17, 1944; "Gen. Wilson Issues Call to French," Aug. 16, 1944; "German 'Disengagement' Started Two Years Ago," Aug. 15, 1944; "Jeep on a French Road Shows Invasion Success," Aug. 16, 1944; "Landings Going Well," Aug. 16, 1944; "Latest MAAF Report," Aug. 15, 1944; "More Paratroopers Dropped in France," Aug. 17, 1944; "National Uprising in France Urged," Aug. 15, 1944; "Paratroopers Casual as if on Practice Jump," Aug. 16, 1944; "Riviera, Once Gay, Now Battleground," Aug. 17, 1944; "Southern France Fighting Day Ahead of Schedule," Aug. 19, 1944; "Strategic, Tactical Planes Support Land Operations," Aug. 15, 1944; "U.S. Sure of Invasion Success," Aug. 17, 1944; "Yanks Cool, Calm, Confident on Way to Hot Southern France," Aug. 17, 1944.

E. GERMAN MANUSCRIPT SOURCES

Bieringer, Ludwig, The Invasion of Southern France in the Saint Rapheël-Le Muy-La Motte-Saint-Tropez Area from 15, 16 August 1944 as Seen from the Point of View of the 800 District Commander at Draguignan (dated Feb. 1947), Archival File #B-402.

Blaskowitz, Johannes, German (OB Southwest) Estimate of Situation Prior to Allied Invasion of Southern France (dated Mar. 1947) Archival File #B-421.

——, German Reaction to the Invasion of Southern France (dated July 25, 1945) Archival File #A-868.

Fretter, Pico, 148 Infantry Division May–Sept. 1944 (dated Aug. 7, 1946) Archival File #B-203.

Kniess, Baptist, Comments on the History of the U.S. Seventh Army (undated) Archival File #B-376.

——, Report on the Guiding Principles Followed in Southern France (dated May 4, 1946) Archival File #A-888.

Pflaum, Karl, Activities of the 157th Reserve Division in Southern France (dated Sept. 12, 1952) Archival File #B-237.

——, Report on the Employment of the 157 Mountain Division from Sept. 8th to Sept. 15th 1944 (dated Oct. 8, 1946) Archival File #B-331.

Wiese, Friedrich, The 19th Army in Southern France (1 July to 15 Sept. 1944), Remarks and Opinions of the OB of the 19th Army (dated Apr. 11, 1948) Archival File #B-787.

Wilnetzky, Horst, Battles of Southern France (to Mid-Sept. 1944) (dated May 14, 1948) Archival File #A-882.

PUBLISHED SOURCES

A. BOOKS

The AAF in the Invasion of Southern France — An Interim Report, Wings at War Series, No. 1 (Washington: Hq. Army Air Forces, 1945).

Adleman, Robert H., and George Walton, *The Devil's Brigade* (Philadelphia: Chilton, 1966).

————, Rome Fell Today (Boston: Little, Brown, 1968).

Aglion, Raoul, *The Fighting French* (New York: Holt, 1943).

Aron, Robert, *France Reborn* (New York: Scribner's, 1964).

Baldwin, Hanson W., *Battles Lost and Won* (New York: Harper & Row, 1966).

Buckeridge, Justin P., *550 Infantry Airborne Bn.* (Nancy, France: privately printed, 1945).

Burhans, Robert D., *The First Special Service Force* (Washington: Infantry Journal Press, 1947).

Churchill, Winston S., *Triumph and Tragedy* (Boston: Houghton Mifflin, 1953).

Cookridge, E. H., *Set Europe Ablaze* (New York: Crowell, 1967).

de Benouville, Guillain, *The Unknown Warriors* (New York: Simon & Schuster, 1949).

de Gaulle, Charles, *The Complete War Memoirs of Charles de Gaulle* (New York: Simon & Schuster, 1964).

de La Gorce, Paul-Marie, *The French Army: A Military-Political History* (New York: Braziller, 1963).

Dodge, David, *The Rich Man's Guide to the Riviera* (Boston: Little, Brown, 1962).

Doenitz, Karl, *Memoirs: Ten Years and Twenty Days* (Cleveland: World, 1959).

Dupuy, Trevor Nevitt, *Combat Leaders of World War II* (The Military History of World War II, Vol. XVII; New York: Franklin Watts, 1962).

————, *European Land Battles, 1944–1945* (The Military History of World War II, Vol. II; New York: Franklin Watts, 1962).

Ehrlich, Blake, *Resistance: France 1940–1945* (Boston: Little, Brown, 1965).

Goddard, William B., and members of the 7th Army Historical Section, *The Seventh United States Army in France and Germany 1944–1945, Report of Operations, Vol. I* (Heidelberg, Germany: Aloys Gräf, 1946).

Greenfield, Kent Roberts, ed., "Anvil Decision, The," in *Command Decisions* (Washington, D.C.: Office of the Chief of Military History, Dept. of the Army, 1960).

Herald, George W., and Edward D. Radin, *The Big Wheel* (New York: Morrow, 1964).

Karig, Walter (prepared in conjunction with Earl Burton and Stephen L. Freedland), *The Atlantic War* (Battle Report, Vol. II; New York: Rinehart, 1946).

Liebling, A. J., *The Road Back to Paris* (New York: Doubleday, Doran, 1944).

Lochner, Louis P., ed. and trans., *The Goebbels Diaries, 1942–1943* (New York: Doubleday, 1948).

Martin, Ralph G., *The GI War* (Boston: Little, Brown, 1967).

Moran, Lord, *Churchill: Taken from the Diaries of Lord Moran* (Boston: Houghton Mifflin, 1966).

Morison, Samuel Eliot, *The Invasion of France and Germany 1944–1945* (History of United States Naval Operations in World War II, Vol. XI; Boston: Little, Brown, 1964).

Mydans, Carl, *More Than Meets the Eye* (New York: Harper, 1959).

Nicolson, Harold, *The War Years 1939–1945* (Diaries and Letters, ed. by Nigel Nicolson, Vol. II; New York: Atheneum, 1967).

"Remy," *La Ligne de Démarcation* (Paris: Librairie Académique Perrin, 1965).

Revel, Jean-François, *The French* (New York: Braziller, 1966).

Robichon, Jacques, *Le Débarquement de Provence* (Paris: Robert Laffont, 1962).

Sevareid, Eric, *Not So Wild a Dream* (New York: Knopf, 1946).

Speidel, Hans, *Invasion 1944* (Chicago: Henry Regnery, 1950).

Stein, Gertrude, "Return of the Native-by-Adoption: Gertrude Stein Describes Her Return to the City of Light," in *Masterpieces of War Reporting*, ed. Louis L. Snyder (New York: Julian Messner, 1962).

Truscott, Lucian K., Jr., *Command Missions* (New York: Dutton, 1954).

United States Army in World War II, Historical Record, the War Against Germany and Italy: Mediterranean and Adjacent Areas.

Walter, Gerard, *Paris Under the Occupation* (New York: Orion, 1960).

B. PERIODICAL ARTICLES

"Champagne Campaign," *Yank*, Mediterranean Edition, Aug. 1944.

"Col. Graves Earns Silver Star; 3 Men Also Cited," *Daily Iowan*, 1944 (month and day unknown).

"Gen. Bowen Shows He Knows Men of 517 Very Well," *Thunderbolt*, Sept. 1964.

Gervasi, Frank, "The French Fight for Rome," *Collier's*, Feb. 26, 1944.

Graves, Rupert D., "Combat Team," *Blue Book*, Feb., Mar. 1948.

"Hey Mac, Kamerad," *Newsweek*, Sept. 4, 1944.

"Iowa Graduate Describes SUI Reunion before 'Take-Off Hour,'" *Daily Iowan*, 1944 (month and day unknown).

"Iowa Graduate Receives Bronze Star in France," *Daily Iowan*, 1944 (month and day unknown).

Jenkins, Reuben E., "Operation 'Dragoon' — Planning and Landing Phase," *Military Review*, Command and Staff College, Aug. 1946.

Lang, Will, "Big Charley's Men," *Life*, 1944 (month and day unknown).

"Letter *Not* to the Editor," unsigned letter from member of the 550th Airborne Inf. Bn., *Saturday Evening Post*, 1945.

Levitt, Saul, "Moving Up," *Yank*, Mediterranean Edition, Aug. 1944.

"Lieut. Howard Hensleigh Describes Drop into France with 'Men from Mars,'" *Daily Iowan*, 1944 (month and day unknown).

Mathews, Sydney T., "The French in the Drive on Rome," Fraternité d'Armes Franco-Américaine, *Revue Historique de l'Armée*, Special Issue, 1954.

Mower, Richard, "Gliders Bring Help," Chicago *Daily News*, Aug. 22, 1944.

"Mower Watches Nazis Run as Glider Men Take Town," Chicago *Daily News*, Aug. 17, 1944.

Pick, Hella, "De Gaulle Makes It 'War' on the Anglo-Saxons," *Manchester Guardian Weekly*, England, Nov. 30, 1967.

Sions, Harry, "Mountain Maquis," *Yank*, Mediterranean Edition, Aug. 1944.
——, "Patriot's Funeral," *Yank*, Mediterranean Edition, Aug. 1944.
Wire, C. Donald, "Southern France Landing," *Blue Book*, Apr. 1948.

C. NEWSPAPERS

Chicago *Tribune*, Combat Reports and Features, Aug. 15–19, 1944.
Dorsey, George, "Beyond Riviera-Roaring Death," *Stars and Stripes*, Mediterranean Edition, Nov. 6, 1944.
"In Command of Forces in Our Region — Robert T. Frederick," *L'Espoire de Nice*, Sept. 6, 1944.
"Le Gouvernement Américain Endend Participer au Ravitaillement Direct de la Région de Nice," *L'Espoire de Nice*, Nov. 21, 1944.
"L'héroïne Américaine, Isabel Pell," *Le Patriot du Sud-Est*, Nov. 26, 1944.
Marshall, Robert, "Riviera Slash Caught Nazis out of Position," *Stars and Stripes*, European Edition, Aug. 15, 1945.
New York *Times*, Combat Reports and Features, Aug. 1–Dec. 1, 1944.
"3 Divisions Stormed South France Beaches One Year Ago," *Stars and Stripes*, European Edition, Aug. 15, 1945.

INDEX

[*289*]